7/20

D0933501

DISCARD

Exploring the History of Childhood and Play through 50 Historic Treasures

Exploring America's Historic Treasures

About the Organization

The American Association for State and Local History (AASLH) is a national history membership association headquartered in Nashville, Tennessee, that provides leadership and support for its members who preserve and interpret state and local history in order to make the past more meaningful to all people. AASLH members are leaders in preserving, researching, and interpreting traces of the American past to connect the people, thoughts, and events of yesterday with the creative memories and abiding concerns of people, communities, and our nation today. In addition to sponsorship of this book series, AASLH publishes History News magazine, a newsletter, technical leaflets and reports, and other materials; confers prizes and awards in recognition of outstanding achievement in the field; supports a broad education program and other activities designed to help members work more effectively; and advocates on behalf of the discipline of history. To join AASLH, go to www.aaslh.org or contact Membership Services, AASLH, 2021 21st Ave. South, Suite 320, Nashville, TN 37212.

About the Series

The American Association for State and Local History publishes the Exploring America's Historic Treasures series to bring to life topics and themes from American history through objects from museums and other history organizations. Produced with full-color photographs of historic objects, books in this series investigate the past through the interpretation of material culture.

Exploring the History of Childhood and Play through 50 Historic Treasures

SUSAN A. FLETCHER

ROWMAN & LITTLEFIELD
Lanham • Boulder • New York • London

Published by Rowman & Littlefield
An imprint of The Rowman & Littlefield Publishing Group, Inc.
4501 Forbes Boulevard, Suite 200, Lanham, Maryland 20706
www.rowman.com

6 Tinworth Street, London SE11 5AL, United Kingdom

British Library Cataloguing in Publication Information Available

Library of Congress Cataloging-in-Publication Data

Names: Fletcher, Susan A., 1980- author.
Title: Exploring the history of childhood and play through 50 historic
    treasures / Susan A. Fletcher.
Description: Lanham, Maryland : Rowman & Littlefield, 2020. | Series: AASLH
    exploring America's historic treasures | Includes bibliographical
    references and index.
Identifiers: LCCN 2019049614 (print) | LCCN 2019049615 (ebook) | ISBN
    9781538118740 (cloth) | ISBN 9781538118757 (epub)
Subjects: LCSH: Toys—United States—History. | Games—United
    States—History. | Play—United States—History. | Children—United
    States—History. | United States—Social life and customs.
Classification: LCC GV1060.5 .F54 2020 (print) | LCC GV1060.5 (ebook) |
    DDC 790.0973—dc23
LC record available at https://lccn.loc.gov/2019049614
LC ebook record available at https://lccn.loc.gov/2019049615

To my Mama
and in memory of my Daddy,
with a grateful heart for a happy childhood.

Also in memory of my friends
Lt. James W. Downing
Donald McGilchrist
and Dr. Bill Mullins.

Contents

Timeline of Artifacts

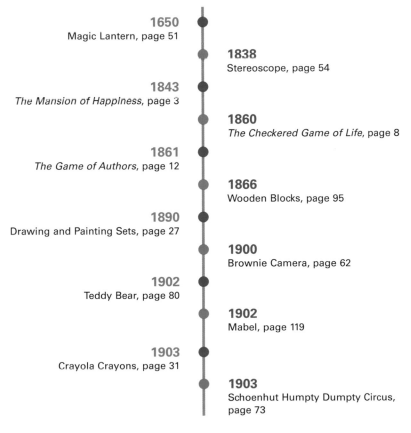

1650
Magic Lantern, page 51

1838
Stereoscope, page 54

1843
The Mansion of Happiness, page 3

1860
The Checkered Game of Life, page 8

1861
The Game of Authors, page 12

1866
Wooden Blocks, page 95

1890
Drawing and Painting Sets, page 27

1900
Brownie Camera, page 62

1902
Teddy Bear, page 80

1902
Mabel, page 119

1903
Crayola Crayons, page 31

1903
Schoenhut Humpty Dumpty Circus, page 73

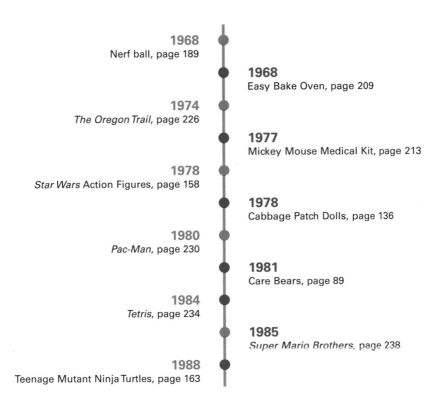

List of Illustrations

Preface

"Childhood lies at the very heart of who we are and who we become."[1]
—Fred Rogers

My mother and I have two different stories about how I got my first Cabbage Patch Doll. My memory of the event goes like this: I'm about five years old, playing downstairs in our house in 1985. My mother comes home from running errands, looking tired and exasperated, clutching a box in her hands. My father asks her what took so long. "I was at Best Department Store and I saw people standing in line for something. I didn't know what they were standing in line for, so I decided to join them to see what they were waiting for," she says. When she finally got to the front of the line, the store employees were unpacking crates of strange-looking dolls with squishy bodies and plastic heads: Cabbage Patch Dolls. She wasn't sure what they were. "But I had stood in line for so long that I decided to buy one." She gave me the doll, which was bald and wore a long christening gown. I named it Tessa.

When I started the research for this book decades later, I discovered that my mother has a slightly different version of the Tessa Origin Story. "Well, Cabbage Patch Dolls were very popular," she told me in an interview in 2018. "And if they got a shipment in, they were gone."[2] On that particular shopping trip, she ran in to one of her friends from church, "and we were both looking for Cabbage Patch Dolls."[3] My mother had been wise to the Cabbage Patch

Doll craze after all! Thus, the hottest toy of the mid-1980s became part of our household.

As a grown-up and a historian of material culture, I look back at my doll Tessa and interpret her through several historical lenses. The doll was a mass-produced object of desire in a culture that had turned young children into consumers. She was the product of an aggressive marketing campaign that spawned one of the biggest toy crazes of the century. She was a gift from a loving mother who wanted her daughter to have a new doll.

But five-year-old Susan didn't know any of that at the time. To me, Tessa was just a companion for my early exploits and adventures. She didn't seem like the usual type of baby doll that needed a lot of mothering attention; instead, she was sturdy enough to drag all over and seemed more like a friend than a real baby that I should probably be taking care of. She fit so well into all my imagination games. When I wanted to play pioneers, I pretended like our sofa was a covered wagon, and I piled Tessa and all my stuffed animals on top of the cushions for the journey westward. When we got a few years older, my best friend Tanya and I played detective with Tessa and all our Barbies, making up convoluted mysteries for them to solve.

I am an only child, so when the neighborhood kids weren't around to play, my toys were acceptable companions. Stuffed animals knew all of my business and were privy to my innermost thoughts. I bonded strongly with my toys, so it's no surprise that I find the material culture of childhood fascinating as an adult.

This book is an exploration of the history of American childhood 1840–2000 through the stories of fifty toys, games, and other playtime artifacts. The book examines change over time with regard to a child's place in the larger story of American history by looking at specific examples of playtime objects. The historical context in which a child grows up significantly influences their playtime. The material culture kids use in play, the locations they play in, their playmates, and the purpose of their play are all deeply embedded in their historical and culture milieu, even if children are largely unaware of that at the time.

Throughout the ten parts, we will explore childhood against the backdrop of culture, politics, religion, technology, gender norms, and parenting philosophies. For example, the entry on the board game *The Mansion of Happiness* looks at the game's relationship to the changing values of American Christianity and consumerism during the nineteenth century. The entry on the Magic Lantern explores the toy's educational value in the field of optics and science, as well as its connection to childhood moneymaking schemes. The chapter on Barbie explores the doll's contested meanings over the decades.

This is a different sort of book than you might be used to reading about the history of childhood and play. There are many other books detailing the history of how various toys and games came to be, including Tim Walsh's excellent work *Timeless Toys* and Scott Eberle's wonderful book *Classic Toys of the National Toy Hall of Fame*. Those books are fascinating, but they don't always include the deeper story of how each object fits into its historical context. Classic academic works on the history of childhood like Howard Chudacoff's *Children at Play: An American History* and Steven Mintz's groundbreaking *Huck's Raft* are superb pieces of scholarship, but they don't examine individual objects of play. This book is different in that it focuses on the material culture of childhood in the context of the large sweep of American history in a format accessible to a popular audience. My vision for this work is to serve as a bridge between these two genres, and to do it in a lively and fun way.

I have decided to focus this work on 160 years of American childhood, 1840–2000. By looking at this time span, we can see significant changes to what it meant to be a kid in this country. A child growing up in the 1990s had a very different cultural, social, technological, theological milieu than a child growing up before the Civil War. Even within shorter timespans of individual decades in the nineteenth and twentieth centuries, we can see enormous change over time. We're starting our exploration around 1840, when the country's identity was finally starting to come into maturity from the early days of its infancy. Our exploration concludes at the turn of the twenty-first century, just before the terrorist attacks on September 11, 2001, cast a dark shadow over the nation.

This book grew out of my early research on American childhood in the nineteenth century. I focused on educational playtime activities among the growing middle class from 1830–1900 and I examined the ways in which toys, games, and playtime activities transmitted intellectual, moral, and social knowledge to children. The material culture of play and prescriptive literature aimed at children during that era directed their leisure toward useful ends. Whereas children in the American colonies would have been encouraged to grow up quickly and gain early maturity, by the mid-nineteenth century ideas about childhood had changed. Adults were beginning to see childhood as a separate phase of life from adulthood. Children in the upper and middle classes were gaining an increasing amount of free time to play without the necessity to work.

Of course, childhood looked very different for a middle-class boy or girl growing up in the urbanized Northeast than it did for children who were in bondage in the South, pioneering the West, or recently immigrating from Europe. Class and geographical location are major factors in the degree to which a child has leisure time at all, the expectations placed upon this leisure time, and the material culture available to fill this time.

This book expands the time frame of my early research to include the twentieth century. Some of the themes from this last century include changes to the level of independence that kids have, an increasing number of mass-manufactured toys and games, a focus on the vulnerability of children, and the impact of urbanization on playtime. Cataclysmic world events also impacted playtime, and we'll learn more about how the Vietnam War forced Hasbro to change how the company marketed G.I. Joe in the 1970s.

HOW TO READ THIS BOOK

This book is comprised of ten categorically arranged parts. Each part focuses on one particular type of toy and game. Each part features five different toys, games, and other artifacts with an exploration of each object. Part 1 focuses on board and card games, exploring themes like shifting American religious values, childhood in the context of war and disease, and the impact of consumerism on play. Part 2 is about art tools and art toys. This part traces the increasing availability of art materials to children over the course of two centuries.

Part 3 is about optical toys and cameras. This part explores scientific education through play, progress in technology, and the invitation for children to document their worlds. Part 4 is about animal toys. By looking at the history of the teddy bear and similar toys, we'll look at popular toy crazes and the marketing schemes that produced them. Part 5 is about construction toys. This part looks at the ways in which construction toys prepared boys to take on the urbanization boom in the early twentieth century.

Part 6 is about dolls. Themes in this part include play as preparation for adulthood and dolls as companionate objects. Part 7 explores action figures and their relationship to war and world events.

Part 8 focuses on physical toys and the sporting life. In this part, we will look at a changing landscape of play and the importance of athletics to masculine and feminine identity. Part 9 is about toys that prepared children for adulthood. Finally, part 10 focuses on electronic games. Themes in this part include changing technology, attitudes about violence, and the universal nature of play.

I realize that not everyone reading this book is interested in the broader themes of the changing nature of childhood over the course of 160 years of American history. Perhaps you picked up this book simply because you want to know more about how your favorite toy came to be. That's ok—this book is for you, and you'll find all of that information here too. You'll also find some funny stories of children of the past and probably plenty of information that will spark a sense of nostalgia for some of the toys that you grew up with.

Each toy in the individual chapters represents an iconic or favorite artifact of childhood that tells us much about the context in which a child was living at a particular moment in time. I chose each of these fifty objects for a variety of reasons. Some of them are iconic toys that almost everyone has heard of like Barbie, G.I. Joe, and *Monopoly*. Other objects have interesting origin stories or maintain an influential presence in childhood well into the twenty-first century. Still other toys in this book are some of my favorite museum objects that have unique and wonderful stories. This category includes the Steiff Elephant that Colorado Springs founder General William Jackson Palmer gave at a Christmas party in 1902. I selfishly included other toys because my friends and I played with them growing up in the 1980s, like Cabbage Patch Dolls and Care Bears. The toys in this book are not necessarily the most "important" objects of their eras, nor do these categories represent an exhaustive list of all the subtypes of toys and games. If your own favorite toy is not included in this book, you can use the model of research in the book to find out more about what you are interested in. We'll be looking at the development of each artifact and then placing it in its historical context.

As I was researching this book, I found the stories of these historic treasures surprisingly moving. There are many stories of inventors turning tragic situations into objects of delight, such as Eleanor Abbott, who created the game *Candyland* to entertain children in the polio ward when she was stricken with the disease herself. Some of these toys inspired children upon their future life paths, like Ted Wasserman, who became a professional artist after buying a set of Crayola Crayons for a hard-won ten cents in 1918. I hope that you will enjoy reading them as much as I enjoyed discovering these stories.

You can read this book in any order that you choose. Although the entries in each chapter build upon one another, you won't do yourself a disservice if you want to skip around to the toys and games that interest you the most. Are you fascinated with *Monopoly*? Flip straight over to that entry. Are you longing to relive a childhood spent playing with Cabbage Patch Kids? You'll find them in chapter 30.

This book is intended for people who love history, toys, and games, and for those of us who have given our lives to working in museums and other public history settings. I write in hopes of making some of the ideas about the history of American childhood that scholars study in the academy accessible to you in a friendly way. And what could be friendlier than the toys that we grew up with?

Acknowledgments

Writing a book about the history of childhood while living in my hometown has naturally caused me to reflect on my own childhood. The first people I need to thank are my parents, Ruth and John Fletcher, and my grandparents Leon and Augusta Brown. I'm so thankful to be part of your family. Thank you for giving me a beautiful, happy childhood and for raising me to be a woman who loves Jesus. Words cannot express how much I love each of you, and how much I look forward to us all being reunited in the world to come.

Because this book is about the history of play, I thank my childhood best friend Tanya Pease. I couldn't have asked for a better companion to grow up with. We played with the usual 1980s and 90s toys, but we also had the best "imagination" games. We were pirates, pioneers, explorers, teachers, and detectives. We did science experiments, art projects, and played outside nearly every summer evening until dark. I'm profoundly thankful that we grew up four houses down from each other. No matter where our lives take us from here on out, you will be in my heart forever.

And now for the friends I met when I grew up. This book is based in part on my master's thesis, and I am grateful to Dr. Annie Coleman for her role as my thesis advisor at IUPUI. I am blessed by her thoughtful attention and all of the ways in which she helped me be a better writer and historian. In 2017, AASLH and Rowman & Littlefield were soliciting proposals for their new

Exploring American History book series. My friend Bob Beatty sent me a note asking, "Wonder if you'd give any thought to repurposing your thesis research on toys & games for a book like this?" I owe him a huge thank-you for starting me off on this journey and for his encouragement along the way.

In 2013, I attended the Seminar for Historic Administration (now HLI), where I met my SHAsome history family. In particular, I want to thank Amanda Bryden, Marc Blackburn, Melissa Prycer, Jenn Landry, and Brett Lobello for their support on this project.

In 2018, I had the great blessing of receiving a G. Rollie Adams Research Fellowship at The Strong National Museum of Play. Ever since I wrote about *The Mansion of Happiness* as a poor grad student, I wanted to see the board game in person, so being at the Strong was a dream come true. I spent a fantastic summer week in Rochester, New York, exploring their collections in the reading room of the Brian Sutton-Smith Library and Archives. My deep gratitude to Christopher Bensch, Nic Ricketts, Julia Novakovic, and Beth Lathrop for welcoming me to their wonderful museum and for all of their assistance. I also thank Patrick Ellis for being a delightful fellow-fellow during our research week in June, and for his thoughtful remarks on my project.

Closer to home, I owe a huge debt of gratitude to my art community at SPQR Art Space and the Modbo Gallery in downtown Colorado Springs. I am profoundly thankful to my friend and art teacher Brett Andrus for helping me set big artistic and personal goals that eventually led to writing this book. After eight years of teaching me about drawing and painting, he became one of my biggest champions as I returned to the world of history-writing. At a critical point in this project when I was feeling discouraged, he helped kick me into high gear. Brett, thank you for giving me space and permission to temporarily step away from the visual arts to focus on research and writing. Your mantra "Plan the Work and Work the Plan" totally works. Thank you for your constant faith in me and for every single thing that you do for the artists in our community.

I also have several of my fellow artists to thank. First of all, my painter friend Lupita Carrasco helped me stay connected to the visual arts world (and to another human) during this process by swapping Instagram messages with me every day showing our daily progress on our work. Having that accountability was helpful, and it was a joy to get to know you through those messages. Thank you also to my friends in my Advanced Studio Classes at SPQR, including Emily Rhoades, Claire Swinford, Elizabeth Selby, April Dawes, and Sophia Hanna. I also thank my friend and Modbo Gallery owner Lauren Cibrowski for sharing her Care Bear stories with me, and for providing a home for the artists in our city.

A big thank-you to my *Springs Magazine* editor Jeremy Jones for bringing me on board his fine publication as a freelance writer. His thoughtful work as an editor has made me a better writer, and I am thankful for his encouragement on this project.

I owe so much to all of my medical champions and healers. Thank you to T. Hedman, D. Hager, Dr. T. Bonack, Dr. A. Liddle, Dr. J. Brinley, and Dr. R. Stringfellow. I am grateful to every one of them for their years of dedication to solving my mysteries and for taking care of me while I wrote this book.

So many people prayed for me while I was writing this book, and I am thankful for each and every one of them. In particular, I want to thank Pastor Katie Fowler, Pastor Jennifer Holz, Bob Beatty, Donald McGilchrist, Paul Lilley, and Ruth Fletcher. Thank you also to my Life Group at First Presbyterian Church: Melissa, Helen and Bill, Joel, Vicki, Christen, and Mason and Maria.

Four of my dear ones passed away over the twenty months in which I was working on the book manuscript, and I want to take the opportunity to acknowledge their influence in my life and work. I miss my uncle Bob's presence in our family, and I am thankful for the opportunity to interview him about his childhood while he was still alive. I am grateful to my friend and American hero Lt. James W. Downing for his brave actions during the attack on Pearl Harbor and for living out the rest of his 104 ½ years with humor, courage, and friendship. Thank you to my fellow historian, friend, and mentor Donald McGilchrist for sharing his vast storehouses of wisdom with me and for being a model of faith, gentleness, grace, and humility. On the day that I submitted the final full submission of this book manuscript, I learned that my beloved former history professor Dr. Bill Mullins had gone home to be with the Lord. He's one of the people who made me want to be a historian, and I owe my career to him. Thank you, my dear friends.

Finally, on a happier note, a huge thank-you to my Paul Lilley for his love and support on this project. Thank you, Paul, for reading over my drafts, making me dinner, and for being my faithful companion. You are a wonderful gift to me, and I treasure you deeply.

Writing a book about toys and games means that your friends and family will be more interested in your scholarly work than they normally are. Thank you to everyone who asked me how the book was going and who said with genuine enthusiasm, "That's a cool project!"

This book is for all of my fellow children of the 1980s and 1990s in fond memory of the time we all spent playing *Oregon Trail*, Care Bears, and My Little Pony. And this book is for a brand-new generation of American children, who my friends are raising right now. May your childhood be blessed, sweet Micaiah, Asher, Phil, Nora, Sasha, and Matthew.

Part I

GAMES

According to *The Nevada Daily Mail*, games help children learn all kinds of academic and practical skills, "but these are not the primary reasons for playing games. The main reason is to have fun. Games make us enjoy being with each other, and they help make the family a unit in which there are many joyful occasions."[2] Americans of all ages enjoy board, table, and card games. In this part, we'll explore five board and card games and their connection to religious virtues, consumerism, education, disease, and the impact of consumerism on play. If you're looking for stories about electronic and video games, they are waiting for you at the end of the book.

Americans have been playing board and card games for centuries. According to historian Howard Chudacoff, during the colonial era and early republic, games were playthings for both adults and children.[3] Many of the games that American children played were imported from Europe or were derivates of European-made games in the early nineteenth century. In 1822, *The Traveller's* [sic] *Tour through the United States* was the first board game published in America. Players tried to reach the city of New Orleans, traversing through the known extent of the United States along the way.[4]

Until the late nineteenth century, holdover Puritan values made parents deeply suspicious about the moral legitimacy of their children's free time. In the colonial era, children were encouraged to grow up quickly. Any free time that they may have had was filled with educational opportunities, lest idle hands lead to the Devil's work. As children gained an increasing amount of free time to spend as they pleased over the course of the nineteenth century, parents soothed their anxieties about the morality of this playtime by continuing to instill educational opportunities into their children's toys and games. This impulse is one of the major themes of this book, and you'll see it returning again in the part on art toys, construction sets, dolls, and objects that helped kids mimic the adult world. But first, we'll start out by exploring this theme as it influenced games. Many of the board and card games that children played with were explicitly didactic. *The Traveller's Tour* taught children about the geography of their young nation. Twenty years later, *The Mansion of Happiness* became a vehicle for communicating moral and religious values.[5] *The Checkered Game of Life* in the 1860s was a tool to teach players about the uncertain nature of life. *The Game of Authors* taught children about literature.

In the twentieth century, games became less explicitly didactic and moved toward being just plain fun. Some of these games included the chance for a player to make a fantasy world for themselves by making money, as in the case of *Monopoly*. As games moved toward a goal of pure fun rather than learning, they became sources of comfort for children in less than ideal circumstances, such as the children who played *Candyland* in polio wards in the 1950s. So, let's put our favorite game tokens—mine is the little dog from *Monopoly*—on the starting space and journey onward to explore the historic context of five of the most beloved games from the last 150 years.

1

The Mansion of Happiness

The Mansion of Happiness
COURTESY OF THE STRONG, ROCHESTER, NEW YORK

Identifying Information:

The Mansion of Happiness: An Instructive, Moral, and Entertaining Amusement

Maker: W. & S. B. St. Ives

Manufacturer: Thayer and Co.

Date: 1843

The Strong Museum of Play, Object ID: 78.412

When you have a game night at your house, chances are pretty high that you chose the games on your table because they are fun and entertaining. Whether you are building your train across the country in *Ticket to Ride*, trying to contain a virus in *Pandemic*, or building your empire in *Monopoly*, most of the games that we play in the early twenty-first century have a high entertainment, strategic, or social value. Game nights during the 1840s would have looked different. Many of the board games that American families enjoyed in the early nineteenth century placed a high value on transmitting educational and moral values to their players in an overt way. One of their favorite games during this period was *The Mansion of Happiness*, which billed itself as "An Instructive Moral and Entertaining Amusement."[1] In this passage, we'll explore how this game communicated Christian values during the era of the Second Great Awakening.

George Fox, an English author and designer, created *The Mansion of Happiness* in 1800. Its spiral design was similar to that of many other European games of this era and previous generations, including *The New Navy Game* from France and *The New Game of Emulation* from England.[2] St. Ives started printing *The Mansion of Happiness* in the United States in 1843. Although St. Ives billed it as "the first board game published in America," that honor actually fell to *The Traveller's Tour through the United States* published in 1822. *The Mansion of Happiness* may not have been the first board game published in America, but it certainly did mirror the changing theological milieu in the United States during the 1840s. After a period of declining interest in religion during the late eighteenth century, the Second Great Awakening reinvigorated Americans' love for God. Revivalism swept the country from 1800 through the 1840s. Church membership soared, with the Baptists and Methodists making the most gains in attendees. Parents who renewed their commitment to religion sought ways to transmit theological values to their children, often choosing to do so through playtime activities. In 1842, Ellis Lewis wrote, "the term education . . . comprehends a proper attention to the moral and religious sentiments of the child."[3] During the first half of the nineteenth century, learning about Protestant Christianity and its incumbent virtues comprised a large portion of a child's playtime experience.

The Mansion of Happiness represented an early nineteenth-century Christian recipe for success. The game taught children to cling to virtue while avoiding vice. Players start on a space marked "Justice" and then progress around the board's spiral. They land on spaces ranging from "Humility" to "Ruin," until the winner reaches the middle of the board, which represented the Seat of Happiness. It was hard to miss the moralistic point of the game. The rulebook from a reprint edition stated:

> At this Amusement each will find
> A Moral fit to improve the Mind;
> It gives to those their proper Due,
> Who various Paths of Vice Pursue;
> And shows (while Vice Destruction brings)
> That Good from every Virtue springs;
> Be virtuous then and forward press
> To gain the Seat of Happiness.[4]

In the religious fervor of the early nineteenth century, parents wanted their children to learn abstract Christian virtues such as temperance, love, and purity. *The Mansion of Happiness* and other games of its kind taught children that they could win in life if they cultivated these traits.

The game represented the course of a child's life and served as a guide to making good choices by explicitly showing them the consequences of their actions. Being virtuous creates forward progress for the players. The child who "possesses" Piety, Honesty, Temperance, Gratitude, Prudence, Truth, Sincerity, Humility, Industry, Charity, or Humanity goes forward six spaces toward the center of the board.[5]

On the other hand, vices hampered a child's journey toward happiness. Less severe infractions included Immodesty and Ingratitude. However, players who come across Idleness move backward into Poverty; landing on Cruelty, Ruin, or Prison sends a child back to the beginning of the game. Punishments take place at The Whipping Post, The Stocks, and The House of Correction. Children also encounter nefarious characters on the journey including the dreaded Sabbath Breaker, a Perjurer, and a Cheat. Spaces named The Road to Folly and The Summit of Dissipation show children the depths that they can descend to unless they are careful.

The gospel of grace is present in the game, however, because no one is ever totally out of the game and even players who get sent all the way back to the beginning have a chance to start over again. Everyone has a chance to reach paradise.

During the latter half of the nineteenth century, however, the source for moral authority began to shift away from the family and religious institutions and toward the marketplace, teaching children values associated with materialism. After the Civil War, Protestant Christianity began to lose its hold on the moral conscience of America. With the advent of a pessimistic pre-millennial eschatology, one that stressed the utter depravity of humanity and the inability to bring about the return of Christ through human measures, the middle class began to believe that achieving moral perfection on earth was impossible. Churches found themselves competing with the stock market and the workplace as the new centers of morality. By the 1880s and 1890s, a new morality became dominant—one based on material success rather than abstract Christian values. According to historian William Ketchum, "Games professing to show the way to Heaven were superseded by pastimes such as *The Game of Business, or, Going to Work* (1895) and *Speculation for Young Children*."[6]

The look of *The Mansion of Happiness* changed alongside this shift. The 1840s version published by St. Ives depicts the Christian journey as peaceful and pastoral, with the seat of happiness illustrated as five women dancing underneath a bower in a rural scene of nature. McLoughlin Brothers republished the game in 1895, and the illustration on the box cover depicts an "opulent Taj Mahal"[7] with a well-dressed boy and girl sitting nearby. This change reflects

Americans' growing interest in the accumulation of riches. No longer content with resting on the cool lawn of the 1840s seat of happiness, the Gilded Age middle class wanted a *real* mansion. The increasingly secularized middle class did not entirely abandon religious morality, but it did begin to substitute a workplace ethic for Christian service and the quest for riches for a journey to piety.

The Mansion of Happiness remained in production for many years, and Parker Brothers produced a version in 1926. By the 1920s, however, society had changed and the game no longer held a grip on American imagination. In the subsequent entries in this section, we will trace these changes and learn whether or not the simple recipe for virtuous living produced the happiness and success that *The Mansion of Happiness* promoted.

2

The Checkered Game of Life

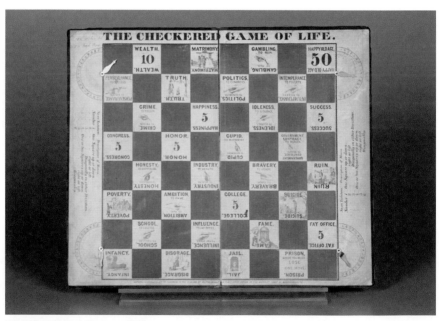

The Checkered Game of Life
COURTESY OF THE STRONG, ROCHESTER, NEW YORK

Identifying Information:

The Checkered Game of Life and *The Game of Life*

Maker: Milton Bradley

Manufacturer: Milton Bradley Company

Date: 1860

The Strong Museum of Play, Object ID 114.5535

After you read this passage, you can sound smart at parties by asking your friends this question: What does Abraham Lincoln's beard have to do with *The Game of Life*? Unless you're at a party with a bunch of other historians who already know the answer, you can dazzle your pals with this bit of trivia. Abraham Lincoln's decision to grow a beard during the 1860 presidential election led to the invention of a game called *The Checkered Game of Life*, which in turn led to the design of *The Game of Life*. Both *The Checkered Game of Life* and *The Game of Life* offer a window into the changing cultural values of Americans over the course of 150 years. Invented on the eve of the Civil War, *The Checkered Game of Life* reflected a mid-nineteenth-century recipe for success. One hundred years later, the anniversary edition called *The Game of Life* reflected a very different America during the 1960s.

All kinds of historical factors influence the development of toys and games, even Abraham Lincoln's decision to grow out his beard. In 1860, a Springfield, Massachusetts, lithographer named Milton Bradley received a commission to print lithographs of clean-shaven presidential candidate Abraham Lincoln.[1] Bradley printed the images, which sold well, and everything seemed terrific for a while. Just before the election, however, something terrible happened that threatened Bradley's business: Lincoln grew a beard.

Ironically, it seems that a child influenced Lincoln's decision. In a letter from October 15, 1860, eleven-year-old Grace Bedell of Westfield, New York, wrote Lincoln to say, "I have got 4 brothers and part of them will vote for you any way and if you will let your whiskers grow I will try and get the rest of them to vote for you, you would look a great deal better for your face is so thin. All the ladies like whiskers and they would tease their husbands to vote for you and then you would be President."[2] (Remember, this was seventy years before women got the right to vote. Girls and women had to influence the men in their lives to vote for their favorite candidates because they couldn't do that themselves.)

Lincoln did grow out his whiskers. Unfortunately for Milton Bradley, however, the ladies liked Lincoln's beard so much that they no longer wanted pictures of him clean-shaven. Bradley's lithograph sales of the presidential candidate plummeted.

Bradley tried to figure out what to do next, and he decided to use his printing press to create a new board game, which he called *The Checkered Game of Life*.[3] The game had a checkerboard pattern, with the alternating spaces bearing the names of virtues, vices, victories, and defeats. Players won the game by attaining "Happy Old Age" when they accumulated one hundred points. The rule book stated that the game "is intended to present the various virtues and vices in their natural relation to one another—the whole embodied in an attractive and entertaining amusement."[4] Bradley "thought it was like the design of his life and the life of nearly everyone he knew; checkered, hazardous, uncertain in its outcome,"[5] according to historian James Shea.

The checkerboard represented a life spent in pursuit of mid-nineteenth-century success. Like *The Mansion of Happiness*, players can land on virtues such as Honor or Industry, but this game added the extra element of worldly success. Toward the middle of the nineteenth century, the moral tone of games changed as industrialism, capitalism, and consumerism began to influence American morality. *The Checkered Game of Life* is an excellent example of this change. While the game taught children virtues such as honesty and warned them against vices including intemperance, the game itself is based on material success. According to historian Margaret Hofer, the game represents "the marriage of spiritual values and worldly achievement."[6]

The spaces explicitly show children the consequences of each action. If a player lands on Ambition, he goes directly to Fame. Perseverance leads to Success. Crime leads straight to Prison, Industry leads to Wealth, Idleness leads to Disgrace, and Gambling leads to Ruin. Virtues allow players to gain success by attending college, attaining a government contract, getting elected to Congress, and marrying well. Combined, all of the virtues and life milestones result in a life well lived and Happy Old Age. In *The Mansion of Happiness*, players reach the seat of happiness simply by displaying virtues. In *The Checkered Game of Life*, however, moral behavior allows them to engage in the business and social world of the day, and these material milestones are what lead to old age and happiness.

The game was instantly popular. During the Civil War, soldiers in the field played a light-weight, portable version of the game that Bradley made for them.[7] The Milton Bradley Company reprinted the game in 1866, the 1870s, and 1911. Generations of families bought *The Checkered Game of Life*, and the company appealed to nostalgia in its marketing campaigns. In a reprint edition, an advertisement that came with the rulebook stated, "Those who are now at the head of families purchase it for their children, because of the pleasant remembrances of the game they played themselves when young."[8]

The moralistic tone of the game was its undoing in the early twentieth century. Americans discovered that life didn't always turn out the way they hoped it would. With financial panics in 1873 and 1893, it was painfully evident that Perseverance didn't always lead to Success. Life just didn't work in a positive, formulaic way. Americans lost interest in the game around the turn of the century, and the Milton Bradley Company stopped reprinting the game.

For the one hundredth anniversary in 1960, however, the company resurrected the game to honor their founder. However, the details of American lives had changed drastically over one hundred years, and the game needed some updates to make it appealing to a modern audience. According to historian Tim Walsh, "Puritan principals in the 1960s. Some things just don't mix."[9]

So, the company redesigned the game, now calling it *The Game of Life*. This new game had a far more circuitous path through life with more decisions to make than the original. Instead of attaining Happy Old Age by accumulating points, the player who won this version of *Life* had accumlated the most paper money. Rather than the nineteenth-century recipe of success gained through morals and hard work, this new version reflected a 1960s version of material success. Children don't achieve anything through honesty or truthfulness—in the new version, everything is achieved by either *doing* or *buying*. The marketing campaign for the new game was very clear about the game's purpose: "You will learn about life when you play the Game of Life."[10] *The Game of Life* continues to be a popular amusement in the early twenty-first century, and it continues to communicate a prescribed life script and the values of our society.

3

The Game of Authors

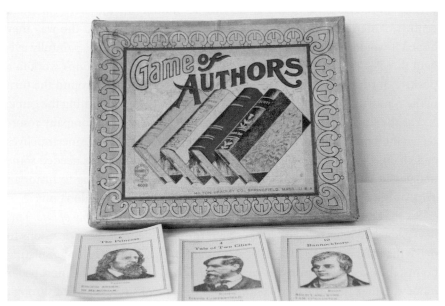

Game of Authors, Milton Bradley

Identifying Information:

The Game of Authors

Manufacturer: Milton Bradley

Date: c. 1890

Collection of Susan A. Fletcher

"A ny one of our young readers may at any time be taught, by practical experience, that knowledge is power and ignorance weakness," [1] wrote the authors of *The American Boy's Book of Sports and Games*. Intellectual education during playtime was part of the middle-class experience in the mid- to late nineteenth century. Just like *The Mansion of Happiness* and *The Checkered Game of Life* taught children religious virtues and how to navigate the tumult of life, games also taught children academic principles. In this passage, we'll look at *The Game of Authors* as an example of intellectual education during playtime.

After the Civil War, literacy was the foundation for nearly every other type of education that a child would undergo. They learned about religion and morality by reading the Bible and other sacred texts; etiquette books taught them about proper gender behavior; and handy books transmitted scientific knowledge. In the late nineteenth century, Americans were highly literate people. By the 1880s, 90 percent of native-born white Americans were literate. According to historian Jean Ferguson Carr, literacy furthered "moral and political agendas." [2] Nineteenth-century author William Thayer advocated for reading as an alternative to "killing time," proclaiming, "what an opportunity for mental culture and religious improvement." [3] Many playtime activities taught young children how to read and, in turn, children spent their leisure hours reading for pleasure and knowledge.

The Game of Authors was a perfect combination of education and amusement, wherein "increased literary knowledge was a bonus that served to legitimatize the questionable practice of playing cards."[4] August Smith invented the game while he was a teacher at a female seminary. He wanted his girls to learn literary lessons while they were amusing themselves. He made a deck of cards divided into suits: one author card and three book cards. The objective was to match the author with their significant works. G. M. Whipple and A. A. Smith published the game in 1861.[5] *The Game of Authors* enjoyed enormous popularity, especially among church groups, in school rooms, and in the parlor; all settings where regular card-playing and dice games smacked of sin.

By 1900, there were many different versions of the game. In 1897, Parker Brothers published *The Game of Authors Illustrated* that featured famous authors of the late nineteenth century including Oliver W. Holmes, James Fenimore Cooper, and Charles Dickens. Children playing the game would learn that Nathaniel Hawthorne penned *Blithedale, The Scarlet Letter*, and *Twice Told Tales*. Charles Dickens is pictured alongside his books *Oliver Twist, Pickwick Papers*, and *David Copperfield*. Another version of the game was McLoughlin Brothers' *Queens of Literature,* which highlighted famous female authors of the day including Charlotte Brontë and Elizabeth Barrett Browning.

Whatever version of *Authors* a child played, the images of the writers would remain in their memories for a long time. Sometimes this influenced their future career choices. According to English professor Kevin J. Hayes, "In my mind's eye I can still see them . . . Mark Twain has a bushy white mustache, bushy white eyebrows, and shock of white hair: America's foxy grandpa, John Seelye calls him."[6] Author Don Webb states, "I loved the game as a child and wound up as a writer because of it."[7]

Monopoly

Monopoly
CREDIT: SUSAN A. FLETCHER

Identifying Information:

Monopoly

Maker: Charles Darrow

Manufacturer: Parker Brothers

Date: 1935

Collection of Susan A. Fletcher

During the early twentieth century, the board and card games that taught intellectual facts and transmitted moral values gradually gave way to games that added in amusement for amusement's sake to their design. By the time the 1930s rolled around, the game *Monopoly* transmitted economic theory but was also just plain fun in a way that *The Mansion of Happiness* and *The Checkered Game of Life* never were. *Monopoly* taught children and adults about property rights, monopolies on industries and utilities, real estate, and the uncertain nature of life while giving them the chance to make money. *Monopoly* flipped the rules of many early nineteenth-century games on their heads. Rather than attaining the Seat of Happiness and enjoying Happy Old Age by following a prescribed set of life circumstances, the winner of *Monopoly* was the person with the most money, gained by smart business dealings. In this passage, we'll explore the mythology of *Monopoly*'s creation, along with the impact of the Great Depression upon childhood in the 1930s.

Monopoly has a false origin myth that seems like a perfect example of the American dream. Here's how the myth goes: An out-of-work man named Charles Darrow was at his economic breaking point during the Great Depression in the early 1930s. In his third year of unemployment, Darrow had a young child and another baby on the way, so he tried to make a living by doing odd jobs and selling homemade jigsaw puzzles. He invented a game called *Monopoly*, in which players traversed around the board, accumulating property and money. He cut out a circular piece of oilcloth to make the playing board. Darrow produced handmade copies of the game and offered it to Parker Brothers.

When the company turned him down, he decided to produce the game himself, printing 5,000 copies at his own expense. He successfully sold the game at Philadelphia department stores and in FAO Schwarz in New York City. Soon, the popularity of the game convinced Parker Brothers to take a chance on it, and in the first year, the company sold half a million copies. The game made Darrow a wildly successful man, and he retired at 46.[1] Parker Brothers played up this story and gave sole credit of the game's invention to Darrow. According to journalist Calvin Trillin, the Darrow myth is a "nice, clean, well-structured example of the Eureka School of American industrial legend."[2]

The reality of the game's invention is much more complicated. In 1904, a Quaker named Elizabeth Magie invented *The Landlord's Game*. Magie was a supporter of political economist Henry George's teachings on the single tax system. In the grand tradition of nineteenth-century didactic games, Magie wanted her board game "to be educational in nature."[3] According to the patent, "The object of the game is not only to afford amusement to the players but to illustrate to them how under the present or prevailing system of land tenure, the landlord has an advantage over the other enterprises and also how the single tax system would discourage land speculation. The player who first accumulates $3,000 wins the game."[4] According to historian Tim Walsh, the game was "a practical example of the immorality of rent gouging, land monopolies, and other corporate monopolies."[5]

The Landlord's Game was popular among a niche audience of academics who liked using it in their economics classrooms. Magie's friend Ruth Hoskins enjoyed the game too, and she introduced it to her friends. One of these players, Charles Todd, reportedly introduced the game to a couple named Esther and Charles Darrow of Philadelphia in 1932.[6] Darrow liked the game and adapted it to create *Monopoly*. According to Walsh, "Charles Darrow didn't invent *Monopoly* but he developed it just like real estate, and in doing so made it more valuable."[7]

No matter who actually invented the game, *Monopoly* represents a tragic era in American childhood: the Great Depression. To anyone playing *Monopoly* during this era, it was painfully obvious that life didn't follow a simple path of success based on how well you behaved. The simple recipe for success that *The Mansion of Happiness* had taught a century before was not helpful in the 1930s.

Fate dealt harshly with families in the Great Depression, with unemployment skyrocketing to 12.5 million in 1932. One-fourth of American families didn't have an employed wage earner living in their household. The average income fell 40 percent from 1929 to 1933.[8] The Dust Bowl forced entire populations living in the plains states to move west. Families lost homes, farms, and hope.

The effect of the Great Depression on American children was devastating. With parents no longer able to reliably provide for their families, children frequently took care of themselves. Many of the gains that children had made in the late nineteenth and early twentieth century in terms of increasing leisure time and a rising standard of living disappeared in the economic crisis. Children of the Great Depression faced significant responsibilities at home, and many left home to make money for themselves.

First Lady Eleanor Roosevelt became the nation's mother-figure, and children sent letters pleading for her help. In October 1936, a teenager from Stillmore, Georgia, wrote Mrs. Roosevelt to explain her situation. The girl's father lost his grist mill in 1933. He became abusive and kept his daughters out of school. The girl was considering running away from home. She asked the First Lady for $100 to buy clothes and to help fix her decaying teeth because "my daddy hasn't the money to fix them, and he only says teeth are supposed to come out sometimes, but this is the only teeth I'll ever have."[9] In 1938, a nine-year-old girl from Boston told Roosevelt about the struggles her father was having to keep their grocery store open. "I'm always sorry because I'm still young and I can't help much . . . I thought if I wrote to You, maybe You would help us, with a little money and then with Your help I can help my father."[10]

In the context of desperate poverty, families entertained themselves at home. For parents who had enough money to afford to buy *Monopoly*, the game was a welcome release from the pressures of everyday life. Players could land financial windfalls, even if it was just with pretend money. The rules stated this plainly: "The object of the MONOPOLY game is to become the wealthiest player through buying, renting and selling property."[11]

The game has been hugely influential on generations of players. For early twenty-first century children who, for the most part, are used to having more than enough money to provide for their needs, *Monopoly* may not be quite the economic fantasy world that it would have been for kids in the 1930s. However, the game is still lots of fun. As of 2009, *Monopoly* had sold 250 million games, been translated into 37 languages, and was played in 103 countries.[12]

5

Candyland

Candyland
CREDIT: SUSAN A. FLETCHER

Identifying Information:

Candyland

Maker: Eleanor Abbott

Manufacturer: Milton Bradley

Date: 1949

Collection of Susan A. Fletcher

In the years following World War II, an epidemic of poliomyelitis gripped parental hearts with terror. During the baby boom of the 1940s and 50s, polio had a significant impact on childhood. In 1952 alone, nearly 60,000 children were infected, and 3,000 died.[1] The disease respected neither class nor race, and children from well-heeled families were just as likely to contract the virus as children of poverty. The symptoms started out mimicking those of a simple cold, but the progression of the disease sometimes resulted in paralysis and death. In this chapter, we'll explore how this childhood epidemic produced one of America's most beloved board games.

During the height of polio hysteria, the landscape of where children could play changed dramatically. Parents were anxious to shield their children from the disease, and they encouraged their kids to play inside where it was safe. Children's play ceased being largely outdoor-based and moved indoors, both to accommodate fragile victims of polio and to shelter the not-yet-infected from the disease. To curtail the spread of polio, public swimming pools closed. Movie theater patrons were encouraged to sit far apart from one another, enforcing a sense of isolation and fear. According to historian Samira Kawash, "the fear of polio in the late 1940s and early 1950s curtailed children's free play."[2]

Adults could contract the disease too. Between 1949 and 1954, adults made up 35 percent of the number of polio victims.[3] In 1948, a California teacher named Eleanor Abbott was one of these adult victims, stricken in her late thirties. She was hospitalized in a polio ward in San Diego. She made friends with her fellow patients, many of whom were children. To ease their boredom and help them recover, Abbott began making simple games for these young patients. According to historian Scott Eberle, "The ideal kind of play for these sick children would delight them with the prospect of sweeter days, captivate them without taking their physical reserves and kept them playing without making play a chore."[4] Abbott drew a racing game that featured two young children traversing through an idyllic land made of candy. Journalist Alexander B. Joy remarks, "In theme and execution, the game functions as a mobile fantasy. It simulates a leisurely stroll instead of the studied rigor of therapeutic exercises. . . . The game counters the culture of restriction imposed by both the polio scare and the disease itself."[5]

Abbott drew her game on butcher paper, and one of her friends sent the sketches to the Milton Bradley Company. The company published the game in 1949. Young children who could not yet read or even count could play the game; all they needed to know was their colors and how to match the candy pieces. So, the company marketed the game to children ages 3–6.[6]

During the late 1940s and 50s, there were not very many toys or games targeted to children in this age group. According to Kawash, "The idea of age-appropriate children's games was a product of the new emphasis on children and child-centered leisure."[7]

The game was also a product of changing demographics and the postwar economic boom. According to Kawash, "In its overt orientation toward the youngest child, Candy Land was part of a larger phenomenon: the postwar baby boom and the attendant flourishing of toys, games, and entertainment fueled by the indulgent spending of parents and grandparents."[8] The inexpensive game was affordable to most postwar families and became common in many households around the country.

The rules of the game were simple and easy enough for most young children to master quickly. At the beginning of the game, players draw one card that may feature a color or a picture. Players traverse along the board, going both forward and backward. They pass the landmarks of the Gumdrop Mountains, Lollipop Woods, and the Molasses Swamp on their quest to be the first player to reach the gingerbread-style cottage called Home Sweet Home. This wasn't exactly the pastoral Seat of Happiness, which had been the goal of *The Mansion of Happiness* one hundred years before, but Home Sweet Home was a worthy goal for sick children in the 1950s. For a child in a 1950s polio ward, a return to his or her cozy home was the ultimate dream.

After she recovered from polio, Eleanor Abbott used the profits that she made from her game to improve the lives of the children around her. She purchased equipment and supplies for schools and contributed to children's charities.[9] *Candyland* remains a perennial favorite. Between 1975–1995, the game sold 23 million copies, and it continues to be among the first board games that young children learn how to play.

Part II

ART TOYS

Through various playtime activities, children in the nineteenth and twentieth centuries learned how to cultivate their art skills. The pieces they created cultivated the initiative and creativity befitting citizens of a vigorous, expanding nation. As young Lucy Larcom of New England learned in the 1820s and 30s, "it was our duty to develop any talent we might possess . . . to do some one thing which the world needed, or which would make it a pleasanter world."[1] There were practical barriers to making the world better through art, however. Both art-making supplies and practical art instruction were expensive in the early nineteenth century, which often put art education out of reach for most families. This part will explore the expansion of the availability of art supplies for children.

During the nineteenth century, middle-class American parents wanted their children, especially their daughters, to have an aesthetic education. Artistic ability was a marker of class status; it showed that parents had enough resources to educate their children beyond the basic subjects. In an age where understanding culture was essential to social progress, a child who could converse intelligently about the fine arts or create art pieces could achieve upward class mobility during adulthood. A nation of citizens actively contributing to the fledgling American art and music scene could secure a place of respect in the Western world. Patronizing the arts legitimatized the middle class, showing that this young nation was just as sophisticated as its European counterparts.

In the 1830s, future author Lucy Larcom decided that she wanted to be an artist when she grew up to make the world better through beauty. She recalled, "A slate and pencil, to draw pictures, was my first request whenever a day's ailment kept me at home from school; and I rather enjoyed being a little ill, for the sake of amusing myself in that way."[2] Unfortunately, art teachers were hard to find in Massachusetts during this time, and her parents could not afford one anyway. She recalled, "If I could only make a rose bloom on paper, I thought I should be happy! Or if I could at last succeed in drawing the outline of winter-stripped boughs as I saw them against the sky, it seemed to me that I should be willing to spend years in trying. I did try a little, and very often."[3] She taught herself how to draw with the assistance of her older sister Emilie, who supplied a set of pencils and a paint box. The girls also took inspiration from nature in their learning process.

As the century progressed, creative children had more options for real artistic instruction. Horace Mann implemented drawing as a core subject in Massachusetts schools as part of his education reform movement.[4] Soon, a new industry arose centered around art books and kits for children. One of the first drawing books created for this audience was *Drawing for Young Children* in 1838. The book had pictures of fruit, flowers, animals, and toys for children to copy. Other publications and kits followed. *Slate Pictures for the Useful Self-Employment of Young Children* had cards with pictures of objects for children to draw. The *Little Folks Color Kit* likewise had scenes for children to copy as well as a book of instructions, but it added tubes of watercolor and oil paints, as well as drawing pencils.[5] Professional artist Louis Prang published a series of *Art Textbooks* for the serious young student.

An education in art history was important too. For this subject, parlor games were an acceptable substitute for families who could not afford to send their children to see the great painters of Europe. In the late nineteenth century, the Picture Study Movement encouraged both children and grown-ups to study the masterworks of famous painters.[6] The game *Gems of Art* provided five ways that children could learn about Western artwork from Hellenic pieces to the Impressionists.[7]

This part will explore the development of children's art materials and art toys from the 1850s through the 1980s. Over the course of 130 years, art-making became increasingly accessible to most children in America. The advent of nontoxic paints meant that young kids could use watercolors without fear of the dangerous minerals that professional-quality paints contained, like cadmium and barium. The invention of Crayola Crayons put affordable art materials in the hands of most children, regardless of economic status. Play-Doh turned an everyday household product into one of the most iconic children's toys of all time. The Etch A Sketch followed active children of the 1970s wherever they wanted to go. Lastly, the Spirograph sneakily taught mathematical principles in the guise of a fun art toy.

6

Drawing and Painting Sets

PLAQUE.

(Doulton and Co.)

Vintage engraving of The Young Creatives, nineteenth century. Little boy painting and little girl holding pan pipes.

CREDIT: DUNCAN1980 CREATIVE #1093611110 COLLECTION: DIGITAL VISION VECTORS

27

Identifying Information:

Drawing and Painting Sets

A ccording to anthropologists Barbara Wittmann and Christopher Barber, "Since the establishment of drawing as an autonomous artistic practice in the Italian Renaissance, and especially since drawing materials became increasingly available around 1800, children's drawings have been created in growing abundance."[1] Drawing and painting provided children outlets for their creativity and imaginations. By the end of the nineteenth century, a variety of manufacturers marketed art supply sets and instruction books to children.

Drawing and painting education in the United States was born of European influence in the early nineteenth century. In 1843, Horace Mann traveled to Prussia while honeymooning with his wife, Mary. According to art historian Elizabeth Dunford, "While in Prussia, he was impressed with the way educators there used drawing as a type of language, as an aid to teaching writing, and as a means of appreciating beauty."[2] When he returned home, Mann implemented drawing as a core subject in Massachusetts schools. He thought art would help children develop moral and practical sense, all of which were vital to producing the best American citizens possible in the nineteenth century. In *The Common School Journal*, he wrote,

> Teaching a child to draw, then, is the development in him of a new talent—the conferring upon him, as it were, of a new sense—by means of which he is not only better enabled to attend to the common duties of life, and to be more serviceable to his fellow-men, but he is more likely to appreciate the beauties and magnificence of nature, which everywhere reflect the glories of the Creator into his soul. When accompanied by appropriate instruction of a moral and religious character, this accomplishment becomes a quickner to devotion. With

the inventive genius of our people, the art of drawing would be eminently useful. They would turn it to better account than any other people in the world.[3]

Despite Mann's enthusiasm about drawing education, acquiring proper art supplies during this period was challenging. Drawing tools and paints were hard to come by in the early republic, especially for children who lived away from urban centers. Almost all of these supplies had to be imported from Europe, and the minerals they contained made them dangerous for kids.

Professional artist Louis Prang did something about that. Born in present-day Poland, he studied art in Bohemia. He came to the United States in 1850 as a political refugee and settled in Boston. Prang believed that every child should make art because it quickened their imaginations and that they deserved access to proper supplies.[4] Prang had a young daughter and was concerned that the art supplies available to her in the mid-nineteenth century were toxic. Hazardous pigments like cadmium and barium comprised the watercolors that adult artists were using. It was nearly impossible to find paint that was safe for young children, who might eat the colors instead of putting them on paper.

In 1856, Prang entered a business deal with the American Crayon Company to manufacturer watercolor sets that were formulated for kids. The "No. 8" paint set included pans of carmine, gamboge (yellow), ultramarine, Hooker's green, violet, warm sepia, orange, and charcoal gray. This invention made paint sets available to most children—not just professional artists.[5]

In the 1860s, Prang began publishing drawing instruction books and drawing cards that children could copy. His fascination with Transcendental philosophy and a love of nature influenced his famous Art Textbooks. In the Prang Book II, students were instructed to "Come out of doors with paint-box and brush! Come to a clear little pool in a meadow! The world is dressed in blue, yellow and green."[6] The company continued to publish art instruction books well into the twentieth century, such as 1910's Progressive Drawing Books.

Watercolor and drawing developed into a favorite leisure activity for nineteenth-century children as access to materials and instruction increased. After she taught herself to paint, Lucy Larcom enjoyed using her newfound skills: "I went on writing little books of ballads," she recalled, "which I illustrated with colors from my toy paint box, and then squeezed them down into the cracks of the garret floor, for fear that somebody would find them."[7]

Soon, other manufacturers got into the art supply and instruction business. Milton Bradley produced the Little Folks Color Kit in 1890. The box cover depicts a young lady creating a masterpiece at her easel. These art sets were marketed to girls because an aesthetic education was an essential part of girlhood in this era. The kit came with watercolor cards that depicted scenes of nature, a paintbrush, and compartments for paint tubes.[8] In 1880, the McLoughlin Brothers published the first coloring book: *The Little Folks Painting Book*.[9]

In the late nineteenth century, academics working in art history, psychology, and the child study movement "discovered children's drawings as objects of knowledge."[10] For the first time in history, children's art was taken seriously as a window into their inner world. In Europe, librarian and art historian Corrado Ricci began a study of children's drawings in the context of art history. Psychologists examined drawings as a means to analyze the young artist's emotional well-being.

Starting in the early twentieth century, a variety of other art tools and art toys became available for children. Pretty soon, Crayola Crayons and Play-Doh would join nontoxic watercolors and pencils in a child's toy box. We'll learn more about these in the rest of this chapter.

Crayola Crayons

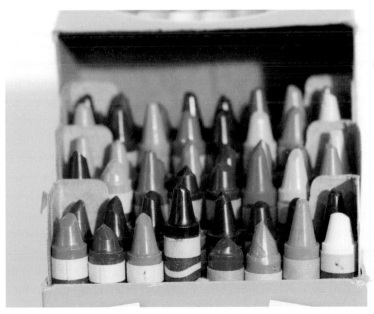

Crayola Crayons have allowed children to express their creativity for almost 120 years.
CREDIT: SUSAN A. FLETCHER

Identifying Information:

Crayola Crayons

Maker: Binney & Smith Company

Manufacturer: Binney & Smith Company

Date: 1903

Collection of Susan A. Fletcher

In the late 2010s, adults returned to their childhood roots and began to color again. With the publication of Johanna Basford's intricate coloring book *The Secret Garden*, a grown-up coloring phenomenon swept the world. *Smithsonian Magazine* called the trend "a childhood pastime retrofitted for frazzled grown-ups."[1] Basford, a graphic designer, remarked, "for years my clients ha[d] been telling me when they see my illustrations that they wanted to color them in."[2] For these grown-ups, the impulse to color stayed with them long past childhood. In a social media post on Facebook in 2015, National Public Radio asked readers, "Are you an adult who likes to color?" User Helen Nieuwenhuis commented, "I love to color! I have great memories as a kid, my mom would bring out the construction paper, tape, crayons, glue, etc., and it was ON. I still color, and I am almost 60."[3] Coloring is a transcendent part of American childhood—made possible by Crayola Crayons.

It's hard to imagine a world without a bright yellow Crayola Crayon box in every household. In the early 1900s, business partners and cousins Edwin Binney and C. Harold Smith manufactured pigments for paint. They had created a special kind of carbon black.[4] They used this carbon black to create a black marking crayon out of paraffin wax. They used this crayon to mark shipping boxes for their company Binney & Smith Co.

Edwin and Harold knew that teachers frequently complained about the messy and dusty nature of chalk, so the business partners started making dustless chalk and other art supplies for classrooms. When their staff visited teachers to sell these products, they noticed students using professional European artist crayons. These crayons were messy, very expensive, and hard to obtain in many areas.[5] So Binney and Smith transformed their black box-marking crayon into the solution to these problems. Their new crayons would be affordable, tidy, and easy to use.

Edwin's wife Alice came up with the name for this new product, combining the French words *craie* (chalk) with *oleaginous* (oily) into the now famous name Crayola.[6] In 1903, they manufactured the first boxes of Crayola Crayons in eight colors: black, red, orange, yellow, green, purple, brown, and blue.[7] They were marketed for "educational color work"[8] and the yellow boxes sold for only five cents.

Crayola Crayons were affordable, clean, and portable. They appealed to a broad age range: high school art students could use them in the classroom, while their toddler siblings clutched them in their chubby fingers at home. Crayolas also transcended language and communication barriers—children who couldn't read at all could use them just as well as their older siblings. Immigrant children who spoke little English could use crayons to express themselves.

Crayola brought art supplies to working-class families who had previously struggled to afford these kinds of materials. In 1917, seven-year-old Ted Wasserman saw his first box of crayons at a cousin's house. Ted fell in love with the crayons and wanted a box of his own, but even at ten cents per box, they were still pricy for his impoverished family. A few months later, a kind aunt gave him a dime, which he spent on a box of his very own Crayola's. He still couldn't afford real drawing paper, so he drew on brown grocery bags and sandwich wrappers. The crayons gave him the tools and experience he needed to launch a professional art career.[9]

Crayola eventually produced eight more colors in addition to the originals. Then, in 1949, the company produced forty-eight colors, followed by the famous sixty-four pack in 1958. The new color names followed historic events of the twentieth century. Burnt Sienna was popular after WWII when browns were popular in interior design. Carnation Pink came out in the 1950s when bathroom fixtures and kitchens were bright pink. During the Civil Rights movement, the Flesh-colored crayon had its name changed to Peach.[10] Aquamarine followed in the 1960s, and then neon colors came out in the 1970s.

By the 1990s, urban children had lost their connection to America's rural past. Adults were concerned that kids were staying indoors all day and not playing outside anymore. They weren't even making mud pies. When Crayola made a crayon called Dirt in 1995, newspaper columnist Henry Wolff used the crayon as a way to talk about this unfortunate state of being. He sarcastically wrote, "I'm just not sure a dirt crayon will solve the problem, children being as starved as they seem to be for dirt, but at least it will give some children an opportunity to see what dirt is all about."[11]

Although the color names of Crayola Crayons have much to do with change over time in American history, the multitude of colors represented something else altogether for the children using them. They meant total freedom. Children could draw anything they wanted to in whatever color their heart desired. This freedom often subverted adult expectations of how things ought to look. In 1983, the "The Upper Room" newspaper column recounted the story of a parent who purchased a box of sixty-four Crayolas and a drawing pad for a young daughter. One day, the parent looked in the girl's sketchbook. The author remarked, "I was shocked and puzzled. On the page was a bright, rainbow-colored elephant . . . in my mind I had set limits as to what she could do with her crayons. In her mind, she was determined to use *all* crayons; there were no limits. It was her drawing pad, her crayons, her choice."[12]

Crayola Crayons served as the gateway to the larger world of art for many children. Binney & Smith Co. implied that using their product would allow the genius of the great masters of the past to inhabit the modern-day student. They produced one pack of crayons that they called "Rubens' Crayola Crayons," with an image of the Flemish master Peter Paul Rubens on the box.[13] Maybe genius did flow from Rubens to modern-day children; many professional visual artists got their start by using Crayolas. In 1905, fourteen-year-old art student Grant Wood drew a picture of oak leaves for a Crayola coloring competition, winning third place.[14] In the 1930s, grown-up Wood secured his place in American art history when he captured the iconic image of a farmer and his sister in *American Gothic*.[15]

Crayola has done exceptionally well for itself over the last 116 years. In that time, Crayola has produced 600 shades of colors and sold more than 100 *billion* crayons all over the world.[16] Children use on average 730 crayons by the time they turn ten.[17]

What became of Ted Wasserman, who bought his first crayons in 1918? He had a long career as a professional artist himself. During the Great Depression, he helped paint work-relief murals. After World War II, he became a well-known figure painter in Utah. In the 1970s, Wasserman and his wife met a wealthy woman named Dorothy Palmer. After a few years of friendship, Palmer asked Wasserman how he became an artist, so he told her the story of how he got started in art with Crayola Crayons. He was surprised when she started crying. She said, "You need to know that my maiden name is Binney and my father invented Crayons and Crayolas! Neither he nor I ever dreamed that one small box of Crayons could help launch such a splendid career!"[18] She later surprised the couple with a big check and a note that read, "I hope, Ted, this will make up for the candy you had to give up as a child in order to buy Crayons."[19]

8

Play-Doh

Play-Doh provides a wonderful creative outlet for children.
CREDIT: SDI PRODUCTIONS CREATIVE # 866452962 COLLECTION: E+

Identifying Information:

Play-Doh

Maker: N. W. McVicker

Manufacturer: Kutol Products/Rainbow Crafts/Kenner/Hasbro

Date: 1955

What is the first thing that comes to mind when you peel open a jar of Play-Doh and inhale the distinctive scent of its contents? For blogger and designer Alexa Westerfeld, "When I opened it up and smelled that Play-Doh smell it took me back. I can fondly recall the days of sitting on the brown carpet in my Grandmother's den, playing with the Play-Doh factory tool and making strings of spaghetti."[1] There's a reason why the scent of Play-Doh vaults us back to our childhoods. In a wonder of neurobiology, our brains process smell and memories in a similar region of the brain, which means that scents are often linked to time-and-place recollections. According to historian Tim Walsh, "The pleasant aroma of Play-Doh can move us and yes, restore our lost balance to mind, body, and soul."[2]

Like Crayola Crayons, Play-Doh began its life as an industrial product. Before World War II, most American homes were heated with coal, which created a cleaning nightmare for homeowners. Black soot on the wallpaper couldn't be washed off with soap and water lest the wallpaper be ruined. So, homemakers made cleaning dough out of water, salt, aluminum sulfate, kerosene, and flour. These homemade mixtures were crumbly and sometimes created bigger messes than what they were intended to clean. Soon, companies began to manufacture their own versions of this cleaning dough. In newspaper advertisements, Clean Wall Paper Cleaner billed itself as "the genuine, non-crumbling wallpaper cleaner. Always firm—always pliable—doesn't get tacky."[3] So, how did a commercial cleaning product become a children's toy?

Kutol, a small soap company from Cincinnati, Ohio, got into the wallpaper cleaning business after some rocky financial years. The company was making powdered soap in the early 1930s, but because of the Great Depression things were not going well for them. In 1933, Kutol's parent company sent Cleo McVicker to shutter Kutol. Upon arriving, instead of closing the factory, McVicker decided that he was going to try saving it. He thought of other products they could sell, looking for ways to solve existing needs. Kroger Grocery Stores told him that they needed more wallpaper cleaner, and McVicker entered a deal to sell them some.[4] The only problem was that he didn't know anything about making wallpaper cleaner! He told his brother and plant manager N. W. McVicker to figure out how to manufacture and produce 15,000 cases of the cleaner, which he did. Soon, Kutol Wall Cleaner was available for sale in red tins.

The technological innovations of the late 1940s and early 1950s would soon impact Kutol again. Once oil- and gas-powered heaters replaced coal-burning furnaces in homes, homemakers didn't need to clean soot off their walls anymore.[5] It looked like the product that had gotten them through the Great Depression was going to fail Kutol in the postwar era.

Meanwhile, Joe McVicker's sister-in-law Kay Zufall was having problems of her own. She was a preschool teacher in New Jersey, and one Christmas she decided to make some clay Christmas tree ornaments with her students. Traditional modeling clay wasn't malleable enough for her young students. She read a magazine article about using wallpaper cleaner for this purpose and bought a jar of Kutol at her local hardware store. Her students rolled out the dough and cut it into shapes. She told her brother-in-law Joe, "You can make that stuff into a toy!"[6]

The business partners changed the wallpaper formula to remove the solvents and started marketing it as Kutol's Rainbow Modeling Compound in 1955. They took the product to a national education convention, and it was instantly successful. Kay and her husband, Bob, came up with a better name for the product: Play-Doh, "the CLEAN modeling compound for young children."[7]

The new age of television in the 1950s exposed children and their parents to all sorts of products and new toys, which created a big demand for Play-Doh. A television commercial from the late 1950s asserted, "Every child wants Play-Doh. Over 5 million new users every year testify to Play-Doh's quality, and fun. Teachers like Play-Doh for its creative, educational value."[8] The commercial also told children how they ought to be using the product: they could make Christmas ornaments, necklaces, and even figurines made of pipe cleaners. After taking over production of Play-Doh in 1956, Rainbow Crafts produced all kinds of accessories, including the famous Fun Factory. This kit contained an extruder and a set of dies so children could squish the dough into various shapes and strands. They also sold Play-Packs that included a plastic tablecloth, cookie cutters, and rolling pin—everything a child needed to use the product cleanly and efficiently.

Rainbow Crafts started producing the toy in 1956, followed by Kenner in 1970 and Hasbro in 1991. Kenner added different dyes to the product in the 1970s to make brighter colors and continued producing playsets and related items. During the last few decades of the twentieth century, some of these new accessories directed children's play in overt ways. Whereas the Play-Doh ads of the 1950s suggested general categories of things to make such as Christmas Ornaments, the playset products directed children toward making specific things in specific ways. The Dr. Drill-N-Fill and the Fuzzy Pumper Barber and Beauty Shop of the 1970s allowed children to mimic the adult world by playing dentist and barber.

By the late 1970s and early 1980s, Baby Boomers who grew up using Play-Doh in the mid-century had children of their own. Play-Doh marketing tapped into this sense of nostalgia in many of their commercials. In the early 1980s, one ad depicted a mother talking to Play-Doh Pete saying, "Hey, I remember you!" to which Pete replied, "I remember you too!"[9]

For parents who didn't want to buy commercially manufactured Play-Doh, making it at home was (and still is) a good alternative. When I was little, my grandma used to cook up a batch of homemade Play-Doh to take to the Sunday School class that she taught every week to three-year-olds. The students who decided to eat the compound were greeted with a surprisingly salty (yet still safe to eat) mouthful. The real-deal Play-Doh continues to be one of the most popular toys in American history though. According to Hasbro, over 700 million pounds of Play-Doh have been produced since 1955, with 100 million cans selling annually.[10]

Etch A Sketch

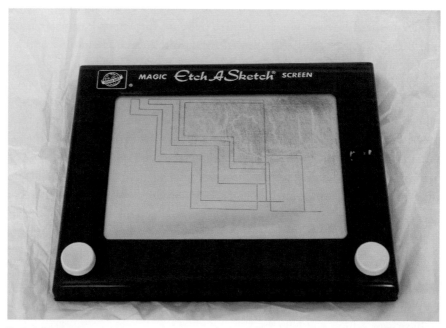

Etch A Sketch
CREDIT: SUSAN A. FLETCHER

Identifying Information:

Etch A Sketch

Maker: Andre Cassagnes

Manufacturer: Ohio Art

Date: 1959

Collection of Susan A. Fletcher

A writer who grew up in the 1970s recalled, "The Etch A Sketch seemed like magic to us kids, like something you'd see in Willy Wonka's factory, conjuring images out of nothing. I remember thinking, 'is it drawing *on* the screen or taking something *off* the screen?'"[1] The Etch A Sketch is an art toy that combines mechanical engineering with the allure of mysterious functionality. In the late twentieth century, it followed children wherever they went and allowed even the most untalented child to create art.

This self-sufficient device allows its user to create art using nothing but the toy. The Etch A Sketch allowed children of the late twentieth century to use it in all sorts of places that other art supplies like a watercolor set couldn't go. A 1973 Etch A Sketch commercial invited kids to "Draw anything your mind conceives anywhere you have to be."[2] The TV spot showed girls and boys using Etch A Sketch while getting a haircut at the barbershop, in the car, and before bedtime. The child of the 1970s had so many more places to go than a child of the 1870s—and the Etch A Sketch served this extended geographical range.

In 1959, a French electrical technician named Andre Cassagnes invented a mechanical toy he called the *L'Ecran Magique* or Magic Screen. One day, "while fitting a plate over an electric-light switch, he noticed that pencil marks he had made on the protective decal were transferred to the other side when he took it off."[3] It was a self-contained drawing screen, and inside it held static-charged aluminum powder and plastic beads.[4] Historian Tim Walsh gives a lesson on the internal mechanism:

> Once in motion, static electricity causes the powder to stick to the underside of the glass screen, giving the Etch A Sketch surface its silvery appearance. Next, the white knobs act to move two rods (which are connected to a stylus) by a system of pulleys threaded with nylon string. Twisting one knob controls horizontal lines and twisting the other controls vertical lines by dragging the tip of the stylus across the underside of the screen. The powder drops to the bottom of the casing and—tada—a black line or "etch" appears.[5]

Cassagnes couldn't afford the fee to patent his invention, so he found an investor named Paul Chaze to help. Chaze finally hired an American agent, who put him in touch with Ohio Art. William Killgallon of Ohio Art loved the toy and renamed it Etch A Sketch.[6] Cassagnes collaborated with Ohio Art's chief engineer Jerry Burger to perfect the invention. Unfortunately, Cassagnes never received the fame that he was due for inventing the toy, but he did live an amicable life making kites for children and taking strolls in France before his death in 2013.[7]

Ohio Art produced the first Etch A Sketch in July 1960, which happened concurrent to the rise of children's television and commercials. The toy's design resembles a television with a blank screen. It was up to the child to draw the picture that they wanted to see on the screen. Moreover, it was through the television that the Etch A Sketch exploded in popularity. Ohio Art created an immediate demand for Etch A Sketch and its sister product Magnasticks through a blitz of commercials. By Christmas 1960, it was the must-have toy for every child in America.

In 1967, Ohio Art hailed Etch A Sketch as the "favorite drawing toy of the century!"[8] The marketing campaign appealed to a generation of parents who were deeply invested in their children's futures, proclaiming that the Etch A Sketch was "for people who love children."[9] Ohio Art made sure parents knew the toy was "appealing to all ages, challenging, creative, entertaining, original, educational, travel-perfect, relaxing, timeless in value, and intriguing."[10]

The toy did inspire some children to become professional artists. Young George Vlosich used the Etch A Sketch to draw a picture of the Capitol building in Washington, DC, on a family vacation when he was ten years old. Later, he enrolled as a student at the Cleveland Institute of Art and has since made a career out of the medium.[11] During the 2012 presidential campaign, Mitt Romney's advisor Eric Fehrnstrom likened the fall campaign shake-ups to an Etch A Sketch, so Vlosich took advantage of the moment and created a portrait of Romney using the toy.

The key to making a piece of Etch A Sketch art last forever is to disable its most prominent feature: the ability to erase by merely shaking. After creating a satisfactory piece, artists drill holes in the Etch A Sketch to drain out all of the aluminum powder and beads—thus destroying the capacity to erase the drawing. For children, though, there is something charming about being able to start all over again when they make a mistake.

Etch A Sketch remains a favorite toy in 2020, and Ohio Art has produced over 100 million worldwide.[12] It was inducted into the National Toy Hall of Fame in 1998. In an interview with *Tech Times*, Ohio Art President Martin Killgallon remarked, "We like to say Etch A Sketch . . . it's easy to play with, but it's not easy to master, so I think that's a clear reason why it's thrived for 55 years."[13]

Spirograph

Spirograph Art

Identifying Information:

Spirograph

Maker: Denys Fisher

Manufacturer: Hasbro/Kenner/Kahootz Toys

Date: 1965

For Christmas one year, I received a Spirograph kit and spent the rest of the day playing with it. My pens went around and around in the plastic cogwheels, making colorful swirls. Little did I know that this toy was teaching me *math*. For art-loving children of the late twentieth century, Spirograph was an introduction to engineering, science, and mathematics.

Spirograph is a Vietnam War–era toy derived from the German Kinematic models of the late nineteenth century. In the 1880s, math educators in the United States used slices of wooden cones to demonstrate parabolas and hyperbolas. Kinematic models helped students understand principles involving motion. The Martin Schilling Company produced many of these educational tools, including a set of metal cogwheels that helped students understand straight-line motion and trochoids. The National Museum of American History explains that trochoids are "curves that are generated by tracing the motion of a point on the radius of a circle as it rolls along another curve."[1]

In 1907, the E. I. Horsman Company produced a drawing model called The Wondergraph, which used these same principles to help people draw curves and lines. An advertisement in the 1908 Sears catalog proclaimed, "The Wondergraph makes, as if by magic, beautiful designs, such as no artist could draw. A child can operate it. . . . This not only will teach the youngest child how to design very beautiful patterns but will suggest to a draftsman patterns which he had never thought of before."[2] In the 1930s, a similar product called the Dizzy Doodler came out, followed by The Magic Designer in 1949. It's hard to know how many children played with these toys, but they never were the cultural phenomenon that Spirograph would soon enjoy in the 1960s. According to historian Tim Walsh, "Spirograph proved to be the right toy at the right time."[3]

While working with NATO to design bomb detonators, British engineer Denys Fisher decided to create a drawing toy based on the principles of hypocycloids.[4] In his work, he used a series of metal cogs and a pen to depict sine and cosine waves. He hoped to market this new method of drawing as a useful tool for draftsmen. He promoted his kit as "Pattern Drawing by Revolving Stencils."[5]

He took this kit to the 1965 Nuremberg Toy Fair, where Kenner Toys acquired the rights to produce the toy in the United States.[6] Kenner sold the first Spirograph set in 1967. It came with twenty-seven pieces including gears, rings, and pens with colored ink. The company sold over 5.5 million sets in the first year of production.

The Spirograph came on the market in the United States during the Vietnam War and the social upheaval of the late 1960s. So much was changing, but the predictability and logic of Spirograph seemed like a haven of control and certainty amid a cloudy American future. Design professor John Bowers received his Spirograph at the beginning of the war. He recalls,

> Soon my brother would receive his draft lottery number. Perhaps the Spirograph offered a bit of rationality and order to the chaos. It was predictable and socially safe. Any combination of templates and color would result in a Spirograph manual "sanctioned" design. The toy gave the illusion of counterculture experimentation, yet furthered the establishment adherence to staying the course.[7]

The timing of Spirograph's release also coincided with the psychedelic art movement of the late 1960s and early 1970s. A Spirograph commercial from 1973 positioned the toy in the lingo of the art world: "Groovy designs, super designs . . . get the fever, the fabulous fever of Spiromania."[8] The toy inspired some children to become designers themselves. Artist Martin Venezky recalls, "It combined two of my loves, mathematics, and drawing, and I can still feel the physical balance between freedom and structure that the toy provided."[9]

In addition to inspiring art students, the Spirograph rolled along as a source of mathematical education. Math teachers across the United States used Spirograph in the classrooms as a tool to help their students understand parametric equations. In 1999, students in Connecticut teacher Dennis Ippolito's class used their graphic calculators to simulate the curves of the Spirograph.[10]

Over time, the toy declined in popularity. Outside of its historical context of the chaos of the 1960s and the psychedelic art movement, it made sense only as a drawing toy. By the 1980s, Hasbro no longer marketed the toy to girls and boys interested in math—it merely became a method of keeping young children entertained. "It became less of a drafting kit and more of a toy for young children," according to Brent Oeschger, cofounder of Kahootz Toys.[11] Hasbro stopped marketing the toy in the late 1990s. In the mid-2010s, Ann Arbor-based Kahootz Toys convinced Hasbro to bring Spirograph back for a new generation of children and is manufacturing it as of 2020.

Part III

OPTICAL TOYS AND CAMERAS

Twenty-first-century children spend much of their days in front of glowing screens, watching television and playing on their "devices." We tend to think of this phenomenon as the scourge of our modern age, but optical devices have always fascinated American children, from the colonial era until today. In the 1700s, Enlightenment philosophy fostered a reverence for science and logic in the American colonies. In the late 1820s, William Clarke, author of *The Boy's Own Book,* proposed that "the science of optics affords an infinite variety of amusements, which cannot fail to instruct the mind as well as delight the eye."[1] Clarke promised that his optical amusements would enable children to comprehend the marvels of heaven and earth.[2] Nineteenth-century children learned the principles of optics through hands-on learning. They made their own camera obscuras, magic lanterns, kaleidoscopes, thaumatropes, and cosmoramas. These objects brought the faraway world close to home and enabled children to document their lives.

Such forms of technology connected children's playtime to current events. With optical technology rapidly changing during the nineteenth century, children needed to understand discoveries like photography. In *The American Boy's Handy Book*, Daniel Beard likened his version of the phantasmascope to "the instantaneous photographs taken nowadays of people, horses, and other animals in motion, [which] opens a new field for investigation and one which, with the aid of the simple toy described, will be found very entertaining as well as instructive."[3]

This part explores three optical toys and two cameras. The Magic Lantern gave late nineteenth-century children opportunities to make money by hosting lantern shows. The stereoscope brought faraway places closer to home via three-dimensional photography, as did the View-Master. The Brownie Camera and home movie cameras gave children a way to document the intimate world around them.

Magic Lantern

Magic Lantern
CREDIT: MANX_IN_THE_WORLD CREATIVE #93439416 ISTOCK/GETTY IMAGES PLUS

Identifying Information:

Magic Lantern

In November 2000, a dancer named Jody Sperling had a tribute show to nineteenth-century dancer Loie Fuller. In a small studio in New York, she reconstructed Fuller's famous "Serpentine Dance." Sperling projected Magic Lantern images from Hans Christian Andersen's "Little Mermaid," and drawings of Presidents Washington and Lincoln on the wall behind her as she danced. The Magic Lantern is good for creating authentic nineteenth-century special effects for modern audiences. The Magic Lantern was also good for helping children living the real nineteenth century to earn money, as this chapter will explore.

The name "Magic Lantern" sounds very exciting, doesn't it? What exactly is this device? According to T. H. McAllister's catalog of lantern slides, "a Magic Lantern consists essentially of: 1st, a source of light; 2d [sic], a case to enclose the light; 3d, [sic] condensing lenses; 4th, object glasses." The Magic Lantern used the light of a candle or lamp to project images from a glass slide onto a blank wall or screen. Alternatively, the images could be projected onto a cloud of smoke if a child wished to create ghostly "phantasmagoria" images.

The magic lantern in general is a very old device, likely invented in the 1660s by Christiaan Huygens.[1] In the eighteenth century, the toy was a popular teaching tool in England. By 1840, magic lanterns were widely available in the United States. Parents who were anxious to infuse education into their children's playtime loved magic lanterns. According to McAllister's *Catalogue of Stereopticons, Dissolving-View Apparatus, and Magic Lanterns,*

"No other optical instrument has ever caused so much wonder and delight." For centuries it was regarded as a mere toy for the amusement of children, but in time, its capabilities as a means of education and intelligent entertainment were recognized . . . and as a result, the Magic Lantern has been raised to the position of a scientific instrument, of vast service in the instruction of youth, and the entertainment of the family circle.[2]

As an entertainment device, the Magic Lantern gave nineteenth-century children business opportunities. In 1886, *Ladies Home Journal* bribed kids to enlist new subscribers to the magazine. For only ten new subscribers to the *LHJ*, children received a Magic Lantern Show Kit, complete with the lantern, slides, show-bills, and tickets.[3] The magazine promised, "Any person who gets a lantern [will] give delightful evening entertainments in churches, school rooms, and their own homes, charging an admission of 10 cents or more, and make $5 and upwards on each exhibition."[4]

The idea of a child earning money purely for his or her amusement was new in the late nineteenth century. Although kids of the laboring classes still worked to supplement the family economy, middle-class children had gained freedom from the necessity to work, along with increasing amounts of leisure time. The lantern shows were opportunities for these middle-class children to cultivate their entrepreneurial skills. An advertisement in the 1904 *Journal of Education* proclaimed, "There is no form for entertainment more instructive or more pleasing than a good magic lantern or stereopticon exhibition. . . . Now when the long winter evenings are at hand, there is a good opportunity to make money by giving exhibitions of this kind."[5] As film historian Meredith Bak observes, "Domestic shows with toy lanterns allowed children to perform as curators, showmen, and audience members. This play naturalized such home entertainment as a commodifiable experience."[6] Kids could charge admission to these shows and earn their own money, presumably to spend on whatever they wanted to buy.

The Magic Lantern gradually fell out of popularity. Cameras and movies eventually supplanted the Magic Lantern in the American imagination. By the 1930s, mentions of the Magic Lantern had faded from newspapers except for a brief mention about one being donated to Barnard's German department to help educate students.[7] In this rest of this chapter, we'll explore a few more optical devices that captivated children over the course of the nineteenth and twentieth centuries.

Stereoscope

Stereoscope viewer and cards
CREDIT: SUSAN A. FLETCHER

Identifying Information:

Stereoscope Viewer and Cards

Manufacturer: Underwood and Underwood, New York

Date: Late-1800s

Collection of Susan A. Fletcher

If you visit a Victorian house museum, you'll probably see a stereoscope viewer and its accompanying cards laying on a table in the parlor. This simple device turned two-dimensional photographs into a three-dimensional world, creating the illusion that the viewer was standing inside the scene. Just like Magic Lantern slides, stereoscope images brought the big, bright world a little closer to American children. This expanded the horizons of nineteenth-century children and allowed them to experience places they might never have the opportunity to visit themselves.

The stereoscope operates under the principle of depth perception. This phenomenon is created when our eyes receive two slightly different images at the same time. Euclid discovered this principle in AD 280. During the Renaissance, Leonardo da Vinci and Johannes Kepler did more work with depth perception and used the concept in some of their experiments. In 1838, Sir Charles Wheatstone discovered that if he drew pictures of the same image from different perspectives and put those two pictures side by side, something interesting happened: the human brain puts the two images together, and the viewer perceives the scene as three-dimensional.[1] Wheatstone coined the term "stereoscope" in 1838 at the Royal Society and created a special viewing device for his side-by-side drawings.

In 1849, scientist David Brewster improved upon Wheatstone's stereoscope viewer and created a device that contained prisms, which merged the two images. Photographic technology was advancing rapidly during this era. Brewster discovered that if he pasted two photographic images of the same scene on a card, taken a slight distance apart, his viewing device would render them in three dimensions. A French company manufactured the first commercially available stereoscope viewer based on Brewster's model. This new stereoscope viewer debuted at the Great Exhibition in London in 1851. Apparently, Queen Victoria tested it out and loved it.[2]

Oliver Wendell Holmes liked the technology too and helped invent the Holmes-Bates stereopticon viewer. He mounted side-by-side photographs to stiff gray and tan cards and inserted these cards into a metal slot on his viewer, which he would move forward and backward to focus the 3-D images. This is the model of stereoscope viewer that really took off in the Victorian age because it was very light and portable. Seeing photographs in 3-D was a mind-bending experience to Americans of the mid-nineteenth century. Holmes quipped, "The mind feels its way into the very depths of the picture. The scraggy branches of a tree in the foreground run out at us as if they would scratch our eyes out."[3]

By 1856, the stereoscope was one of the most common sources of entertainment for citizens in both Europe and North America. That year, the London Stereoscopic Company had 10,000 scenic stereoscope cards available to its customers.[4] During the American Civil War, residents of both the North and South could buy stereoscopic cards that had images of the war, bringing the conflict home in horrific detail. Only a few decades earlier, the only way to experience battle scenes would have been to view them through the artists' canvas or sketchbook. Now, people could see these events in three-dimensions.

Holmes prophesied the stereoscope's ability to bring together people from all parts of the world, remarking, "The stereoscope is to be the card of introduction to make all mankind acquainted."[5] A 1909 advertisement declared, "The best way to acquaint children's minds with foreign objects and foreign modes of living, next to letting them actually visit the different places of interest, is with the Stereoscope."[6] The technology was affordable to most middle-class families. Viewers sold for sixty-nine cents and cards were five cents each in 1909.

Although Victorians played with the stereoscope as a form of amusement, the devices were educational too, and that appealed to parents who wanted their kids to use their leisure time well. In his catalog of stereoscope and Magic Lantern views, T. H. McAllister stated: "In the education of youth, the value of pictorial illustration is accepted as the most efficient mode of fixing ideas in the mind."[7] Underwood and Underwood, a stereoscope manufacturer, published several books describing how to use each of their view cards in the classroom. If a child couldn't travel to Paris or see a famous monument in Asia, she could look at a stereoscope and feel as though she was there. "The best substitute for the real object is undoubtedly the stereograph, which gives a life-size representation with abundance of detail that rivals nature itself. Using stereographs is not play; it is work."[8]

Stereograph views were helpful tools in Western boosterism. During the 1870s and 80s, stereoscope cards of gorgeous Pikes Peak and Cheyenne Canyon attracted both tourists and potential residents to the new community of Colorado Springs. A card that featured Balanced Rock in Garden of the Gods had side-by-side images of a woman pretending to "hold up" the gravity-defying rocks. Who wouldn't want to travel to the Pikes Peak region to attempt the feat themselves?[9]

Stereoscope cards also showed children how they ought to be playing. Images of other children playing with dolls and carriages exposed kids to the array of material objects available to them, and how they ought to be using these toys. For the first time, children compared their playtime lives not just to their siblings or the kids in their neighborhood, but now to children living in a faraway scene. Viewing another child's toys could be a source of jealousy or pride, depending on how you looked at it.

As with the Magic Lantern, the stereoscope declined in popularity during the early twentieth century due to the invention of moving images. However, the novelty factor of the stereoscope continued to fascinate children well into the future. In the summer of 1945, New York City schoolchildren discovered a collection of 600 stereoscope cards at a small branch of the Brooklyn Public Library. A *Brooklyn Daily Eagle* article remarked that the kids had found "entertainment possibilities rivaling the movies. In fact, the youngsters, whose tongues twisted on 'stereoscope,' referred to the machines most frequently as 'movies.' They are also called 'cameras' and 'telescopes.'"[10] The children of the 1940s didn't know what the old technology was called, but they loved it anyway. Viewing the old-fashioned cards at the library became all the rage that summer. Eventually, the librarians had to set aside certain days of the month to handle the crowds. "The problems of distributing the stereoscopes, keeping the various groups of slides intact and warding off conflicts threatening between those using the machines and those waiting in line for them have kept the librarians busy."[11]

13

View-Master

View-Master with reels

Identifying Information:

View-Master

Maker: William Gruber and Harold Graves

Manufacturer: Sawyer's, GAF, View-Master Ideal, Tyco Toys, Fisher-Price

Date: 1939

Collection of Susan A. Fletcher

By the 1930s, the rage for communal stereoscope and Magic Lantern viewing parties had ebbed. Adults and children no longer needed glass plates or stereoscope cards to see exotic lands and current events—now there were newsreels and movies to entertain them. Families put their old-fashioned stereoscope viewers away, leaving them for later generations to discover. However, this old technology would soon be revived in the form of the popular View-Master.

In 1938, stereoscopic photography reemerged in a new format. That year, piano tuner and photographer William Gruber came up with a plan to use movie film to produce stereoscopic images. He invented a small wheel that held seven tiny views of stereoscope photographs shot with Kodachrome movie film. [1]

While on vacation to Oregon Caves National Monument, he met fellow photographer Harold Graves. Graves was the president of Sawyer's Photographic Services. The two men quickly became friends. They worked together and perfected a small plastic disc that could hold the reels of film. In 1939, Sawyer's produced the first View-Master and introduced it at the New York World's Fair.

The first View-Master looked like a pair of binoculars attached to a flat disc. Viewers inserted the photograph reels and advanced the images by sliding the metal lever. They created a sense of nostalgia for the stereoscope viewers of the Victorian age, but they had a special 1930s twist: color film. "Remember the stereoscope of grandfather's day?" asked a 1942 View-Master manual. "Sawyer's View-Master is a modern-day stereoscope device that brings you realistic, three-dimension photographs of scenic attractions in full-color Kodachrome."[2] The View-Master was an instant hit. People loved the colorful 3-D images.

The original View-Master pack included fifteen reels featuring beautiful scenery of places like Pikes Peak in Colorado. Just as stereoscope viewers could consume images from this region in the 1870s when the city was in its infancy, the View-Master continued to attract visitors to the area in the 1930s.

The View-Master served the same educational purpose that earlier optical devices had. Just as Magic Lantern slides were used to recruit young men into the navy in the late nineteenth century, in the 1940s the US military used View-Master slides to train pilots and sailors. Biblical scenes were favorites for the View-Master too, just as they had been in Magic Lantern slide shows of the Victorian era.

View-Master slides also served as pure entertainment. In 1951, Sawyer's acquired their chief competitor the Tru-Vue Company, along with the rights to license Disney characters in the slides. From then on, View-Master became a children's toy primarily. For the first time, the three-dimensional images that children consumed became directly tied to child-centric popular culture. Children viewed images of Mickey and Minnie Mouse, turning them into lifelong Disney consumers. Other View-Master reels included Rin Tin Tin and the Roy Rogers Show.[3]

The View-Master was more suited to individual play than to group activity. Only one child at a time could look through the plastic device, whereas a room full of kids could be entertained at a Magic Lantern show. Historian Scott Eberle argues, "As play became more individual, drawing inward rather than looking outward, the experience became more internal rather than a friendly stereoscopic gathering."[4] Play had changed a lot since the nineteenth century. For one thing, children of the late twentieth century often played by themselves because of declining birth rates and changing neighborhood structures, whereas kids were much more likely to have sought communal play a century earlier.

Later in the twentieth century, View-Master helped export American culture to other parts of the world. In 1984, President Ronald Reagan visited Beijing, where he gave The Fusuijin Street Neighborhood Committee a set of art supplies and a "View-Master with six sets of slides showing scenes of the United States."[5] This exchange was a crafty bit of cultural diplomacy during the tense Cold War years.

Although the View-Master has changed over the years to appeal to a changing audience into the twenty-first century, the reels are still the same shape and size, meaning that a reel from the 1930s will still work in a modern viewer. This perpetuates a strong wave of nostalgia for the generations of people who have used these toys. A 2018 View-Master commercial depicts three generations playing with the toy together—grandparents reflect on the images they had seen in the 1940s, while parents remember looking through their plastic red View-Masters in the 1980s.[6]

14

Brownie Camera

Brownie Camera
CREDIT: JENNIFER MCGLINCHEY SEXTON

Identifying Information:

Brownie Camera

Maker: Frank Brownell

Manufacturer: Eastman Kodak

Date: 1900

Collection of Jennifer McGlinchey Sexton

The turn of the twentieth century brought something very exciting to America's children: the ability to create their own photographs. After passively consuming visual imagery in the form of stereograph cards and Magic Lantern slides during the nineteenth century, the Eastman Kodak Brownie Camera offered children an alternative to images that grown-ups had taken. Here was a chance for a girl or boy to document the world around them. Although photography in its various forms had been around since the 1820s, during the majority of the nineteenth century, cameras were strictly tools that adults used. The Brownie put children behind the lens.

George Eastman, a bank clerk from Rochester, New York, was an amateur photographer on a mission to make photography more affordable and accessible to the masses. In 1884, he patented a way of coating strips of paper to make camera film, thus kicking off the revolution in popular photography. In 1888, he introduced the Kodak camera, which sold for $25. This portable handheld camera came with one hundred shots. According to journalist Clive Thompson, "Suddenly photography became unmoored in space. People took the camera out into the sunshine—and were immediately entranced by the ability to capture lively, goofy, everyday motion."[1] Kodak introduced photography as a hobby for Americans. Now the average person could take pictures, not just professionals with studios and expensive equipment.

The Eastman Kodak Company produced both cameras and film. The Kodak Camera cost around $645 in today's money, which was attainable for ambitious members of the middle class, but still too expensive to find its way into every home. In a brilliant marketing scheme, Eastman decided that inventing an affordable camera would help them sell more film. We'll read more about this marketing technique in our passages about Barbie and G.I. Joe in chapters 29 and 33. Companies in the twentieth century became adept at selling one object of desire cheaply and then churning out expensive accessory products for that object that the owner would need to continue buying forever.

In 1900, Eastman asked Kodak designer Frank Brownell to make a cheaper camera to perpetuate these sales cycles. Brownell obliged and created a small camera that came in a sturdy square box. It was light and rugged. The little camera sold for $1—about $29 today—making it reasonably priced for most families. He named his invention the Brownie after the spirited characters in Canadian illustrator Palmer Cox's works. According to Cox, "BROWNIES, like fairies and goblins, are imaginary little sprites, who are supposed to delight in harmless pranks and helpful deeds. They work and sport while weary households sleep, and never allow themselves to be seen by mortal eyes."[2] Just like the Edwardian children who admired the characters, the brownies went to school, rode bicycles, and got into mischief.

Eastman hoped to instill an early love of photography in kids, thus guaranteeing that film sales would continue long into the future.[3] Kodak used the brownie sprites in an ad campaign targeting children. Kids were used to seeing the brownies hawk a variety of products including soap because Palmer Cox had licensed his characters to several companies.[4] Kodak licensed the characters too, and soon the brownies got into the business of selling cameras to kids. The packaging for The Brownie had an illustration of a little sprite holding the camera. In 1902, Eastman Kodak published an origin story for the camera; it was a decree from the Brownie Queen.

The clever marketing scheme and significant price reduction on the camera worked to make photography a hobby for children. The company sold 150,000 cameras in 1900. Just five years later, one-third of all American households owned a Brownie.[5] In *The Youth's Companion*, one advertisement declared that the camera could be "operated by any school boy or girl."[6] In 1904, an advertisement in the *Brooklyn Daily Eagle* listed the camera under hints for Christmas presents for children.[7]

The portable Brownie could follow active kids almost anywhere they wanted to go, which coincided with an increase in the amount of leisure time available to both grown-ups and children. Summer vacations were becoming popular. A portrait at The Science Museum Group in the UK features a young girl by the seaside, excitedly holding her Brownie Camera.[8] The *Brooklyn Daily Eagle* held a contest for boys and girls to enter their favorite vacation photographs taken with their own cameras. The winners would have their pictures printed in the newspaper that summer.[9]

Children also used the camera to capture minute details of their everyday lives. Until the acquisition of the Brownie Camera and its knock-offs, children recorded the story of their lives through diaries, sketches, and paintings. Now, they could freeze moments in time through a photograph. Children could capture their seaside vacations, pets, toys, and friends, creating a visual record of their existence.

The impulse to create these visual records became ingrained in American identity. According to historian Marc Olivier, this impulse is symbolized in Palmer Cox's 1904 book entitled *The Brownies in the Philippines*. In the book, one of the brownies totes his namesake camera around on a trip to Asia. Olivier argues, "The appearance of this new figure both indicates and spreads a growing anxiety about the undocumented life. Sprites once content with a quiet and invisible domesticity learn to seek photographic proof of their expedition. Similarly, potential consumers, especially women and children, learn that their own previously invisible lives need mediated expression."[10]

Before the introduction of the handheld camera, a family in the nineteenth century would have hired a professional photographer to document big life events such as a child's birth, a large family gathering, or a wedding. Now, every moment of the childhood was eligible for documentation, either by children themselves or their eager families. Kodak's 1943 book *How to Make Good Pictures* encouraged parents to create "an intimate snapshot diary covering the entire period from cradle days to full manhood or womanhood."[11] The ubiquity of these snapshots from 1900–2000 changed how historians understand childhood. In studying children living in previous centuries, historians looked to their diaries, writings, and paintings. Now we can *see* the toys that they played with, the homes they lived in, the woods they ran in, and the friends they interacted with. This evidence is sometimes tricky to interpret, however.

Clive Thompson reminds us that people's behavior started to change as they purposely made their lives camera-ready.[12]

The Brownie Camera evolved as the twentieth century progressed. Kodak issued new models frequently, such as the 1946 Brownie Reflex Camera. A flash was added in 1950. In 1955, the Brownie became a movie camera, allowing users to capture moving images of their lives.[13] In the next chapter, we'll explore the ways home movies impacted childhood.

15

Home Movies

Girl Playing with a Super Eight Home Movie Camera.
CREDIT: ERICMICHAUD CREATIVE # 92251421 COLLECTION: E+

Identifying Information:

Home Movies

With the invention of small, portable movie cameras in the 1930s, almost every aspect of a family's daily life could be recorded for posterity. Just like the Kodak Brownie Camera revolutionized how children of the early twentieth century interacted with photography, home movie cameras changed children's relationship to film. Home movie cameras also gave power to minority children and their adults to tell the truth about their own lives.

It's a little bit hard to pinpoint exactly who invented the first movie camera. During the 1870s and 80s, several people experimented with cameras that took a rapid series of images. Some of these early moving-images pioneers include Wordsworth Donisthorpe, Louis Le Prince, and William Freise-Greene. In 1891, William Kennedy Laurie Dickson, an employee of Thomas Edison, invented the Kinetograph Camera, possibly inspired by one of Greene's inventions.[1] These new moving-images cameras were very expensive, and only the wealthiest Americans could afford them. Technological advancements to both cameras and film in the early twentieth century introduced home movie cameras to a broader range of consumers. In 1933, Kodak introduced 8mm film, which could be used in cheaper and lighter cameras than its 16mm predecessors.

As the economy stabilized after the Great Depression, more American families were able to buy these newly affordable home movie cameras, like the Cine-Kodak Eight. Soon, people of all ages, classes, and races started making home movies. According to film historian Rick Prelinger, "We see film shot by families of color, by working-class families, by people living in rural areas, and by children and students."[2]

These cameras gave minority families the power to document their own lives. According to Prelinger, "While many images of African American people shot by white photographers still reproduced the same negative stereotypes, African Americans themselves also picked up cameras to document their own lives, families, and communities."[3]

According to Dr. Jacqueline Stewart of the University of Chicago's South Side Home Movie Project, "Although home movies are often dismissed as 'amateur' photography, these and other community films contain a wealth of information about the ways in which people represented themselves and their views on the world."[4] This project collects mid-century home movies from Chicago's South Side. The films in this archival collection also document locations, people, and events "that are not always captured in official histories."[5] Some of these archival movies include a collection by the Maxwell family, who documented their lives in the South Side. One of their home movie reels features a mother and father proudly showing off their infant daughter. In another reel, the Maxwells visit the zoo, where they eat cotton candy and look at the seals. In yet another reel, the children open their Christmas presents to find a Soda Pop Maker and pajamas.[6]

These home movies are vital to how historians understand childhood in African American communities in the twentieth century. According to Stewart, "I think that one of the reasons why marginalized communities don't get the same kind of historical attention is because we don't have the same kind of presence in the official archival record. One of the really valuable things about collecting visual materials, whether that's photographs or films in our case, is that it opens up a realm of documentation beyond the written word."[7]

Part IV

ANIMAL TOYS

Toy animals are some of the world's oldest and most beloved playthings. According to Antonia Fraser, the impulse to play with them stems from the desire to "imitate the pets of real life in a toy animal."[1] Ancient children played with toy porcupines and toy lions in Persia, wooden tigers and crocodiles in Egypt, and toy horses in Greece.[2] Children in North America enjoyed playing with animal figures too. Lakota children made animal figures out of clay and bones, while Plains tribes used sun-dried mud to replicate horses and buffalo.[3] Colonial American children brought their animal toys from Europe. In this part, we'll explore five animal toys from the twentieth century, starting with the Schoenhut Humpty Dumpty Circus in 1903 and ending with Care Bears in the 1980s. Some of the historical themes to watch out for include America's obsession with the circus in the early twentieth century, westward expansion, Jewish immigration, and the psychological role that stuffed animals play.

For much of the nineteenth century, the most popular commercially produced animal toys in the United States were Noah's Ark sets. Intricately carved wooden arks came with pairs of giraffes, lions, and other animals depicting the biblical story of Noah and the flood. Children liked these toys because they could play with them on Sunday—a day they couldn't do much else. While formal legislation protecting the Sabbath never passed on a national level, parents throughout the century recognized the value of a day of rest.

G. Stanley Hall declared that observing a day of rest "gives seriousness and poise to character and brings the saving fore-, after-, and over-thought into the midst of a hurrying objective and material life . . . it teaches self-control, self-knowledge, and self-respect."[4] Among the conservative middle class, amusements usually tolerated during the week became taboo on Sunday. For kids, this was especially tiresome; no running around outside, no social calls. Fortunately, there was a loophole in the Sabbath rules: children who spent their Sunday afternoons learning about God during their playtime had a legitimate outlet for fun. Noah's Ark playsets were popular Sunday toys because they taught kids about the Bible and allowed them to play quietly indoors.

In the late nineteenth century, stuffed animals became the new favorite things for quiet play. In 1880, Margarete Steiff, a German toymaker, began making soft animals out of felt. Americans imported these Steiff stuffed animals, and children loved them. In 1902, a hunting trip that Theodore Roosevelt took inspired the creation of the century's most beloved toy: the teddy bear. Soon, stuffed animals became an indispensable part of childhood.

Toy animals have been favorites for thousands of years because they encourage imaginative play. A stuffed bear, for instance, can serve any role in a child's play script. These toys often serve as transitional objects that aid a child's psychological development as he or she moves away from total dependence on their mothers to become their own separate being. They provide comfort and security in times of anxiety, and they help children learn to love something apart from themselves. These toys also help children develop language skills, rehearse emotions, and encourage socialization. Animal toys are frequently a child's introduction to the natural world, and playing with these objects encourages children to learn about nature.

This part explores five animal toys. First, the Schoenhut Humpty Dumpty Circus reflects America's obsession with the circus in the late nineteenth century. A small Steiff Elephant that made its way from Germany to the United States tells the story of childhood in the American West. Third, we will learn about the origin stories of the teddy bear and how the nation went crazy for the cute little bears. Fourth, a toy monkey once owned by German immigrant Gert Berliner tells the story of the Jewish refugee crisis in the 1930s and 40s. Last, Care Bears of the 1980s assuaged parental guilt and helped children express their emotions.

Schoenhut Humpty Dumpty Circus

Elsa Juhre plays with her Schoenhut Circus set.
CREDIT: ELSA JUHRE SCHMITZ

Identifying Information:

Schoenhut Humpty Dumpty Circus

Maker: Albert Schoenhut

Manufacturer: A. Schoenhut Company

Date: 1903

Collection of Rogers Historic Museum, ID1997.54.3.1 & 3-7.

In March 1921, the Ringling Brothers Circus came to Bridgeport, New York. According to an article in the *New York Times*, "the percentage of small-boy truancy in the neighborhood of Pier 7, North River, took a big jump."[1] Boys skipped school to see the Bengal tigers, polar bears, elephants, camels, and zebras. During the height of the late nineteenth- and early twentieth-century American circus-craze, children all over the country had the rare opportunity to see exotic animals in the flesh. In 1903, the Schoenhut Humpty Dumpty Circus let kids reenact the circus by playing with a menagerie of wooden animals.

In the late nineteenth and early twentieth century, Americans went crazy for the circus. During the Gilded Age, impresarios P. T. Barnum and James A. Bailey reluctantly joined forces to create the hugely popular Barnum and Bailey Circus. The Ringling brothers started their circus in the 1880s, and by 1907 it had become the world's largest railroad circus.[2] Although those two circuses are the most familiar to us living in the twenty-first century, there were smaller shows that traveled the country entertaining people like the Adam Forepaugh and Sells Brothers show. These extravaganzas featured daring circus performers, trained animals, and over-the-top showmanship.

A circus train coming to town was one of the biggest events of the year in many communities. The circus brought exotic animals to all parts of the country, allowing children to gawk at creatures they had only seen in photographs or drawings. In 1868, the Dan Rich Great Show featured a "school of educated animals," including "a pair of monster royal Bengal tigers," a "South American Tapir, White or Polar Bear," and "the Australian Kangaroo."[3] In 1906, the Adam Forepaugh and Sells Brothers Enormous Show advertised that it was bringing a "TREMENDOUS all-embracing OMI-ARK MENAGERIE OF All The World's Wild Animal Life."[4] For children living in the far West, rural south, or plains states, zoological parks were few and far between; the circus was a rare opportunity to see real-live lions, leopards, and elephants.

Animal toys of the early twentieth century reflected this obsession with the circus. Between 1903 and 1935, toymaker Albert Schoenhut developed a line of products called the Humpty Dumpty Circus. His initial set featured a jointed wooden clown with a chair and ladder. He soon started making animal figures too, including horses, elephants, and a lion. The wooden animals were posable, so children could reenact scenes from a real circus.[5] "They allowed children to re-create the fantasy of the circus long after the show left town."[6] The Humpty Dumpty Circus eventually included an array of animals like a giraffe, alligator, leopard, and bear.

In 1918, young Elsa Juhre's parents purchased the starter set of the Humpty Dumpty Circus. Her family lived in Rogers, Arkansas, where her father owned a meat market. Their neighbor George Bingham was a photographer, and he took Elsa's picture with her Humpty Dumpty elephant, clown, and donkey. Bingham occasionally borrowed the circus set to use as a prop when he photographed the other children in town. Elsa donated these toys to the Rogers Historical Museum when she grew up.[7]

Parents who wanted their children's playtime to be productive loved the toys. In 1928, promotional material for the Humpty Dumpty Circus remarked that the toys trained the eye and the hand, encouraging children to "work out their own ideas by means of the figures."[8] The company also noted that "boys that started to play with the Humpty Dumpty Circus toys in the early years of 1903-4-5 [sic] are men now, some of great prominence, Doctors, Lawers [sic], Judges, Manufacturers, Merchants, etc., etc., and many of them refer to the Happy Days they spent with Schoenhut's Humpty Dumpty Circus Toys."[9]

17

Steiff Pull Elephant

Steiff Elephant, gift of William J. Palmer to Charlotte and Leo Wolgamood.

CREDIT: COLORADO SPRINGS PIONEERS MUSEUM, OBJECT ID 2000.0030.0002

Identifying Information:

Steiff Pull Elephant

Maker: Steiff

Date: c. 1907

Colorado Springs Pioneers Museum, Object ID: 2000.00300002

During the late nineteenth and early twentieth centuries, children on the Western frontier had very different playtime lives than their counterparts in the Northeastern United States. Nature was their playground, and children roamed forests, waded through streams, and rode horseback. Many children on the frontier helped their families on farms and went to work early in mining camps. The gains in free time that children of the Northeast were getting in the late nineteenth century didn't always extend to these rural kids. Additionally, in the remote West, children did not have easy access to the commercially produced toys that were becoming popular back East.

Nevertheless, such toys sometimes did find their way to the frontier. In 1907, a small stuffed elephant by the German company Steiff was a Christmas present from the founder of Colorado Springs to his young friends Leo and Charlotte Wolgamood, who were the children of his carpentry foreman. This toy elephant tells the stories of the international toy trade and childhood on the Western frontier.

During the nineteenth and early twentieth centuries, many of the commercially produced toys that American children played with were imported from famous toymakers in Europe. You will learn more about this exchange in part 4 when we talk about dolls. Many years before the Wolgamood siblings received their stuffed elephant, Margarete Steiff was born in Giengen, Germany, in 1847. When she was a little girl, she contracted polio and became paralyzed. Margarete remained active despite her disability. When she was seventeen, she trained to be a seamstress. Her father built a dressmaking workshop in their home, and Margarete made a living selling clothing. In December 1862, she saw a pattern for a pincushion shaped like an elephant and decided to make one herself. She crafted this adorable elephant out of felt. Margarete sewed more of the little elephants and soon noticed that local children were playing with them as toys.[1]

She started making stuffed children's toys based off of this original elephant design. She founded her company Steiff Manufacture in 1880. Her nephew Richard Steiff joined her in 1897, and the pair, along with their workshop staff, made all kinds of stuffed toys. In the Steiff catalog from 1901, the company displayed a photograph of its menagerie, which included stuffed dogs, birds, horses, lions, monkeys, pigs, and a camel.[2] Steiff used high-quality material to create her toys. The company motto was "For children, only the best is good enough!"[3]

Many of these stuffed animals—including the elephants—were mounted on small metal wheels, designed for a child to pull along. Animals pull toys have been around since ancient times, and they were trendy in the United States after the Civil War. In the early 1900s, one particular Steiff pull-toy found its way from Germany to a boy and girl in Colorado Springs, Colorado.

Childhood in young Colorado Springs was more civilized than in many other Western communities. City founder and Civil War veteran General William Jackson Palmer ensured that the people living in his city had access to good schools, churches, theaters, and culture. General Palmer loved kids and did many things to make childhood in his city joyous and magical. In the early 1900s, he and his young adult daughters Elsie, Dorothy, and Marjory hosted Christmas parties every year at their home Glen Eyrie for both the town's children and their employees' families.

For one party in early January 1903, Palmer sent his carriages to pick up the town children. Servants escorted the kids from town across the snowy landscape to the glittering warmth of the "castle" at Glen Eyrie.[4] One girl recalled, "It took one solid hour to drive across the Mesa, and the children behaved much as they do in a modern carpool. We loved every minute of it. I can shut my eyes and see the castle, the shining floors, and fires burning in the enormous fireplaces, the lovely smell of English lavender and burning pines."[5] A giant Christmas tree lit with candles and ornaments greeted the guests. They had a beautiful evening of games, piñatas, a moving-picture show, and refreshments. The most exciting part of the evening was when Palmer gave a Christmas present to each child.

In 1907, Palmer gave Charlotte and her brother Leo a stuffed pull-toy elephant by Steiff, which he had imported from Germany. It came on a set of wheels and had a red circus blanket and two long tusks. The children loved it. Eventually, the little elephant found its way into the collections of the Colorado Springs Pioneers Museum, where it helps local historians interpret the history of childhood in the Pikes Peak region.

18

Teddy Bear

Ruth Brown Fletcher's teddy bear
CREDIT: SUSAN A. FLETCHER

Identifying Information:

Teddy Bear

Date: 1902

Collection of Ruth Brown Fletcher

The teddy bear is one of the most beloved artifacts of childhood. Perhaps you had a favorite bear yourself. This passage will explore the development of the teddy bear by exploring the childhood of Theodore Roosevelt, the man who inspired the toy's invention, along with the cultural impact of the toy.

Theodore Roosevelt was born on October 27, 1858. He grew up in New York City. In his autobiography, Roosevelt recalled, "I was a sickly, delicate boy, suffered much from asthma, and frequently had to be taken away on trips to find a place where I could breathe."[1] He was also terribly nearsighted. Before the twentieth century when American schoolchildren began receiving routine vision tests, it took a while to figure out why Theodore often stumbled into things and was having a hard time studying. When he was thirteen, he finally got some glasses. In Roosevelt's words, being able to see "literally opened an entirely new world to me. I had no idea how beautiful the world was until I got those spectacles."[2]

While he was convalescing from asthma and before he got his glasses, young Roosevelt often played indoors. While his peers had fun outside, he found many pursuits to fill his time inside. He was a great reader and particularly enjoyed Thomas Mayne Reid's books, which inspired him to pursue a life of big adventures. His family subscribed to *Our Young Folks*, a popular children's magazine. He also enjoyed Longfellow's poems.[3]

When he got older, he decided to strengthen his asthma-weakened body after a bullying incident left him feeling physically helpless. He learned how to box, and his father installed a home gym for Theodore to do gymnastics and weight lifting. When Roosevelt was stronger, he took up the physical activities common to boys of his day, including swimming, hiking, and horseback riding. Roosevelt pursued this active life during the time the Muscular Christianity movement was becoming popular in the United States.

When he was a grown-up, Roosevelt continued dealing with tough situations. After his mother, Martha, and first wife, Alice, both died on the same day in 1884, Roosevelt fled to the American West. He lived on a ranch in the Dakota Territory, hunted big game, and drove cattle. He then went on to serve as lieutenant colonel of the Rough Riders during the Spanish-American War, and became Governor of New York in 1898.[4] Roosevelt became be the twenty-sixth president of the United States in 1901 after the assassination of President William McKinley.

While serving as president, he continued to pursue hunting as his great passion. In the late nineteenth century, hunting gained new popularity as middle-class men sought to emulate the rugged virility they saw in the disappearing frontiersman and the lower classes. Popular fiction such as *The Boy Hunters; or, Adventures in Search of a White Buffalo* promoted the idea that "white men (or boys) prove their manhood by fighting and vanquishing Indians and wild beasts."[5] Roosevelt made hunting part of his identity to create an image of himself that was virile and powerful.

On November 14, 1902, Roosevelt went on a bear hunting trip in rural Mississippi at the invitation of the state's governor, Andrew H. Longino. He was exhausted from a year of dealing with the United Mine Workers Strike. After negotiating a deal between the mine workers and the union, he decided to get out of Washington, DC, and take a vacation in the countryside. He visited Longino, and the pair traveled to the lowlands of Mississippi for the hunt. Although the other members of the party saw bears during the trip, Roosevelt was the only one who didn't see any bears at all the first day.[6]

This is the story that got reported to the public and that launched a million cuddly toys: Trying to help Roosevelt, his guide Holt Collier went out with his hounds to look for a bear. The dogs tracked and cornered the bear. The men tied the bear to a willow tree and called for the president. When Roosevelt arrived and saw the captured bear, his assistants told him to shoot it. Roosevelt refused. Killing a captured animal was unsportsmanlike. Although he was well-known for his game-hunting escapades, he did have his standards. Members of the press, who were also part of the hunting party, spread the news of Roosevelt's moment of compassion.[7]

The real story is far more gruesome. According to Holt Collier, his hunting dogs tracked a bear for miles. When they closed in, the bear swiped at the dogs and mortally wounded one of them. Collier butted the bear in the skull with his rifle to make the creature release his prized dog. Although Collier could have killed the bear himself to protect the dogs, he knew that his job was to save the kill for the president. Collier intervened in the bear/dog fight by lassoing the massive bear and tying it to a tree. When Roosevelt arrived, he refused to shoot the gravely injured bear. However, Collier and his men recognized the extent of the bear's injuries and knew it would not survive, so they killed it with their knives.[8]

News of the first, more sanitized version of the story spread across the nation. Clifford Berryman, the cartoonist for the *Washington Post*, drew a caricature of the president refusing to shoot a scared, adorable bear cub. The public fell in love with the little creature. New York shop owner Morris Mitchom saw the cartoon and asked his wife Rose to sew a stuffed bear just like the one in the comic. Rose used plush velvet for the fur and shoe buttons for the eyes.[9] They called the creatures "Teddy's bears" and sold them for $1.50 each.

Mitchom reportedly sent a letter to Roosevelt asking him if they could officially use his name for their toys. Roosevelt said yes, and soon a teddy bear craze swept the nation. Interestingly, at the same time the Steiff company was already manufacturing stuffed bears based on the animals at the Stuttgart Zoo.[10]

No matter who invented the teddy bear, everyone wanted one in 1906. At the shops and resorts on the Jersey Shore, little boys and their parents went crazy for the bears. According to historian Gary Cross, "The boardwalk, even more than the new downtown shopping district, was an ideal place for novelty toys. Here a crowd appeared, eager to stand out and to blend in, a perfect setting for the frenzy of playful innovation and imitation."[11]

The teddy bear craze of 1906–1907 was the predecessor of all toy crazes of the twentieth century. An advertisement for "Teddy Roosevelt Bears" in the *Pittsburgh Press* ballyhooed, "We advise you to BUY NOW as we can't promise how long the present supply will last. Both the imported and domestic kinds—well put together—the biggest novelty in years."[12]

The toy appealed to everyone. Cross notes that it appealed to girls because it was cuddly and soft, and to boys because it was manly. Grown-ups loved teddy bears too. Adult women used the bears as surrogate babies and pets.[13] Teddy bears helped parents love their children. According to Cross, "the teddy bear gave adults special feelings about their children. Parents had photographs taken of their children hugging teddy bears because this made them see their offspring as loveable like bears."[14]

Not everyone was a fan of the bears, however. Teddy bears supplanted dolls as girls' favorite companion toys, which upset a clergyman in Michigan who objected to girls abandoning their motherly roles. *New York Times* responded to this controversy saying that the clergyman "permits his own supersenstiveness to get the better of his judgement . . . the Teddy bear is merely one of the humors of the day. As a toy, it is cheap and safe. It will soon pass, however, to the limbo of the Uncle Sam dolls, the walking dolls and talking dolls, and the other toys of the past, now forgotten."[15]

The teddy bear, of course, did not pass into the land of forgotten toys. The height of this particular craze ended in 1908, but teddy bears had entered children's hearts forever.

19

Stuffed Monkey

Gerhard Berliner's Stuffed Monkey
JEWISH MUSEUM BERLIN, ACCESSION 2004/46/0, GIFT OF GERT BERLINER, PHOTO: JENS ZIEHE

Identifying Information:

Toy Monkey

Date: c. 1935

Owner: Gert Berliner

Jewish Museum Berlin Object I.D.: 2006/46/0

In 1939, fourteen-year-old Jewish teenager Gert Berliner fled Nazi Germany. Berliner packed a few of his possessions, including his toy monkey, into a suitcase. He said goodbye to his parents, Paul and Sophie, and boarded the train for Kalmar, Sweden. Upon reaching Sweden, he was taken in by a local family. In 1943, his parents were sent to Auschwitz, where they were killed, leaving Gert an orphan. After the war, Berliner left Sweden. He came to the United States in 1947 at the age of 22, bringing his toy monkey with him.[1] Berliner's toy monkey tells his personal story, as well as the story of other young Jewish refugees who fled to the United States during the 1930s and 40s.

Berliner was born in 1924 in Berlin, Germany. As a child, he clipped his toy monkey to the handlebars of his bike, which he rode all over the capital city.[2] When Adolf Hitler and the Nazi party rose to power in Germany in 1933, life changed dramatically for Gert and his fellow Jews. That year, Nazi persecution of Jews began by barring Jewish citizens from holding public offices or civil service positions and excluding them from employment in many areas. In 1935, Hitler announced the Nuremberg Law, which stripped Jews of their civil rights as German citizens. For Jewish families hoping to flee the country, options were increasingly limited. However, Gert was able to escape on the *Kindertransport*, an organized effort to evacuate Jewish children from Nazi-controlled Germany to England, Sweden, and other European countries from 1938–1940.

In the United States, US Secretary of Labor Frances Perkins proposed to bring 250 Jewish refugee children to the United States. According to historian Bat-Ami Zucker, "Jewish leaders believed the plight of children would arouse less antagonism, perhaps even some sympathy; since children would not compete with other Americans for jobs, they might more readily gain admission."[3] The German Jewish Children's Aid (GJCA) hand-selected the potential young refugees and raised funds to bring them to America. The first ten children arrived in November 1934. The GJCA provided a $500 stipend to the families housing each child, making the hosts promise they would let the kids stay in school until they turned sixteen.

The resettlement program was a complicated, contested political situation. After the *Kristallnacht*, President Franklin D. Roosevelt decided that the United States needed to respond to the refugee crisis, so he extended German-Jewish visitor visas to at least six months. That same year, the Jewish fraternal organization Brith Sholom commissioned Gilbert and Eleanor Kraus, a wealthy couple from Philadelphia, to evacuate Jewish children from Austria. The Krauses selected refugee families who were near the top of the waiting list for United States immigration visas.[4] They found American families to take them in. The Wagner-Rogers Bill proposed that 10,000 German refugee children would enter the United States in 1939 and 1940; however, the bill was withdrawn.

In 1940, Nazi Germany invaded Belgium, the Netherlands, and France. With peril looming for Great Britain, the Children's Overseas Reception Board evacuated British children to Commonwealth countries and the United States. Many of the original *Kindertransport* children who had been sent to England were part of this second wave of resettlement. Eight-year-old John Lang left Berlin in January 1939 on a *Kindertransport* train to London. He recalled, "Toward the end of 1940, much earlier than I would have believed, the American Embassy in London informed me that my quota number had been reached and I could now proceed to the United States. . . . The North Atlantic voyage was perilous, and we never knew whether we might be torpedoed by a German submarine, as so many other ships had been."[5]

The United States never welcomed Jewish refugees in significant numbers for a variety of complicated reasons including rampant anti-Semitism and the political climate of the day.[6] However, for the few Jewish children who were able to evacuate to the United States during this period, their resettlement in this country likely spared them from death in Europe. In a letter to the

Washington Post, Thea Lindauer, wrote, "I was one of those children because my father was astute enough to see what the future would hold. The experiment was, I believe, discontinued because most parents, unlike my father, did not foresee the horrors that lay ahead."[7]

Lindauer settled in the Chicago North Shore area. Her host families gave her a good education, and eventually, her parents were able to join her in America.[8] For Edith Schumer, who left Germany when she was twelve, the cultural barrier was hard to overcome. "After you get here and the excitement wears off, it gets pretty depressing because you're living by a whole new set of rules,"[9] she said seventy years later. Many of the refugee children spoke no English, and often their American hosts didn't speak German. It was "total confusion," in the words of Kurt Rothschild, who escaped from Germany when he was fourteen.[10]

Gert Berliner left Sweden after the war and came to the United States when he was twenty-two years old in 1947. As a grown-up, Berliner became an internationally famous photographer, filmmaker, and painter. In 2003, Aubrey Pomerance, archivist at the Jewish Museum Berlin, came to New York to ask Berliner for a donation to the museum. He wondered if Berliner had an artifact from his childhood in Germany that visitors could relate to on a personal level in the museum exhibits. Berliner "eventually decided that the toy monkey should go back out into the world where it would do more good as a little ambassador to history."[11] So he donated the monkey to the museum. The monkey is a visitor favorite at the Jewish Museum Berlin, where it tells the story of Jewish children during World War II. In November 2018, Berliner's son Uri, a correspondent with National Public Radio, did a story about his father and his toy monkey, which you should listen to when you have the opportunity.[12]

Care Bears

Care Bears

Identifying Information:

Care Bears

Maker: Elena Kucharik

Manufacturer: Those Characters From Cleveland, Kenner

Date: 1981

Collection of Jennifer McGilnchey Sexton

If you were a little girl in the 1980s, chances are pretty good that you had Care Bear toys somewhere in your home. The bears were everywhere, appearing in the form of stuffed animals, on tumblers, on bedsheets, and more. The omnipresence of Care Bear products echoed other toys crazes of this era that were based on fictional characters, including Pac-Man, Strawberry Shortcake, and the Teenage Mutant Ninja Turtles. The Care Bears tell the story of an emphasis on good feelings and emotion in childhood in the late twentieth century.

The Care Bears began their lives as illustrated characters on American Greetings Card Company (AGCC) products before they were toys. The card company was famous for turning cheerful illustrations into profitable consumer products. In the 1970s, American Greetings put their character Holly Hobbie on stationary, serving trays, and lunchboxes. They did the same thing with Strawberry Shortcake in 1980. They called the development of Strawberry Shortcake "Project I." Their secret follow-up "Project II" was the Care Bear.[1]

The adorable bears were the brainchild of a dream team of artists including Elena Kucharick, Muriel Fahrion (who had illustrated Strawberry Shortcake), and Susan Trentel. The company intended the loveable bears to follow a path similar to Holly Hobbie and Strawberry Shortcake: transforming from illustrated greeting card characters into toys and subsequently movie stars.

In 1981, Jack Chojnacki, the President of AGCC's licensing division Those Characters From Cleveland, got Kenner Toys involved.[2]

Kenner Toys started the Care Bear line in 1981 with ten stuffed bears, including Birthday, Cheer, Funshine, Good Luck, Love-A-Lot, Tenderheart, Bedtime, and Wish Bear. Chojnacki recalled that the bears had a "high aaaaaah factor,"[3] the sound of little girls gushing over the adorable creatures. Other species soon joined the happy bear family including Brave Heart Lion, Bright Heart Raccoon, and Gentle Heart Elephant in 1984.[4] The company licensed over four hundred products including Care Bear–themed sheets, lamps, glasses, and clothing. The bears had their own book of poems too. This marketing blitz echoed the teddy bear craze of 1906.

The Care Bears came about in a season in American history in which children were encouraged to examine their feelings. The vice-president of Care Bears' advertising firm stated, "In the case of Care Bears, we believe we tapped into a need for kids to deal with emotions. Children need to understand what is happening interpersonally in the world around them."[5] In the 1980s, the outside world seemed confusing and complicated; parents wanted their children's toys to create a safe, happy environment. A newspaper article in 1984 proclaimed, "Adding proof to the theory that kids like to hug and be hugged is the big rush for the loveable, huggable Care Bears."[6]

The advertising campaign for Care Bears alluded to the role of stuffed animals as transitional objects for children. A Kenner television advertisement stated, "Cheer Bear makes you feel real swell, Grumpy Bear knows whenever you're blue, and Champ Bear's always rooting for you."[7] For kids who often felt misunderstood by the adults in their lives, a toy that understood their inner world was appealing.

Kenner marketed the Care Bears to grown-ups as a way for them to express tender feelings toward their children, much like the teddy bear craze of 1906. A 1986 television marketing study noted the decline in birth rates and the increase in mothers working outside the home. The reporter remarked that parents "may have more money, but they have less time to spend with their children. To compensate, they may buy more things for their children."[8]

Kenner knew exactly what to do with that information: capitalize on parental guilt to sell more toys. The company created a television advertisement depicting a father giving his daughter Bedtime Bear, presumably as a way to make up for an unexplained extended absence. The ad states: "Give a soft, cuddly Care Bear and share your special feelings today."[9]

The same ad shows a grandmother giving her granddaughter a Tender Heart Bear. This corresponds with an increase in the number of toys that grandparents were buying for their grandchildren in the 1980s. Historian Howard Chudacoff notes, "Because grandparents often reside at some distance from their families, they do not always know a grandchild's practical needs in terms of clothing, school supplies, and the like. Consequently, grandparents, as well as aunts and uncles, are more likely than ever to treat and seek affection from grandchildren by buying them toys."[10]

The Care Bears hit the market at a unique time in American history. In the late 1980s, toy companies could appeal straight to children through TV cartoons, turning very young kids into consumers. Historian Natalie Coulter notes that in the 1980s "Madison Avenue had clearly detected the rise of young girls in the nation's stores and in true capitalist spirit recognized this."[11] Gary Cross notes that the Care Bears were part of an "interconnected industry that encompassed movies, T.V. shows, videos and other media forms along with toys, clothing and accessories."[12] The Care Bears existed in many dimensions: on TV, on the movie screen, in books, and as stuffed animals. As one reviewer of the 1985 Care Bears movie stated, "I couldn't help being bothered by the blatant commercialism of this whole venture. . . . One wonders if such products as Care Bears and Cabbage Patch dolls, with their accompanying philosophies of sweetness and light, aren't trying to take the place of religion."[13]

Care Bears also offered children tough lessons on personal ownership and responsibility. In the 1980s, children owned more toys than any other generation in American history. Sometimes it was hard to keep track of your things. American families took road trips, and kids often forgot their toys in hotel rooms or restaurants. Joanna Knighten recalls, "I left my beloved Love-A-Lot in New Mexico, at a hotel. My parents chose this to be the 'you need to look after your things' lesson. I saved all my pennies and replaced her with a Care Cousin because they were on sale at Kmart. Hence, I learned somethings are worth paying full price for and you can't just replace a stuffed friend. It doesn't work that way."[14]

Part V

CONSTRUCTION TOYS

In a 1963 television commercial for the Gilbert Erector Set, a boy remarks, "I don't usually think of it as a toy . . . it's more like a whole world, I guess."[1] Construction toys have been the raw materials in world-building and imaginative play. In the early twentieth century, these toys were strategic tools to prepare boys for future careers in architecture and engineering. According to Gary Cross, "They taught boys to admire the technologies of the future and allowed them to imagine themselves in control of modern power."[2]

By the turn of the twentieth century, middle-class boys between ages 14 and 19 had gained increasing amounts of free time. Although their counterparts in the laboring classes still had to work out of economic necessity, for the first time in American history middle-class males of what we now call the "teenage years" had the freedom to play and experiment. Urban infrastructure was expanding rapidly in this era, and construction toys became popular in response to the building boom. It was clear that the country needed smart young men who could build the America of the future, and construction toys gave children an opportunity to gain practical skills in engineering and architecture on a small scale. Tinkertoy, Erector Sets, and Lincoln Logs were all invented in the first fourteen years of the twentieth century, and they remained influential toys for decades.

Construction sets gained newfound popularity in the late twentieth century as American parents became anxious about their children's place in a global society. The National Science Foundation responded to these fears by promoting education in science, technology, engineering, and math (STEM). According to science historians Susan Blackley and Jennifer Howell, "In the U.S., the rhetoric about STEM is founded in political reactionism to the potential deposition of the U.S.' global superiority."[3] With China and the United States' other rivals making huge scientific gains, politicians and parents grew worried that American children were unable to compete with their international counterparts. Returning to practical education in formal settings and in playtime seemed like the answer to the problem. Construction toys have promoted these STEM skillsets all along, even before this kind of education got its catchy acronym.

Erector Sets, Tinkertoys, Lincoln Logs, LEGOs, and other toys of their kind encourage cognitive thinking skills by employing principles of math, engineering, design, and art. For younger children, these toys help develop fine-motor skills. According to science writer Gwen Dewar, children who spend time playing with blocks score higher on tests of spatial ability than kids who don't play with them. [4]

Researchers have also found that boys from higher socioeconomic classes outperform both boys and girls from lower classes on these tests. The researchers theorize this may be because the wealthier boys have "greater access to expensive construction toys and more social encouragement to play with such toys."[5] This disparity in access to mass-produced toys like construction sets is a reality for many families around the country. Just because LEGOs give children all kinds of skills, that doesn't mean every family can afford to buy them.

In this part, we'll look at five construction toys. First, wooden blocks in the nineteenth century taught children spatial and literary skills, and they continue to help modern American children develop their fine-motor skills. Next, we'll move on to the Big Three construction sets of the 1910s: Erector Sets, Tinkertoys, and Lincoln Logs. Last, we'll look at the development of LEGO and how the toy influenced mid-twentieth-century children.

21

Wooden Blocks

Wooden Blocks

Identifying Information:

Wooden Blocks

In 1970, a preschool teacher at the Discovery Center in Hempstead, New York, led her students through a lesson using wooden blocks. The teacher would "hold up a colored wooden alphabet block and ask a child a question about it. The child, handling the block and answering questions, might learn something about letters, colors, size, shape, and texture."[1] For 150 years, toy blocks have helped children build their fine-motor skills, learn their letters, and develop spatial awareness.

American children have been playing with blocks since the Colonial Era. In 1693, philosopher John Locke told parents to help their children learn how to read by giving them "dice and playthings, with the letters on them to teach children the alphabet by playing."[2] Locke believed that education and play went hand in hand. Architecture historian Witold Rybczynski notes that Maria and R. L. Edgeworth mention building bricks in their 1798 work *Practical Education*. According to Rybczynski, these rational toys "were intended to teach children about assembling many small and different parts into a whole, about gravity and physics, and about how buildings were made."[3] American author John Ruskin said that he played with wooden blocks in his youth in the 1820s, which taught him "the laws of practical stability in towers and arches."[4]

In the 1830s to 1850s, Friedrich Wilhelm August Froebel, a German museum curator and pioneer of the kindergarten, created toys designed to educate children while they played. Froebel thought that play was the work of children. His system of *Spielgaben* (play gifts) included puzzles, blocks, and other manipulative toys. Froebel's blocks consisted of smooth wooden rectangles, cylinders, and cubes. They taught children to manipulate the space around them and aided their cognitive development. Milton Bradley later popularized these blocks by mass producing his own version of them.

A few decades later, children could build their language skills by playing with Crandall's Blocks. In the 1860s, woodworker Charles Crandall had two young sons who were convalescing from scarlet fever. While they were recovering, he built them a set of blocks out of croquet boxes, pasting letters to each one. He patented his invention on February 5, 1867, giving America a toy that would help generations of children learn their alphabet. P. T. Barnum found the toys so ingenious that he exhibited some in his museum.[5]

There were many varieties of alphabet blocks in the late nineteenth century. The 1877 edition of *American Agriculturist* listed several varieties of Crandall's blocks, including Crandall's Wide-Awake Alphabet and the Illuminated Pictorial Alphabet Cubes. The catalog boasted, "Nothing has ever been invented that more fully combined amusement and instruction and proved more truly an almost endless means of making the little ones (and the great ones) happy than Crandall's Blocks for Children."[6] In 1882, educator Adeline Whitney patented a system of curved blocks that would form three-dimensional alphabet letters when assembled correctly. In the 1890s, the R. Bliss Manufacturing Company made lithographed wooden spheres with beautiful script letters.[7]

Blocks have influenced generations of American children. Architect Frank Lloyd Wright used a version of Froebel blocks when was little. He recalled, "I sat at the little kindergarten table top and played with the cube, the sphere, and the triangle . . . I learned to see in this way, and when I did, I did not care to draw casual incidentals of nature. I wanted to design."[8] We'll learn about how Frank Lloyd Wright's son John invented Lincoln Logs later in this section.

Erector Set

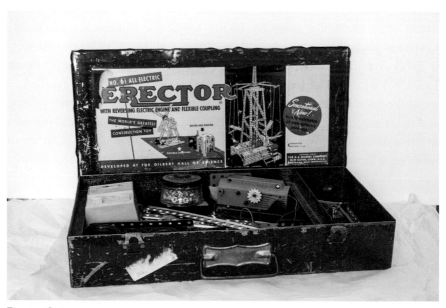

Erector Set
CREDIT: SUSAN A. FLETCHER

Identifying Information:

Erector Set

Maker: Alfred C. Gilbert

Manufacturer: Mysto Manufacturing Company/A. C. Gilbert Company

Date: 1913

Collection of John and Ruth Brown Fletcher

Like many boys in the 1950s, Bill Beutel enjoyed building things with Erector Sets. He recalls, "My most vivid Erector Set memory is liking to put gears on the wrong (back) side of the motor, which allowed much faster motion with the projects vs. the 'safe' side with the gearbox."[1] Bill became a civil engineer when he grew up, inspired by his childhood hobby. He wasn't the only boy who went to work in the sciences after playing with the toys. A visitor to a recent museum exhibit honoring the legacy of Erector Sets remarked, "My first exposure to my friend's Erector Set inspired me to become a mechanical engineer."[2] The Erector Set was an influential part of boyhood in the early and mid-twentieth century. The toy prepared boys to build the America of the future.

Erector Set inventor Alfred Carlton Gilbert grew up in Oregon and Idaho in the 1880s and 90s. In this era, the philosophy of Muscular Christianity made it cool for young men to be athletic and outdoorsy. (You'll learn more about Muscular Christianity and late nineteenth-century athleticism in our passage about football in chapter 38.) Like many boys of this period, Gilbert spent much time playing outside and running around. He loved hunting, gymnastics, and pole-vaulting. When he was a boy, he broke the world record for climbing a twenty-five-foot rope in seven seconds.[3]

As a young adult, Gilbert was interested in all sorts of things, and he was good at everything he did. He attended Yale University, where he ran track and field while earning a medical degree.[4] In 1908, he became part of the United States Olympic Team at the London Olympics. He competed in the pole-vaulting competition. So, how did a pole-vaulting doctor become one of the most influential toy makers in US history?

In 1909, Gilbert graduated from Yale and decided to start his own business. Instead of practicing medicine as his family expected him to, he decided to sell magic sets and founded The Mysto-Manufacturing Company.[5] On his commute to work each day, he noticed the bones of a new urban infrastructure spring up all around him. He was inspired by steel girders, towers, trains, cranes, and other wonders of the early twentieth century. He decided to create a toy construction set that featured steel parts, working motors, and other metal components. Gilbert wanted boys to mimic the construction boom happening in the real world. He called this toy the Erector Set—"The Toy Like Structural Steel."[6] He quickly changed his company's name to the A. C. Gilbert Company.

Early advertisements prophesied all the reasons why the Erector Set would soon take America by storm. A Christmas ad in 1913 proclaimed, "The boys are delighted with Erector because it is fascinating fun to build strong bridges, high skyscrapers and hundreds of other big steel models. Father likes Erector because it teaches boys the principles of engineering and construction. And mother thinks it's fine because it keeps the boys happy and contented."[7] This marketing language targeted parents who wanted their boys to have future careers in engineering. These advertisements also turned children into consumers themselves. "Hello boys," the ad proclaimed, "You'll have the time of your life if your Christmas gifts include the Erector Set No. 4."[8]

As I mentioned in the chapter introduction, older boys and young men had increasing amounts of leisure time during the early 1900s. Gilbert's Erector Set was the perfect toy for this awkward age of boyhood. It gave them something useful to do, and they had fun using it. The practical engineering knowledge that they gained did seem to set them up well for the future. In 1922, almost a decade after the Erector Set first appeared, another advertisement linked this childhood amusement to a solid, well-prepared future: "Boys Today—*Men Tomorrow!*"[9] In this ad, A. C. Gilbert testified, "Thousands of young men from 20 to 30 years old, who are today making great strides in engineering, chemistry, and other sciences were Gilbert Toy boys just a few years ago. I have watched their progress with intense interest and I will tell you that I am mighty proud that my engineering toys have started these boys on the road to success."[10]

The A. C. Gilbert Company produced numerous other products that would similarly prepare boys for their futures, including chemistry sets (see the entry on chemistry sets in chapter 43), microscopes, tool chests, an inventor's lab, and the famous American Flyer Trains.[11]

Gilbert capitalized on the importance of educational toys to keep selling his products during the First World War. In 1917, the United States entered the conflict. The Council of National Defense diverted the nation's resources to the war effort and banned the manufacture of nonessential products, dooming the children's toy industry. A. C. Gilbert served as the chairman of the Toy Association's War Service Committee, and he decided to show the government that educational toys *were* essential items.

He attended a meeting of the Council of National Defense. Gilbert brought some construction toys with him to prove his point.[12] He gave the council a lecture on the importance of toys and play: "The greatest influence in the life of a boy are his toys. . . . It is because of the toys they had in childhood that the American soldiers are the best marksmen on the battlefields of France."[13] Soon, the grown-up government officials in the meeting were playing with the toys themselves. His plea worked, and the *Boston Post* called A. C. Gilbert "the man who saved Christmas for the children."[14]

23

Tinkertoys

Bruce Trotman and his father Dawson Trotman play with a Tinkertoy set during Chrismas 1938.

Identifying Information:

Tinkertoys

Maker: Charles Pajeau

Manufacturer: Tinkertoys of Evanston

Date: 1914

The Navigators Archives M002 Dawson Trotman Collection

For Christmas 1938, Bruce Trotman received a Tinkertoy set. After the Trotman family opened their presents, his father Dawson helped him build a windmill using the wooden spools and rods.[1] A few years later, on a sunny Christmas Day in Los Angeles in the 1940s, Bruce's younger siblings Ruth, Burke, and Faith got their own Tinkertoy sets. Now, he and his siblings could combine their resources and build all kinds of wonderful things together. Tinkertoy sets were well-loved in the twentieth century for their value in boosting a child's career potential.

In the early 1900s, stonemason Charles Pajeau of Evanston, Illinois, was unhappy running his father's stone monument business. To ease his boredom, he turned to inventing. He watched children playing with sticks, pencils, and empty spools and that sparked an idea for a construction set. According to Patricia Hogan, former curator at the Strong Museum of Play, "Pajeau based his design on the Pythagorean theorem, making the size of his wooden sticks the correct length to form the 90-degree triangles that strengthened the towers, windmills, and houses kids built."[2]

In 1914, Charles and his business partner Robert Petit produced the toys. Pajeau sold them in Chicago stores, creating window displays to entice potential buyers. The next year, Pajeau took his invention to the American Toy Fair in New York City. The exposure at the show was just what the pair needed, and within the year they sold one million sets.[3] The business partners continued to improve upon and expand the Tinkertoy lines. In addition to the now-iconic spools and colorful sticks of a basic Tinkertoy set, colorful pull-toys like Drag-on Tinker and Pony Tinker soon joined Pajeau's catalog.[4] Tinkertoy capitalized on the newfangled small electric motors available in this era, and they included them in some of their special sets. Soon, children could make toys that moved by themselves, such as electronic-powered windmills.

As a child of the late nineteenth century himself, Pajeau had likely been indoctrinated by his own family on the importance of educational toys and games. This philosophy is evident in the wording on the Tinkertoy packaging in 1928, which declared that the product "holds attention indefinitely; never becomes tiresome; develops originality and application, and is much appreciated by parents on this account."[5]

Parents valued the toys for their educational and preparative nature. In a 1916 Christmas advertisement in *The Owosso Daily Argus*, the D. M. Christian Company told parents, "Do not overlook the important fact that the children want toys and the toys demanded today are 'Toys that Teach.'"[6] The advertisement stated that Tinkertoy "teaches invention and designing"—for the low price of 50 cents. Ten years later, an advertisement in 1927 proclaimed, "Tinkertoys are the ideal toys for children . . . made for play, education, and to provide mothers more leisure."[7]

No wonder Tinkertoy found its way into the Trotman household in California in the 1930s and 40s. They had been popular toys for fifteen years before the oldest baby Bruce was born, and parents Dawson and Lila would have had plenty of opportunities to encounter the toy, perhaps even in their own childhoods. The marketing of Tinkertoy aided in this product recognition and created an impulse to buy it for the holidays. An advertisement in *Junior Home* in 1928 declared, "Tinkertoys will gladden the hearts of thousands this Christmas. . . . Fortunate indeed are the boys and girls whose Christmas brings them Tinkertoys."[8]

Tinkertoy became such an iconic part of American culture that it influenced all kinds of professional adult fields, from architecture to military operations. In 1950, the Navy Bureau of Aeronautics and the National Bureau of Standards had a secret project code-named "Project Tinkertoy." The Navy was concerned about the shortage of electronics that occurred during WWII and the Korean War because of the bottlenecks in supply created by a shortage of skilled electronics workers. The government hoped this would never happen again during future national emergencies. The goal of Project Tinkertoy was to make electronic parts so easily recognizable and interchangeable that anyone without an electronics background could figure them out and they could be "arranged as easily as a child's building toy."[9] "Project Tinkertoy" aimed to produce parts that were electronically connected for use in "guided missiles, radar sets, proximity fuses, and electronic fire control and communication methods."[10] Perhaps the men working on this secret project had grown up playing with Tinkertoys themselves and were inspired by their toys.

Given this connection to war, interestingly, Tinkertoys themselves were part of a pacifist toy movement during the 1960s. During the Vietnam War, Tinkertoy designer Jack Wright stated, "I don't believe American manufacturers should sponsor the idea that war and horror are fun."[11] Wright's sentiment was reflective of an increasing queasiness over the manufacture of war toys during the conflict (see G.I. Joe and Green Army Men for more details about war toys).

Tinkertoy enjoyed the height of its popularity in the early and midtwentieth century when construction sets were the must-have things for boys. Toward the end of the century, the various companies who bought and sold the rights to manufacture Tinkertoy needed to target new generations of children. In so doing, these companies relied on parental nostalgia for the days they had spent playing with the toy themselves. In the next passage, we'll take a closer look at how nostalgia for the past helped market another construction toy: Lincoln Logs.

24

Lincoln Logs

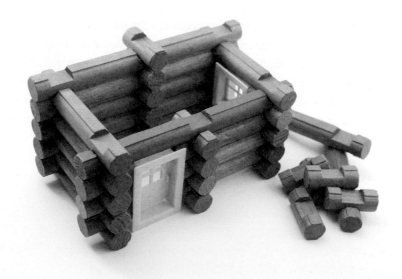

Building a cabin with Lincoln Logs
CREDIT: JOJI CREATIVE # 181895006 COLLECTION: ISTOCK/GETTY IMAGES PLUS

Identifying Information:

Lincoln Logs

Maker: John Lloyd Wright

Manufacturer: Red Square Toy Company/J. L. Wright Manufacturing

Date: 1916

Whereas Erector Set allowed children to construct buildings and toys that celebrated the modern use of steel and metal in the growing cities of the early twentieth century, Lincoln Logs called to mind another era in American history. They celebrated the frontier spirit. Created in 1916 by architect John Lloyd Wright, Lincoln Logs married Japanese architecture with the simple materials of the American West. The toys helped children idealize their pioneer past and taught them practical building skills. In this passage, we'll take a look at Wright's childhood and how his toys influenced children in the twentieth century.

John Lloyd Wright had an extraordinary and challenging childhood as the son of world-famous architect Frank Lloyd Wright. Born in 1892, John grew up in the Wright home in Oak Park, Illinois, with his brothers and sisters. His mother, Catherine, taught kindergarten for the kids in the neighborhood. In an era in which men didn't always spend very much time with their children, John's father played an active role in his early life. Frank taught John how to box, gave him a horse, and introduced him to music. John played in his father's library and studio, which influenced his decision to become an architect himself when he grew up.

As the child of a luminary figure, John had access to some very interesting toys. For Christmas one year, he and his siblings got a mechanical donkey that jumped up and down, and a toy monkey that climbed a string. The children had a playroom that Wright designed for them. John later wrote that inside this playroom, "the oak floor marked off with kindergarten arrangements of circles and squares were always strewn with queer dolls, building blocks, funny mechanical toys, animals that moved about and wagged their strange heads."[1]

Just like many other parents of the late nineteenth century, Frank Lloyd Wright was adamant that his children be well-educated in art and music. John played the violin, his brother David played the flute, sister Frances played the piano, and his little sister Catherine "sang and sucked her thumb."[2]

In addition to the creative playtime that John and his siblings enjoyed indoors, John was also a very active little boy who had some exciting escapades outdoors. He liked to climb up things, which often got him into trouble. He managed to fall out of trees and off the roof of the playroom, and once he even toppled head-first into a barrel of his father's creosote stain.[3]

Unfortunately, this happy childhood did not last long. Frank Lloyd Wright abandoned his family just after the birth of youngest child Robert Llewelyn in 1903. He left in the middle of the night without saying goodbye to his kids, which resulted in a profound sense of humiliation and loss for John. After his dad left, he would hide in his room after dinner, listening to the gramophone.

John had a complicated relationship with his father for the rest of his life. However, their relationship led to the development of one of the most iconic toys in American history. John eventually decided that he wanted to be an architect too. In 1916, he worked alongside his father to design the Imperial Hotel in Tokyo. The hotel's foundation was earthquake-proof, comprised of interlocking beams in the traditional Japanese style. This style of architecture fascinated John.

After his father fired him from the project, John went back to Chicago, humiliated and unsure of what to do next. According to historian Andrew Clayman, "He observed the recent successful introduction of Tinkertoy (invented by Charles Pajeau in nearby Evanston) and Erector Set and set forth combining the budding trend of cheap model construction toys with some of the concepts he'd acquired in Japan."[4] Wright decided that his toys would be comprised of interlocking redwood beams. He named his invention Lincoln Logs and patented this building set in 1920.

The marketing campaign for Lincoln Logs appealed to a sense of nostalgia for the frontier past. Although it's unclear if he named his product after his father's real middle name or after President Lincoln, it was hard to miss the connection to nineteenth-century America. According to Taylor Horst of History Colorado, "The log cabin harks back to a mythic, preindustrial America when the West was still a frontier brimming with unknown opportunities. John Lloyd Wright's toy allowed the next generation of children to live out this same Lincolnian dream."[5] The marketing materials made this connection explicit. "The very '*Spirit of America*' is typified by the creative possibilities of LINCOLN LOGS,"[6] proclaimed one advertisement.

At least one child who played with Lincoln Logs in the 1920s and 30s would end up making her contributions to the Spirit of America and the real American West. John Lloyd Wright's own daughter Elizabeth played with Lincoln Logs as a young girl. When she was a grown-up, Elizabeth became an architect too. Elizabeth Wright Ingraham settled in Colorado Springs after World War II. She designed 150 buildings in the state, elevating the built environment of Colorado and the surrounding region.[7]

For many boys and girls growing up in the twentieth century, cabins and forts constructed with Lincoln Logs were set pieces for imaginative play involving other kinds of toys. Eventually, the Lincoln Log product catalog included expansion packs that included farm animals, cowboys, Indians, and even Royal Canadian Police.[8] When nostalgia for the Western frontier reached an all-time high in the 1950s, Lincoln Logs fit in alongside the cap guns, coonskin hats, and other Western-themed toys that children gobbled up during this period. Lincoln Logs also served as elaborate set-pieces for imaginative play with other toys. Historian John Coats recalls, "I spent a good deal of time creating the settings for my play: inside with those blocks and Lincoln Logs (always good for the Alamo), outside, preferably, with a dirt pile. I'd say I likely spent more time in construction than in actual play fighting. I do remember, for a time, using blocks, thrown at high velocity, to attack Lincoln Log forts, but the damage to the sheetrock ended those experiments."[9]

Although Lincoln Logs never reached the toy-craze level that Erector Sets and later LEGOs would, they did entertain children throughout the twentieth century. John Lloyd Wright sold Lincoln Logs to Playskool around 1943, and today K'Nex continues to sell the toys. From 1916–2004, over 100 million sets were sold. In 2016, the company came out with a hundredth-anniversary tin honoring John Lloyd Wright and the children who played with Lincoln Logs over the last century.

25

LEGOs

LEGOs have been entertaining children for decades.
CREDIT: ATLMODERN CREATIVE #637266678

Identifying Information:

LEGOs

Maker: Ole Kirk Christiansen

Manufacturer: LEGO

Date: 1958

The year 2018 marked the sixtieth anniversary of LEGO. In honor of the occasion, adults who grew up with the toys shared their favorite memories around the blogosphere. "LEGO to me means curiosity," recalled Sam Rowland. "As a kid, anytime my LEGO's broke I could put them back together, or it would inspire a new use for the pieces. I think that was one of the most valuable lessons I ever learned . . . and I learned it from a plastic brick."[1] LEGO has been teaching valuable life lessons and delighting children for decades.

LEGO came to American children from Denmark. In the 1930s, Danish carpenter Ole Kirk Christiansen had fallen on hard times and was looking for a way to stabilize his business. In 1924, his children had accidentally burned down his wood shop. He rebuilt, but a few years later the global economic collapse of 1929 caused financial strife in his small town. He was having a hard time selling his wooden household goods because people couldn't afford them. Christiansen later recalled, "We were in a difficult time—but it was well that we could not see what lay ahead. During the summer we were asked to make toys for Jens W. Olesen, Federica, and as we had no other work, we looked on it as a gift from God."[2] He made inexpensive wooden blocks, cars, and pull toys for the local children. His toys were well-loved, and in 1934 Christiansen started manufacturing toys exclusively.[3] He named his company LEGO, combining the Danish words "Leg" and "Godt," which meant "play well."[4] He was committed to manufacturing high-quality toys.

During World War II, imports into German-occupied Denmark were banned. People were forced to buy Danish-made goods because they couldn't get foreign products, so Christiansen's toy sales doubled.[5] Another fire in 1942 burned down the factory, but Christiansen rebuilt again. After the war, he became interested in the use of plastics in children's toys, and he purchased Denmark's first plastic-injection molding machine.

He acquired the rights to Kiddicraft's Self-Locking Blocks, and in 1949 they started producing the plastic Automatic Binding Brick.[6] In 1953, he renamed these little bricks LEGO, bestowing on the toy bricks their proud company name. The company started producing "The LEGO System of Play" in 1955. With this play system, children could build their own towns and villages. Christiansen passed away in 1958, and his son Godtfred took over the company.

LEGO came to the United States in 1961 through a licensing agreement with luggage company Samsonite. With these play systems, children in America could build modern cities, airplanes, animals, and more. In an early commercial, Samsonite advertised "Hey kids, look—a whole new world to build!"[7] American kids fell in love with LEGO right away, and the toy supplanted Tinkertoy and Lincoln Logs as America's favorite construction toy.

Although most of the construction toys of the twentieth century appealed heavily to boys, LEGO made clear that their products were for children both boys and girls. In a television commercial from 1973, a small girl and her older brother play with LEGOs. The toys were meant for kids of all ages, and the narrator of the TV ad states, "First it's new LEGO preschool blocks for little hands, then LEGO building sets for models for older children . . . LEGO grows from child to child. . . . There's no end to LEGO."[8] What better way to sell more products than to make the toys accessible to families with children of all ages, ensuring that LEGO would be relevant to a child throughout their entire growing-up years?

In 1981, the company produced one of its most iconic advertisements. The ad featured an impish little girl in pigtail braids holding up a LEGO creation that she built herself, overlaid with the words, "What it is is beautiful."[9] The narrative of the ad asks, "Have you ever seen anything like it? Not just what she's made, but how proud it's made her. It's a look you'll see whenever children build something all by themselves."[10] The advertisement made clear that the pride of accomplishment and creativity is what makes girls beautiful, not an outside set of unrealistic beauty standards.

LEGO continued the spirit of mid-century construction toys and extended it well into the twenty-first century.[11] However, Gary Cross argues, "LEGO compromised with the American fantasy industry in the 1980s."[12] Toward the end of the century, LEGO started partnering with television shows and movies to produce *Star Wars* playsets and other fictional worlds. Some parents criticized this move because it seemed to defy the free-play nature of construction toys, replacing it with simple mimicry of fantasy worlds. However, LEGO enthusiast Paul Lilley responds to that criticism saying, "Yes, you build 'the thing' but then the parts all get cannibalized for the next project," allowing even these fantasy tie-ins to be used in imaginative ways.[13]

Despite those criticisms, LEGO remains an impactful toy in 2020. Construction toys like LEGO fit well into STEM-related playtime activities. LEGOs continue to fulfill their educational purpose for many children. Tiffany Tseng, an engineer at MIT, states, "Legos are a good introduction to communicating ideas with physical objects. Putting things together and taking them apart got me interested in how things work, and by the time I was an undergraduate, I knew I wanted to be an engineer."[14]

Part VI

DOLLS

For many American girls over the last two centuries, a doll was the most beloved (and sometimes the only) toy in her possession. Dolls serve as companions for little girls, but they also transmit all kinds of cultural values. In this part, we'll look at five different dolls and explore what they say about play as preparation for the future, racial identity, sexuality, consumerism, and the need for companionship.

Just like animal toys, dolls are some of the oldest playthings in the world. The doll form seems to be as old as time itself. Many ancient cultures produced human effigies for ritual, religious, and funerary purposes. According to Antonia Fraser, "the existence of such objects of magico-religious significance has led some scholars to assert that the doll form existed for thousands of years before the first child took possessions of it."[1] It is hard to know when children adopted dolls as objects of play. We do know that the ancient Greeks made dolls with moveable limbs, and there's documentary evidence to suggest that children were playing with these dolls in at least 100 BC. Roman girls played with dolls and were sometimes buried with them.[2]

Many cultures used dolls as a means of religious education. Parents of indigenous cultures of North America gave dolls to their children to help them learn about the physical and spiritual world. Puebloan people including Hopi, Zuni, and Acoma Pueblo gave their children kachina dolls to educate them about cosmology. The dolls represented the kachina—a spiritual being that can be represented through masks or figurines. The dolls were made for different age groups, including infants and toddlers.[3] Inuit tribes also gave dolls to their daughters to teach them about cultural traditions.

Dolls are the great equalizers among traditions, languages, ethnicity, cultures, and time periods. As the curatorial staff of the Colonial Williamsburg Foundation reminds us, during the eighteenth century, "enslaved children, Native American children, and European-American children of all social levels enjoyed playing with dolls. Dolls taught children how to care for their possessions, how to share, and enabled girls to mimic the behaviors of their mothers."[4]

In the American colonies, girls enjoyed playing with handmade dolls constructed out of cloth and carved wood. Their mothers had access to dolls imported from Europe, but most of those were fashion dolls and not children's toys. Eventually, designers switched to paper dolls for the fashion trade, and these paper figures became favorite toys for little girls.[5]

By the nineteenth century, dolls had become tools to prepare girls for a domestic future.[6] During the first half of the nineteenth century, dolls taught practical domestic skills like sewing. Catharine Beecher claimed that by learning how to make doll clothes, "ever afterward, the cutting and fitting of any article of dress . . . was accomplished with entire ease."[7] In the antebellum period, girls made rag dolls "in an attempt to facilitate sewing skills that integrated leisure with training in the domestic economy."[8]

In the late nineteenth century, class consciousness factored heavily into the adult desire for girls to play with dolls. During the late nineteenth century, the birth rate dropped among middle-class women. According to historian Priscilla Clement, "childrearing authorities hoped that early play with baby dolls would discourage later 'companionate marriages' and 'one-child mothers.'"[9] With the advent of French Bebe dolls in the middle of the century, girls could act out their future maternal role, learning how to dress, cradle, feed, and rock the baby.

Families had an increasing number of manufactured dolls to choose from, most of which were imported. There were porcelain dolls from China, wooden dolls from Germany, or wax dolls from France. Despite the number of goods available, these manufactured dolls were expensive. In an age when the average income in the United States was $486, French jointed dolls could cost upwards of $30. The average middle-class daughter might own one or two manufactured dolls of middling monetary value. Gary Cross argues that "girls received few dolls, and they were often repaired rather than replaced."[10]

This part will explore five dolls and what they have to say about American girlhood. Margaret Woodbury Strong's doll Mabel tells the story of dolls as favorite companion objects for little girls. Next, the SoWee Sunbabe doll tells the story of childhood in the Texas Panhandle. Third, girls learned much about racial identity through their toys, and in the 1950s the SaraLee doll was an attempt to give African American girls a doll that looked like them. Barbie tells a complicated tale of changing gender roles and sexuality in the mid- to late twentieth century. Finally, Cabbage Patch Kids turned young children into consumers in the 1980s.

Mabel

Margaret Woodbury holding her doll Mabel
COURTESY OF THE STRONG, ROCHESTER, NEW YORK

Identifying Information:

Mabel

Manufacturer: J. D. Kestner Doll Factory

Date: c. 1902

Strong Museum of Play Object ID 80.1799

When she was five years old, Margaret Woodbury received a porcelain doll. She named it "Mabel." Margaret was an only child, and, in the absence of siblings, toys became her faithful companions. This passage looks at Mabel and the other toys in Margaret's childhood collection because they give us a window into upper-class childhood at the turn of the twentieth century.

Margaret Woodbury was born on March 20, 1897, to John Charles Woodbury and Alice Motley Woodbury in Rochester, New York. When she was five years old, she received a bisque doll made by the J. D. Kestner Doll Factory in Germany. Mabel the doll wore a pretty white dress and had a delicate, endearing face. At some point, locks of Margaret's blond hair were made into a wig for the doll, forever bonding the child with her favorite possession.

Although imported dolls were still very expensive, a rising middle-class or upper-class family could usually afford to purchase one for their daughters in the early twentieth century. European-manufactured dolls had been popular in America since the colonial era when adult women owned imported fashion dolls. These figures became children's toys in the mid-nineteenth century, when lucky American girls had access to dolls imported from France, Germany, and other centers of European doll-manufacturing.

Around 1805, Johannes Daniel Kestner Jr. of Waltershausen in Thuringia, Germany, started making dolls for the children in his region. Early on, he made dolls out of wood and papier-mache. In the 1850s, Kestner produced porcelain and bisque dolls to his product line, which were all the rage at the time. After Johannes died, his grandson Adolf took ownership of the factory. According to *Collector's Weekly*, "Like every doll maker, Kestner produced a version of the universally popular 'Dolly Face' head, which has the rounded, slightly double-chinned face of a toddler or baby."[1] The Kestner dolls were very popular with well-to-do East Coast families in the United States in the early twentieth century.[2] The wealthy Woodbury parents may have encountered other Kestner dolls in their social circles, prompting them to buy one for their daughter Margaret.

Mabel was one of many toys in Margaret's toy box. The Woodbury family had the resources to buy more manufactured and imported toys than many other families of the day could have afforded. When Margaret was born, she received a silver rattle, a common gift for babies during this period.[3] She owned a black stuffed dog named Dixie who wore a collar and tags around its neck. Dixie and Margaret had all kinds of adventures together. The stuffed dog was once the subject of a photoshoot when tiny Margaret decided to play with her new Brownie Camera.[4]

Dolls soon became an important part of young Margaret's life too. Photographs of her as a baby depict her sitting in a pram with a doll by her side. When she was two years old, she played in the yard by "picking flowers for dolly."[5] By 1899, she had acquired at least four more dolls including two African American dolls (one black rag doll, and one "mammy" doll), along with two white baby dolls. Margaret had a small carriage, which she used to push her dollies up and down the street.[6] She took her dolls everywhere, including to the beach. There she sat her babies on the sand while she played with a bucket in the ocean.[7]

When she got a little bit older, the Woodbury family traveled all over the world. Her parents, who were collectors themselves, encouraged Margaret to bring an empty bag along to gather small objects wherever they went. They traveled to Japan, Hawaii, Colorado Springs, and other exciting places. Margaret acquired interesting artifacts from each of these places. She also brought Mabel along on these trips, and the doll became her favorite companion.[8]

When Margaret grew up, she continued her collecting habit. She married a lawyer and businessman named Homer Strong, and they had a daughter named Barbara. As an adult, she never forgot how much Mabel and her other childhood toys had meant to her, and this sense of joy guided her collecting philosophy. According to the staff at the Strong Museum of Play, "The most serious phase in Margaret's collecting did not start until after the deaths of her daughter and husband. Collecting trinkets, art, furniture, and dolls brought Margaret joy and comfort, and sharing her collections with friends and those who visited her home gave her a sense of purpose."[9] Her collection of dolls grew from 600 to 27,000 between 1960 and 1969.[10]

As an adult, Margaret was an heiress with shares in Eastman Kodak stock, so she had the resources to acquire anything she wanted. She had a particular fondness for ordinary objects of childhood, however. When any of her acquaintances questioned this, she would reply, "Little girls did not look at the marks on the backs of doll heads. . . . There were dolls under every Christmas tree in America, and little girls loved all of them. Just look at the condition some of the poor things are in now from too much loving."[11] Eventually, she had hundreds of thousands of toys in her collection.

Later in life, she set up a trust for her artifacts and created a vision for the Margaret Woodbury Strong Museum of Fascination. After she passed away in 1969, her vision of a museum became a reality. The Margaret Woodbury Strong Museum opened in Rochester, New York, in 1982. In 2003, the museum changed its mission to focus solely on its collection of playtime artifacts. Mabel, the doll who served as Margaret's faithful companion in childhood, is a proud ambassador to the many children who visit the Strong National Museum of Play.

SoWee Sunbabe Doll

Ruth Brown Fletcher's SoWee Sunbabe Doll
CREDIT: SUSAN A. FLETCHER

Identifying Information:

SoWee Sunbabe Doll

Maker: Ruth E. Newton

Manufacturer: The Sun Rubber Company

Date: c. 1946

Collection of Ruth Brown Fletcher

The majority of American children didn't come to be in possession of a large number of manufactured toys until the economic boom of the post–World War II years. The modern toy box that overflows with abundance is a recent phenomenon, fueled by modern consumer culture and a child-focused parenting style of the late twentieth and early twenty-first century. Until that point, girls may have only owned one toy; and that toy was usually a single doll. This passage will look at a rubber SoWee Sunbabe Doll and its role in a girlhood spent on the plains of Texas.

Ruth Brown and her sister Glenna grew up in the Texas Panhandle in the 1940s and 50s. Their father worked at a gas production plant. They each owned one doll, plus an occasional addition to their collection. This girlhood spent with only a few toys was the norm for most children from 1840 through the 1950s. Spending money on lots of toys came into vogue for middle-class families during the economic boom of the 1950s, but this carefree attitude did not extend to working-class families. Brown recalls that when she was young, "I didn't have very many toys. I had a little rubber baby doll. [Mother] made us doll clothes and blankets."[1] She acquired this doll when she was an infant, along with a teddy bear.

Ruth's baby doll was a SoWee Sunbabe Doll made by the Sun Rubber Company in Barberton, Ohio. The rubber doll has molded hair, bright glass eyes, and a tiny bow mouth. The Sun Rubber Company was founded in 1923 as a manufacturer of hot water bottles. Soon they expanded their product line to make rubber dolls and squeaky toys. The company was known for licensing characters to produce in doll-form, including the Gerber baby and various Disney characters. In 1949, the Sun Rubber company manufactured Amosandra, one of the first black baby dolls. The company's artist Ruth E. Newton designed many of their toys, including the SoWee Sunbabe doll.[2]

Ruth treasured her SoWee doll, which she named Jo. She recalls, "For Christmas and birthdays, my mother sewed doll clothes and quilts for little Jo."[3] According to historian Gary Cross, the tradition of sewing handmade doll clothes was "more than an example of old-fashioned thrift. It represented a tradition of craft work that complemented the decision to purchase manufactured dolls. . . . This was merely a natural extension of the custom of hand-sewing the clothing of family members."[4]

Two more dolls entered the Brown household in the 1950s. Ruth and Glenna's father bought a child-size doll for one of the sisters, and shortly thereafter he won a matching version of the doll at a Christmas party at his job. When Glenna was a little bit older, she received one more doll: "My last doll was a bride doll," Glenna recalls. "She was a walking doll—they could walk, and their arms could move. They were two feet tall."[5]

Growing up in the dusty Panhandle, the girls spent much of their time playing outside by themselves and with their cousins. They invented all kinds of outdoor games to play. "Back in that day, we didn't have toy stores where we could get any toys we wanted, and we couldn't afford them. The games we played like Hide and Seek and Red Rover were all games that didn't require any equipment or tools," Glenna recalls. The sisters made mud and sand pies, played with yo-yos, played house, and ran around outside. Ruth recalls, "We climbed trees. We played jump rope and jacks. We had a swing set that Pop made for us."[6]

When they wanted to play indoors, the girls had a variety of amusements. "We played Go Fish and Old Maid, and my dad taught us to play poker. My mother didn't like that—she thought it was gambling,"[7] recalls Glenna. They also played a homemade game that their family members made called Wahoo, along with checkers. The sisters experienced the pop culture of their day through the comic books that they bought for a nickel. They read *Archie*, *Looney Toons*, and *Little Nancy*.

Glenna recalls, "The toys that we had we took care of. We had our dolls forever. They were things that we didn't take for granted."[8] Baby Boomers who grew up during this time period sometimes find themselves in shock over the child-centered consumer culture of the early twenty-first century. It's important to remember that American families have always been limited in what they could (and wanted to) acquire for their children based on economic situation, geographical location, class status, and more. As you read about the fifty different toys and games in this book, keep in mind that up until the late twentieth century it was normal for families to only own a few of these toys at a time, and even more normal for families to manufacture their own playthings at home. The overflowing toy box that many Millennials grew up with in the 1980s and 90s was an entirely new thing in the history of American childhood and has a lot to do with a child-centered culture that developed during this time period. You'll read about that more in the passages on Barbie and Cabbage Patch Kids.

28

SaraLee Doll

SaraLee Doll
COURTESY OF THE STRONG, ROCHESTER, NEW YORK

127

Identifying Information:

SaraLee Doll

Maker: Sara Lee Creech

Manufacturer: Ideal Toy Company

Date: 1951–1953

Strong Museum of Play Object ID 82.2165

D oll expert Debbie Garrett recalls, "Black dolls were not readily accessible during the mid-1950s through mid-1960s in the segregated South of my youth. The available ones, according to my mother, were derogatory. Their exaggerated facial features and unrealistically dark complexions were negative depictions of black people, therefore, unacceptable in our household."[1] For many black families, finding dolls for their daughters to play with was a big challenge. The black dolls that were available perpetuated racial stereotypes; playing with only white dolls was also problematic. This passage looks at the development of the SaraLee doll in 1949, which was an attempt to provide African American girls with a doll that looked like them.

Doll expert Myla Perkins breaks down the history of black dolls into two categories, first, "dolls representing blacks to white children and parents."[2] These objects included porcelain and wax dolls from Europe, topsy-turvy dolls, Beloved Belindy dolls, and Aunt Jemima dolls of the late nineteenth and early twentieth centuries. Most of them promoted negative racial stereotypes for a white audience.

"Dolls made for and marketed to black children"[3] comprise Perkins's second category. These objects include dolls made within the African American community, such as Leo Moss's toys. Moss was an African American doll maker from Macon, Georgia. In the late 1880s and early 90s, he created intricate black dolls, working with reclaimed materials, crafting papier-mache doll heads out of scrap wallpaper. Moss based the figures on his friends and family members, and he let the children in his community play with them.[4]

However, Perkins argues that the "abundance and variety of black dolls as proper playthings for black children diminished greatly by the 1930s."[5] Many of the black baby dolls that were available to little girls by the mid-twentieth century came from the same molds that doll makers used to create white dolls. These objects had features of Caucasian children, just with darker skin. Black girls had very few options to play with baby dolls that looked like them—and this was creating devastating problems.

In 1939, psychologists Kenneth B. Clark and Mamie P. Clark conducted an experiment on racial identification using dolls and other objects. The Clarks wrote, "Because the problem of racial identification is so definitely related to the problem of the genesis of racial attitudes in children, it was thought practicable to attempt to determine the racial attitudes or preferences of these Negro children."[6] They recruited 253 black children for the study. The Clarks gave the children four dolls, all of which were the same except for skin color. Two of the dolls were white, and two were brown.

They asked the children a series of questions: Which doll did they want to play with? Which one was "a nice doll," which one looked "bad," which was a "nice color," and which "looks like you?"[7] Almost all of the children indicated that the brown dolls looked "bad," and most of them indicated a preference to play with the white doll, which they labeled as "pretty" or "nice."[8] According to Kenneth Clark, "And this, we interpreted as indicating that color in a racist society was a very disturbing and traumatic component of an individual's sense of his own self-esteem and worth."[9]

In 1948, Florida businesswoman and activist Sara Lee Creech saw two black girls playing with white dolls. Creech became concerned that the girls didn't have any dolls to play with that looked like them, so she decided to make one. She did extensive research on the history of black dolls in her effort to make one that was "anthropologically correct."[10] Through her research, she came to believe that toys transmitted racial prejudice to children, and she wanted to do something to help.[11]

She enlisted a large team to help make her doll as true-to-life as possible. Creech asked sculptor Sheila Burlingame to design the mold for the doll's head. Burlingame based her work on images of the black children in the Belle Glade community.[12] Creech took the prototypes of the doll to her friend novelist Zora Neale Hurston, who introduced her to influential leaders in the African American community. These associates included Bishop Wright of the AME Church, Ralph Bunche, and Jackie Robinson. One of these connections introduced Creech to former first lady Eleanor Roosevelt, who loved the project and wanted to do what she could to support it.

Helen Whiting of Atlanta University challenged Creech to consider an array of skin colors for the dolls to accurately represent the array of black skin tones. Creech assembled a jury of African American leaders including Bunche and Hurston to discuss which shade the doll's skin should be.[13] According to writer Emily Temple, "The ideal situation, they had decided, was to bring four different dolls to market at once, all presented as siblings, all with different features, hair, and skin colors, so as not to contribute to yet another stereotype, but the Sara Lee doll was the first hurdle."[14]

The Ideal Toy Company manufactured Creech's "Saralee Negro Doll" in 1951. The sixteen-inch doll was made of vinyl and sold for $6.95.[15] The packaging described the doll as "More Than Just a Doll . . . An Ambassador of Good Will."[16] Despite the idealistic triumph of getting the doll through the manufacturing process, the product faced numerous challenges. The Sears company had supported the project early on and was glad to sell it on their shelves. However, other department stores like Macy's refused to sell it. Sales of the doll were disappointing. Furthermore, the doll's vinyl skin started to fade due to an unforeseen manufacturing error. The Ideal executives eventually blocked the production of SaraLee's sibling dolls, and they ceased production of the SaraLee doll itself in 1953.

Despite the commercial failure of the SaraLee doll, it highlighted the need for realistic black dolls for girls to play with. According to Debbie Garrett, "I'm emphatic about a black child having a doll that reflects who she is. When a young child is playing with a doll, she is mimicking being a mother, and in her young, impressionable years, I want that child to understand that there's nothing wrong with being black."[17]

29

Barbie

Barbie wardrobe
CREDIT: SUSAN A. FLETCHER

Identifying Information:

Barbie

Maker: Ruth Handler

Manufacturer: Mattel

Date: 1959

In 2019, Barbie turned sixty years old. Over the last six decades, Barbie has witnessed seismic changes to childhood and youth in America. She was an active player in shifting ideas about girlhood and womanhood. She turned three generations of girls into ravenous consumers. And she's been one of the most controversial toys in American history.

Barbie was a watershed creation in the history of doll play. Until the late 1950s, the majority of dolls that little girls played with were either babies (classic baby dolls) or grown-ups (adult china dolls and fashion paper dolls). As you've already learned in this chapter, doll-play was intended to inspire maternal nurturing skills and to help girls learn the practical skills of homemaking. Barbie was different. She was a teenager who didn't need to be nurtured. She represented a brand-new pause in between girlhood and motherhood: a glorious adolescence wherein a teenager could spend hours on clothes and boys without worrying too much about what lay ahead for her. Gary Cross notes, "Barbie was an early rebel against the domesticity that dominated the lives of the baby boom mothers."[1]

Barbie is based on a sensual object of desire from Europe. In 1953, German artist Reinhard Berthein drew a cartoon figure of a sassy call girl for the Hamburg *Bild-Zeitung*. Her name was Lilli. She was tall, blonde, and buxom. In the cartoon, she accompanied men to dinner and costume parties, and she occasionally went out wearing nothing more than her underwear. The newspaper turned the character of Lilli into a plastic doll, which sold at gentlemen's novelty stores. The doll wore eyeshadow, red lipstick, and stared downward in a suggestive glance.

In 1956, Ruth Handler first encountered the Bild Lilli dolls while she was traveling in Lucerne, Switzerland, with her husband, Elliot, and her children, Barbie and Ken. The Handlers were co-owners of the Mattel Company, which Elliot had founded with his business partner Harold Matson in 1948. Ruth knew how much her daughter Barbie enjoyed playing with paper fashion dolls, and she decided to create a three-dimensional doll that serve the same function as these fashion dolls. Handler transformed the suggestive Lilli doll into the "girl next door."[2] The new version was scaled down slightly and wore a striped bathing suit. Handler named her creation after her daughter. In the first year, the original Barbie doll sold 350,000 units at $3 each.[3,4]

Barbie, her accessories, and her extended family are part of a clever marketing scheme known as the razor/razor blade model. Think about the process of shaving: you can buy a razor handle for a reasonable amount of money, but then you're stuck buying very expensive razor cartridges indefinitely. In this case, Barbie is the razor handle and all of her clothes, accessories, and companions are the razor blades. Barbie can't go around naked, so she needs a closet full of outfits. She shouldn't be lonesome, so her owner should also buy her at least a few more companion dolls. Once Barbie enters a house, all of her accoutrements follow, and out the door goes her owner's money.

This marketing process turned late twentieth-century children into ravenous consumers. Historian Miriam Forman-Brunell reminds us that in the post–World War II years, Barbie "exemplified the ethos of an expanding consumer culture where spending replaced saving."[5] Whereas thriftiness and resourcefulness had saved the day during the Great Depression and the war years, being a good American in the 1950s and 60s meant that you were buying all of the shiny new things available to you in the postwar economic boom.[6] With family size decreasing, many teenage girls no longer had the traditional responsibilities of taking care of their younger siblings. They now had free time to play and the ability to take babysitting jobs outside the home. Earning their own money gave girls the resources to spend on acquiring all the right things for their leisure time. According to historian Howard Chudacoff, "Barbie and her clones proved to be problematic . . . because they fostered a desire to indulge in 'carefree buying,' consumerism that was unattainable to girls from low-income households."[7]

Barbie also changed how girls experienced doll play. Whereas their brothers growing up in the 1950s and 1960s were busy preparing for their futures by playing with chemistry sets and construction toys, Barbie made girls' play quite different. In the beginning, mothers seemed to be in favor of Barbie because she was a significant step away from the notion of doll play as preparation for motherhood that they had grown up with themselves. Playing with Barbie didn't cultivate a nurturing instinct; instead, the doll taught girls about fashion and consumerism. According to Chudacoff, "The objective in the storyline in girls' fantasy toys thus was 'popularity' achieved mainly through grooming and acquisitiveness."[8]

Barbie has always been a lightning rod for differing views on gender and sexuality. Because Barbie was built on the foundations of a sexy call girl, it's hard to separate her from an overt sexuality. During Second Wave Feminism in the 1960s and 70s, activists protested Barbie as a symbol of everything they were fighting against. In 1972, the National Organization of Women passed out leaflets at the annual New York Toy Fair, charging that Barbie "perpetuated sexual stereotypes by encouraging little girls to see themselves solely as mannequins, sex objects or housekeepers."[9]

Although Barbie had a variety of careers over the years, including doctor and astronaut, it's been hard to shake her origins as a busty bimbo. This image of her became painfully evident in 1992 when Mattel released the infamous Teen Talk Barbie. In the early 1990s, toy companies figured out how to put voice boxes in toys to make them "talk." Both Barbie and G.I. Joe gained voices. The Teen Talk Barbie said things like "math class is tough," and "let's go shopping!" among the 270 phrases she was programmed to say. The American Association of University Women were horrified and called for Mattel to pull the dolls from shelves. "Preteen girls most likely to play with Teen Talk Barbie are at the highest risk for losing confidence in their math ability,"[10] said AAUW President Sharon Schuster.

Although Mattel offered to delete the "math class is tough" comment, the fight against the toy wasn't over. In 1993, The Barbie Liberation Organization (BLO) entered the fray by pulling off one of the greatest stunts in toy history. A secret group of activists decided to mock the absurdity of gender-based toys by switching out the voice boxes on Teen Talk Barbie and the talking G.I. Joe action figures. They purchased boxes of both toys from stores all over the country. The BLO performed "surgery" to transplant the Barbie voice boxes into the G.I. Joes and vice versa. The group then "reverse shop-lifted" the toys by stealthily returning them to toy store shelves, just in time for the Christmas season.

The BLO explained, "Before our surgeons performed the operations, Teen Talk Barbie Dolls were programmed to subtly brainwash young minds. The phrases they speak indoctrinate young girls into a system of beliefs and values that seek to subjugate women and provide them with less opportunity than men. The dolls enforce stereotypes and stunt the growth of independent thought."[11] The organization put a label on the back of each box asking the unsuspecting consumer who purchased it to call their local news station.

On Christmas Day 1993, children unwrapped their presents to find some big surprises. Girls found their Teen Talk Barbies uttering guttural phrases like "Cobra, attack!" Their brothers' G.I. Joes were saying, "Let's go shopping!" Confused parents looked at the special labels on the packages and called their local television stations. After a few days, the Barbie Liberation Organization sent a VHS tape to the major news organizations across the country, revealing their plot. The spokeswoman on the video was an image of Barbie with a talking mouth superimposed on her face. "We're an international group of children's toys that are revolting against the company that made us,"[12] she explained.

Although some of the parents who bought the surgically altered toys were understandably upset, many more appeared to be good sports about it. Moreover, some of the children got the message the BLO was trying to send. One local news report featured the reaction of young Hannah Henze and her friend Zak Zelen. Zak remarked about the surgically altered G.I. Joe he accidentally got, saying, "This guy is not as violent."[13] According to young Hannah, "It makes Barbie not so babyish because they made her talk like a kid and she's a grown woman."[14]

30

Cabbage Patch Kids

Victoria Miller with her
Cabbage Patch Doll
CREDIT: VICTORIA MILLER

Identifying Information:

Cabbage Patch Kids

Maker: Xavier Roberts

Manufacturer: Original Appalachian Artworks and Coleco

Date: 1978

Collection of Victoria Miller

The Cabbage Patch Doll is the first toy that I remember getting as a child. As I discussed in the preface, my mother lined up at Best Department Store in the mid-1980s to buy a Cabbage Patch Preemie for me. I named the doll Tessa, and she became a constant companion. This passage explores the development of Cabbage Patch Kids (CPK) and the forces of 1980s consumerism behind them.

The father of Cabbage Patch dolls, Xavier Roberts, grew up in Cleveland, Georgia. His father died in a car accident when he was young. His widowed mother Eula raised Xavier and his five siblings. She supported her family by making quilts and other crafts. After high school, Xavier continued the family's tradition of handcrafts. He was fascinated with the folk-art form of soft sculpture.[1]

The origin of the Cabbage Patch dolls gets murky from here. The official Cabbage Patch history sees Xavier Roberts creating soft-form dolls that he called Little People in 1976. Each one had a sweet face, stubby little hands, and a squishy nose. He showed the dolls at the shop where he worked. One day, a customer walked in the store and asked how much the dolls were. Roberts replied, "They're not for sale . . . but you can adopt them."[2] And the toys took off from there.

However, a lawsuit filed against Roberts in 1980 claims that he visited a craft fair in Berea, Kentucky, in 1976. There he saw vendor Martha Nelson Thomas adopting out some soft-form dolls that she made. Thomas later claimed that Roberts asked if he could sell her toys at his shop in Helen, Georgia. The pair never agreed on a price, and Roberts told her that he'd find a way to sell the dolls whether they were made by her or someone else. Roberts turned out to be that someone else.[3] He later settled out of court with Thomas, his lawyer admitting that her doll inspired Roberts.

His version of the dolls became famous in the region, and the adoption model became the standard way by which the dolls were sold. Roberts opened the BabyLand General Hospital in an old medical clinic in Cleveland, Georgia, and employed more staff to help him make the dolls. After the handmade dolls were featured on television, people from outside the region flocked to the "hospital" to view and adopt the enchanting dolls. The demand was more than Roberts and his team could keep up with, and they sold the manufacturing rights to the dolls to Coleco Industries.[4]

Coleco's advertising firm held market research sessions with adult women and introduced them to the dolls. They asked the women questions to see how they felt about the concept of adoption.[5] The women all responded positively. Historian Howard Chudacoff explains, "Advertisers quickly learned that they could merge a 'backstory' fantasy with a product to create a meaningful relationship between toy and child."[6] Each CPK came with an official adoption certificate and a short story about the doll's identity. This marketing technique worked well beyond anything the company could have imagined.

In 1983, a Cabbage Patch Kid craze swept the nation, similar to the teddy bear craze of 1906.[7] Christmas 1983 was the height of the Cabbage Patch Craze. Public demand outpaced Coleco's rate of production, creating widely publicized shortages of the dolls. The company hired charter planes to fly the toys to the United States from Asia, where they were manufactured. Even this act of desperation couldn't fill the demand. Parents mobbed the few stores that did have the dolls in stock. The JCPenny in Ludington, Michigan, held lotteries to sell the dolls as soon as they arrived on the loading dock.[8] At the Zayre Department Store in Wilkes-Barre, Pennsylvania, a crowd of 1,000 people rushed into the store after waiting in line for eight hours. The store owner armed himself with a baseball bat, and a woman broke her leg when the crowd knocked her to the floor.[9]

Debra Brookhart recalls the night her father returned home after searching for one of the dolls. "I vividly remember he came home hours later with horrible war stories of being smacked and shoved around by people in the stores trying to get a Cabbage Patch Kid. He pulled out the awfullest knock-off Cabbage Patch Kid I'd ever seen. After hours of searching, he finally found it in a gas station."[10]

Although Coleco did target girls in their marketing campaign, it seems that adult women were driving the toy craze. Cabbage Patch Kids were what parents thought they ought to be giving their kids, rather than what the kids were demanding. Gary Cross argues that women bought CPK because they "reminded them of their own baby doll play and their desire that their children share in this experience."[11]

However, Cabbage Patch Kids were also unique in doll-play history. In the 1980s, many parents were no longer raising their girls with a strictly domestic future in mind. Doll play shifted away from play as preparation for the future and toward a companionate model. Coleco commissioned studies on this shift to understand how to market their dolls. Dr. Paul C. Horton told the company that children "need attachments external to themselves to give solace and comfort."[12]

The adoption scheme helped bond children to their new dolls and gave them something outside themselves to care about. Dr. Malcolm Watson of Brandeis University wrote, "The relative uniqueness of each doll, as well as the procedure of adopting the doll and committing to it, increase the child's ease of attachment to the doll and the use of it as a companion."[13] Adopting a Cabbage Patch Kid become a ritual by which adults could enter into children's play. In 1984, Indiana Judge George A. Jacobs started a tradition of holding mock adoption ceremonies in his courtroom for the town children who wanted to "officially" become Cabbage Patch parents. Kids raised their right hands and recited the Cabbage Patch adoption oath: "I promise to love my Cabbage Patch Kid with all my heart. I promise to be a good and kind parent. I will always remember how special my Cabbage Patch Kid is to me."[14]

Cabbage Patch Kids raised awareness of adoption, but this often caused uncomfortable situations for adoptive families in the real world. During the 1980s, attitudes toward adoption had become more open than they had been in previous decades. Parents who adopted children were increasingly likely to discuss their family status openly and honestly. However, adoptive families worried that Cabbage Patch Kids might be giving their children's friends the wrong messages. One father wrote the *New York Times* to say, "Familiarity with the fantasy of doll 'adoption' may breed contempt for the adoption reality. Adoption . . . is a crucial and sacred subject to most adoptive children. Playtime curiosity about doll 'adoption papers' can make light of the real event that the papers symbolize."[15]

The big Cabbage Patch craze only lasted a few years. In 1986, Cabbage Patch Kids had a sales slump. That year, Coleco sold $250 million of dolls, but this was $350 million less than 1985. Stock prices fell from $21.50 a share in 1985 to $8.25 in January 1987.[16] Despite declining sales, the dolls remained part of children's toy boxes for many years. Children who grew up in the 1980s remember their Cabbage Patch dolls fondly.

Part VII

ACTION FIGURES

O n Christmas Day 1987, a boy named Dan ran downstairs at his grand-mother's house to the awaiting Christmas tree and presents. To his sheer delight, "Standing on top of the boxes were Kenner's Real Ghostbuster's Action Figures, the four main Ghostbusters. . . . They all had their proton packs strapped to their backs, and all of them were busting their little companion ghosts that came packaged with them."[1] Action figures were much-anticipated gifts under many Christmas trees in the 1980s. Kids across the country tore open packages of G.I. Joes, He-Man, Ghostbusters, and other action heroes. In this part, we'll look at the development of action figures from the metal toy soldiers of the nineteenth century to the colorful Teenage Mutant Ninja Turtles of the 1980s. Along the way, we'll explore these toys' relationships to war and violence, and the context of late twentieth-century boyhood.

What *is* an action figure, anyway? Are action figures a type of doll, or are they something different? Does an action figure have to move in order to be considered for the category? For the purposes of this book, I like the *Cambridge Dictionary*'s definition: "a toy that is made to look like a soldier or a character from a film or television show."[2] With this definition in mind, I am including toy soldiers and Little Green Army Men into this category because of the type of play that they inspired, along with G.I. Joe, the *Star Wars* figures, and Teenage Mutant Ninja Turtles. Also, although many action figures are related to dolls both in size and the kind of imaginative play that they inspire, I am considering action figures a separate category from dolls.

Action figures in the United States started with metal toy soldiers, which became popular children's toys in the late nineteenth century. Little Green Army Men followed in the 1930s. In the mid-1960s, the world of "toys that are made to look like soldiers" changed forever when G.I. Joe came on the scene. All of these toys helped boys play out games of war in a time when their fathers and older brothers may have been fighting in foreign wars, which bonded fathers and sons.

Global events had a significant impact on how boys played with action figures. For instance, the Vietnam War soured Americans' attitude toward war toys. In 1973, the OPEC oil crisis made petroleum so expensive that toymakers were forced to think of other ways to manufacture plastic toys, especially action figures. In the late 1970s, action figures became popular again thanks to *Star Wars* toys. Those toys shifted war-play away from the real world and toward a fantasy world instead, which made this type of play more socially acceptable. Attitudes toward the military changed again with a wave of patriotism under the Reagan administration in the 1980s, which dovetailed with an explosion of action figures in that decade. These included Transformers, Masters of the Universe, Thundercats, Ghostbusters, and Teenage Mutant Ninja Turtles. By 1985, sales of action figures hit $620 million.[3]

The role of war and violence in boys' play is still a hotly debated topic. According to psychologist Joseph Cassius, "It's not socially acceptable to shoot somebody, but it is socially acceptable to play at it. What's good or bad isn't the point. . . . If the kid has a need to express aggressiveness, he may do this by his selection of a particular toy."[4]

By the mid-1980s, almost every action figure played out battles between good and evil set in a fantasy world. Whereas children of the 1950s played toy soldiers and fought historic battles against the Nazis, action-figure play of the 1980s was much different. The enemy had become an abstract notion of evil as embodied in fictional villains. The Autobots battled the Decepticons, and the Teenage Mutant Ninja Turtles fought against Shredder.

In this part, we'll explore five action figures and learn what they tell us about the historical context in which children would have played with them. Toy soldiers appealed to children and parents because they educated kids on military history. Little Green Army Men became important objects that helped children process real-world violence and war during WWII and the Korean War. Third, G.I. Joe turned boys into young consumers by supplying them with all kinds of accessories to buy, just like Barbie did for girls a few years earlier. The *Star Wars* figures embody a rise in media-influenced toys during the Cold War. Last, we'll look at how the Teenage Mutant Ninja Turtles preached a message of surrogate family during the 1980s and 90s.

31

Toy Soldiers

Painted lead soldiers

Identifying Information:

Metal Toy Soldiers

Science History Institute. *Painted Lead Soldiers*

Men have enjoyed reenacting battles with little military figures for thousands of years. Tiny soldier figures appear in a variety of cultures including ancient Egypt and Rome. These figures were often made of clay, wood, or stone. The metal toy soldiers that we are familiar with today came into being in the 1730s when metalsmiths in Germany began mass-producing tin soldiers. These became useful in war strategy by professional military men.[1] These metal soldiers became cheaper and more easily accessible in the 1890s, shifting them from an adult's possession to a child's toy. Toy soldiers became an iconic part of boyhood in the early twentieth century, introducing boys to the grown-up world of war.

These metal soldiers became popular children's toys in 1893 when English company William Britains revolutionized the toy-making industry by introducing the hollow casting method. This made the little metal soldiers much lighter and cheaper, which made them perfect for children's toys. For the first time, the soldiers were widely available to boys in England and the United States.

Toy metal soldiers became commonly available amid an increase in the amount of playtime available to boys in the early twentieth century. Historian Kenneth Brown argues that "It is important to note that toy soldier games were essentially home-centered, private activities, characteristics which, it has been argued, were becoming increasingly typical of leisure patterns, particularly among the working classes."[2] In 1914, toy soldiers sold for 25 cents per box.[3] The little figures were affordable for a boy who wanted to collect enough of them to build an army. He also likely had enough free time to do so in that time period.

Some play experts were worried that these figures would cultivate an early love of war. One complained, "I have seen toy soldiers given to little boys before ever they had seen real soldiers or even heard of them."[4] However, not every boy was interested in war play. Sensitive, artistic boys found themselves at odds with their war-loving companions. Pablo Casals, the famous cellist, recalled, "I never enjoyed having toy soldiers and when my playmates played at war I would refuse to join in."[5]

Regardless of a boy's views on war, toy soldiers taught children important lessons on military history and sometimes inspired their future career choices. History professor John Coats recalls, "I certainly played with several sets of soldiers when I was a child. These were usually World War II . . . but also a set of Alamo soldiers and generic Vietnam era sets from five and dimes."[6] Public historian Marc Blackburn recalls, "My most vivid memory was a Civil War playset that I got one holiday season. The Union soldiers were blue and the Confederate Grey. It also included some spring-loaded cannon and plastic earthworks. It captured my imagination."[7]

Toy soldiers also cultivated artistic skills and creativity. Boys built elaborate sets and props for their soldiers out of their construction toys. Coats built forts for his soldiers using Lincoln Logs. "The creative aspect of this play is an interesting consideration," Coats recalls. "I painted (and repainted) all of my standard-sized soldiers. . . . I can remember sitting at the kitchen counter, tubes of acrylic in front of me, a palette of tin foil at the ready, and my mom as a reference for how to blend color: cadmium red, titanium white, ultramarine blue."[8]

The collector's market and the booming 1980s economy drove the price of toy soldiers through the roof. No longer a simple childhood toy, they became a display of wealth and power.[9] Magazine publisher Malcolm Forbes amassed a collection of 80,000 toy soldiers by 1982. He kept them in a palace in Morocco. Among his collection were metal soldiers depicting the battle of the Aztec city Tenochtitlan in 1521, Rommel's Afrika Korps from 1941, and a Norwegian polar expedition. When asked if Forbes viewed his collection as a business investment, he said, "Well, that's the sophistry I use to justify paying exorbitant amounts of money for toy soldiers. If you buy enough, you drive up the market price. And then I'd point to the high market price and say to my wife, 'See, these are a good investment, don't be upset with me, honey.'"[10]

32

Little Green Army Men

Bob Beatty's childhood Green Army Men
CREDIT: BOB BEATTY

Identifying Information:

Little Green Army Men

Manufacturer: Bergen Toy and Novelty Company

Date: 1938

Collection of Bob Beatty

For a few years after I bought my house, every time I went into my back-yard, I would accidentally find a Little Green Army Man. The children who lived here before me left the little toys all over the yard. I found plastic soldiers buried in my flower beds and the planters. Above ground, faded green figures lay in the rock piles. These tiny soldiers were cheap and ubiquitous, so the kids who grew up in this house before I bought it presumably owned enough to leave them laying around the yard without much thought. This passage will explore the impact of material technology on the manufacture of Little Green Army Men and the role of the toys in war-play.

Little Green Army Men evolved from metal toy soldiers. In 1938, the Bergen Toy and Novelty Company (aka Beton) started selling two-inch plastic soldiers.[1] The company was already well-loved for their tiny lead-based soldiers, Indians, circus figures, and more. Beton modeled their new plastic soldiers after the WWI US Army Doughboys. They carried rifles, bugles, and spyglasses. The original figures were painted with lead paint, although this practice ended within the first few years of production.[2] In the 1930s, plastic was a newly available material, and many toy companies were experimenting with it to use in children's toys.

When the United States joined WWII, the plastic army men were updated to reflect the modern 1940s military man. The figures came in more extreme action poses and looked like they were frozen in battle. For a whole generation of American boys who anxiously waited for their fathers and older brothers to return from Europe and the South Pacific, they could craft every playtime scenario to make sure the good guys won. Author Charles Garcia recalled that his parents gave him a case of army men for Christmas one year when he was growing up in Pueblo, Colorado. "The little green army men become my constant companions and are never more than a quick reach away. . . . I love these little green army men because I see my father's face on each one."[3]

During the 1950s, the country experienced a boom in the plastics industry. Advancements in manufacturing plastic meant that the material was becoming cheaper. The widespread availability of the material created some competition for the Bergen Toy Company. Soon, the Louis Marx Company, the Multiple Plastics Corporation, and others sold army men figures and play-sets from various historical eras. When the general public became aware of the dangers of lead poisoning in the 1970s, the Little Green Army Men surged in popularity, replacing ubiquitous metal toy soldiers from earlier generations.

The Little Green Army Men figures represented many different roles for a soldier and thus came in all sorts of poses with various accruements. Boys valued each of these pieces in different ways based on their dynamism. They liked the men carrying guns and other weapons but found some of the others baffling or just plain boring. Writer Peter Hartlaub recalls that his mine-sweeper figures "ended up getting a toaster oven court-martial."[4] As for the corpse-figure men, he wonders if they were "included as some kind of anti-war message to kids. Maybe the liberal foreman in the army man manufacturing facility insisted on throwing one dead army man in each package to show indeed, war was stupid."[5]

This anti-war sentiment hit Little Green Army Men hard in the 1970s. Little Green Army Men declined in popularity during the Vietnam era. According to blogger Cam Clark, "When the country is embroiled in an unpopular war, people don't want to play with toy soldiers that remind them of said war, apparently."[6] There was another problem for the army men in the 1970s—this one stemming from a shortage of plastic. The OPEC oil crisis impacted toy manufacturers across the country, and makers of plastic action figures were hit particularly hard. The rising cost of petroleum meant that the commodity was scarce and too expensive to use in plastic toys. This crisis ended the production of G.I. Joe and put many US-based Green Army Men manufacturers out of business.

Although many of the Little Green Army Men manufacturers are overseas now, boys still love playing with the toys.[7] Boys continue playing with them because they are cheap, durable, and allow for spirited play. According to Patricia Hogan, "The green army figures, especially, encourage the open-ended, imaginative play that fosters creativity, learning, and discovery."[8]

Some of the lessons learned while playing with Little Green Army Men inspired kids to become historians when they grew up. Historian Bob Beatty grew up in a family with a military background, the son of a Naval Commander. As part of his "all-American boy attraction to militaria,"[9] Beatty loved reenacting Civil War battles with his Little Green Army Men. "I'm sure the plastic toy soldiers came from a cheapo Christmas or birthday gift—maybe a bag in my stocking,"[10] he recalls. He enjoyed playing war with the toys, "basically taking the toy soldier part and living it out."[11]

33

G.I. Joe

G.I. Joe action sailor, 1964
COURTESY OF THE STRONG,
ROCHESTER, NEW YORK

Identifying Information:

G.I. Joe

Maker: Don Levine

Manufacturer: Hasbro

Date: 1964

The Strong Museum of Play, Object ID 113.6086

During the 1980s, the lyrics to the *G.I. Joe* cartoon theme song echoed in living rooms across the country: "A real American hero—G.I. Joe is there!" For boys in the late twentieth century, G.I. Joe represented the ideal soldier: brave, smart, and always willing to help others win the fight against evil. This passage explores the development of G.I. Joe and the toy's place in the changing culture of childhood during the 1970s and 80s.

In the early 1960s, Barbie had taken the toy world by storm. Mattel's competitors tried to figure out how to replicate this success. Stan Weston, a licensing agent who had pitched a variety of other toys, decided that a toy soldier might replicate the razor/razor blade marketing approach of the Barbie doll. Just as a grown man would buy a razor and then need to continue buying razor blades for the duration of his life, girls who owned Barbie dolls would keep buying accessories for them. He decided that a toy soldier could have similar kinds of accessory products. He pitched this idea to Don Levine, the Vice President and Director of Marketing and Development at Hasbro.[1]

Meanwhile, Levine had seen a wooden art model in a shop window. The way the figure articulated and moved inspired him. Levine recalled, "Tin and plastic soldiers have been favorites of children as long as there have been toys; it seemed to me that this fully articulated man could be a giant step forward."[2] Hasbro developed toys that could articulate just like the art model, and they released the first G.I. Joe action figures in 1964. This fighting man was posable, so unlike regular toy soldiers, children could shape them into combatready poses.[3]

Hasbro named their figures after the generic term for an infantry soldier from WWI and WWII. The 11.5-inch figures represented the four branches of service at the time, with a G.I. Joe Action Marine, Sailor, Pilot, and Soldier. In its marketing campaign, Hasbro appealed to the nostalgia of boys playing with toy soldiers. For the promotional film for G.I. Joe at the 1963 Toy Fair, the team at Hasbro remarked,

> Since the beginning of time, children have always played soldier, with wooden swords, broomsticks rifles, cast lead soldiers, with plastic miniatures. But none of these had the ring of authenticity. None of these gave a boy the feeling that he was playing real soldier . . . to make a boy's dream come true, Hasbro is proud to present G.I. Joe: America's Moveable fighting man.[4]

Like Barbie, G.I. Joe came with a multitude of accessories. The original 1964 G.I. Joes came with "box after box of authentic uniforms and equipment,"[5] so the figure could transform into a Marine, Navy Frogman, or Air Force pilot. The razor/razor blade approach that you learned about in the passage on Barbie worked very well for G.I. Joe too. While their sisters were busy outfitting Barbie in the latest fashions, boys strove to attain all of the G.I. Joe gear and play-sets.

G.I. Joe became one of the biggest toys of the 1960s. According to historian Gary Cross, "It achieved this feat, at first, not by challenging expectations of fathers as Barbie broke with the doll culture of mothers, but by affirming the values and experiences of many fathers."[6] The children growing up in the early 1960s had fathers who likely had fought in either WWII or the Korean War. These dads considered military experience a normative part of life. The action figures encouraged male bonding between fathers and sons, and among the community of boys who played with the toys. Kids could reenact battles and defend their country against all sorts of evil. The first G.I. Joe television commercial in 1964 made the link between the toys and war very clear: "When you get G.I. Joe and the authentic G.I. Joe equipment, you'll have the greatest realism, the greatest fun you ever had in playing soldier."[7]

When the Vietnam War started, however, parents found themselves in a moral quandary over war toys. Experts like Dr. Benjamin Spock actively discouraged parents from buying these toys, and sales of G.I. Joe fell dramatically. Although the boys who were young enough to play with the toys possibly had fathers fighting in the Vietnam conflict, the general spirit of the country had soured toward wartime toys just as they did toward the war itself. In 1966, anti-war groups across the country chose children's toys as symbols of the war they were fighting against. In 1966, a group of mothers in New York carried black umbrellas with the slogan "Toy Fair or Warfare" as they picketed the annual NY Toy Fair. That same year, a newspaper article noted, "In recent years, vocal groups—mainly women—have protested the sale of war toys, claiming children who learn to glorify violence are much more likely to unleash it when they grow up."[8]

The toy industry launched a counter-protest. Jerome Fryer, the president of Toy Manufacturers of the U.S.A., insisted, "Toys don't create war. Wars create toys. Unless you eliminate the adult activity, you can't stop the child from duplicating it."[9]

Amid this debate, sales of G.I. Joes fell dramatically. In 1970, Hasbro responded to this decline by turning the wartime Joes into an "Adventure Team." The new figures were burly and bearded, and their mission had changed from military objectives to those of exploration and discovery. A television commercial for a G.I. Joe play-set in the 1970s explained the spirit of these new Adventure Joes. "This is the rugged G.I. Joe Adventure team. Today's mission: rescue stolen idols."[10] The Stolen Idol play-set came with accessories like the Adventure Team helicopter, a plastic cobra, and a fake idol. Other adventure Joes went on patrols to capture stingrays in the Devil of the Deep play-set, or to look for a missing mummy.

In 1979, Bob Prupis of Hasbro wanted to resurrect military-style G.I. Joe for modern American boys. However, the price of petroleum had increased during the Middle East conflicts under the Carter administration. The same crisis that caused long lines at gas stations caused problems in the toy industry. The cost of petroleum had risen from $15 to $40 per barrel. The raw material needed for plastic children's toys was just too expensive now for most American consumers. Prupis had a solution to the problem: shrink the G.I. Joes to make them cheaper to produce.[11] The original 12-inch figures were out; the new 3.75 figures were in.

   The return of G.I. Joe in 1982 happened during a wave of patriotism during the early years of the Reagan administration. It was evident that Americans were in an all-out good versus evil fight against the Communists. American boys needed something to fight against, and what better way to do so than to give them more action figures. Hasbro resurrected the Joes in similar formats to the famous 3.75-inch *Star Wars* toys. (You'll learn about the *Star Wars* toys in the next passage.) The company spent $4 million on its marketing campaign for the new figures. The new G.I. Joes became the best-selling toy of the 1982 Christmas season. By 1988, G.I. Joes were once again a favorite in toy boxes across the country.[12]

   The release of the new Joes coincided with the launch of Marvel's G.I. Joe comic book series, which created a backstory for the Joes. In 1983, the theme song to the new television cartoon explained: "G.I. Joe is the codename for America's daring highly trained special mission force. Its purpose: to defend human freedom against Cobra, a ruthless terrorist organization determined to rule the world."[13] In giving the G.I. Joes an in-depth story, Hasbro realized that it could create a bond between children and these material objects. Of course, a psychological bond meant that Hasbro was very likely to sell a lot of the toys. This bond, along with changing political times, overrode the anti-war toy movement of the late 1960s and 1970s. In the three years following the rerelease of G.I. Joe and the debut of the TV cartoon in 1983, The National Coalition on Television Violence reported a 350 percent rise in the sale of war-related toys.[14]

   The release of the second wave of G.I. Joes corresponded with a wave of childhood safety panics in the United States. It seemed like there were threats to kids everywhere, from neighborhood molesters to gangs. According to historian Steven Mintz, "In the late twentieth century, American society projected its fears and anxieties onto the young and instituted desperate measures to protect them from exaggerated menaces."[15] The G.I. Joes educated children about these threats through their television show. At the end of each cartoon was a public safety announcement sponsored by the National Child Safety Council. Dr. Robert Selman of Harvard's School of Education and Human Development oversaw each PSA.

   The Joes addressed all sorts of threats that could beset kids of the 1980s.[16] Some of these dangers included age-old perils like drowning, house fires, and drowning in frozen ponds. The PSAs also addressed moral concerns like telling the truth, stealing, and having gumption. However, they also had lessons for the modern-day child who faced perils particular to the new world of the 1980s. G.I. Joe Dusty made sure that kids knew how to put reflectors on their bikes, while Roadblock warned kids against downed power lines. Doc told kids never to take medicine without adult supervision. The PSAs also addressed social concerns like bullying and peer pressure.[17] Each PSA closed with the famous phrase, "Now you know, and knowing is half the battle."

An increasingly large cast of G.I. Joe characters from 1964 through the 90s meant that the Joes were starting to be more racially diverse. During the civil rights movement of the mid-1960s, Hasbro introduced the first African American Action soldier. This was one of the first mainstream toys that represented an adult African American male. This original model was built on the same mold as its Caucasian counterparts, just with darker skin. It wasn't until the 1970s and the release of the Adventurer series that the black G.I. Joes started looking more true-to-life. More African American characters appeared in the 1980s including Stalker, Doc, and Roadblock.

Other ethnic groups were represented too. Zap and Shipwreck were Hispanic, while Clutch was Jewish. Asian characters included Storm Shadow and Quick Kick. Spirit Iron-Knife represented Native Americans. However, he was widely criticized for being much more a stereotype of what white people thought Native Americans were like than being a fully formed character. Nevertheless, in spite of the often cringeworthy depictions of these minority characters, their very presence in a child's toy box and on the television screen had a significant impact. According to a blogger at Action Figure Insider,

> This can be important to a kid in a world where various forms of media expose them predominately to people who look nothing like them, and it's often easier for a child to relate to characters who share not only similar physical traits, but also a similar cultural identity. . . . Asking a non-white child to play in an all-white world will eventually lead to questions that shouldn't *have* to be asked.[18]

G.I. Joes remained popular toys throughout the 1980s and 90s, but they faced stiff competition from other action-figure lines. Boys had plenty of action figures to choose from in this era, including Masters of the Universe, Transformers, and—as you'll see later in the chapter—Teenage Mutant Ninja Turtles.

34

Star Wars

Star Wars action figures
CREDIT: AMBER DELOS SANTOS

Identifying Information:

Star Wars Action Figures

Maker: Mark Boudreaux and Kenner Design Team

Manufacturer: Kenner

Date: 1978

Collection of Amber De Los Santos

"My earliest *Star Wars* memory is a handful of the classic Kenner action figures at our house, all of which had their lightsabers replaced with toothpicks,"[1] recalls writer Josh Modell. In the late 1970s and early 80s, the *Star Wars* toys created a young fan base for the science-fiction movie franchise. Like Little Green Army Men and G.I. Joe, the action figures allowed kids to play at conflict and war, but in a fantasy setting. In this passage, we'll look at the ways in which *Star Wars* action figures influenced a child-centered consumerism of the 1970s and early 80s.

Star Wars and its accompanying merchandise are products deeply embedded in their historical context. George Lucas based much of the film on historic world events and contemporary politics. Lucas said that he conceived of the movie as a reaction to what he saw happening around the country at the time. "It was really about the Vietnam War, and that was the period where Nixon was trying to run for a [second] term, which got me to thinking historically about how do democracies get turned into dictatorships? Because the democracies aren't overthrown; they're given away."[2] Lucas based Emperor Palpatine on Richard Nixon and the Empire on Nazi Germany. *Star Wars* also had much to do with the Cold War. According to historian Christopher Klein, "The tense relationship between the United States and the Soviet Union, with the threat of nuclear annihilation lurking in the background, was hardly history when 'Star Wars' first premiered in 1977."[3]

George Lucas and 20th Century Fox had an ambitious marketing plan for *Star Wars*. They intended to saturate consumers with movie-related products including toys, clothing, and lunch boxes. It was an unprecedented scheme in film history. When Mego, the company that produced the *Star Trek* action figures, turned down licensing to make toys for Lucas's film, Kenner took a chance on the products.

Star Wars hit theaters on May 25, 1977. No was expecting it to be an overnight sensation, but it was. It earned $461 million domestically, which was the highest-grossing film in American history at the time. *Star Wars* was one of the first movies that children went to see in the theater. Parents took kids of all ages—even very young kids—to see it. Although grown-ups loved the movie, it had an extraordinary sway over kids and teenagers. They went to see the movie over and over again. Gwen Ihnat recalls, "I saw *Star Wars* in 1977 in the theater. That summer it was just the thing you did. You might go see *Star Wars* once a week. You might go see it and then get back in line immediately to see it again."[4]

The popularity of the movie took Kenner's executives by surprise. Due to secrecy surrounding the project, Kenner had only six months to design the toys. The company was not prepared to release toys into the market when the movie came out, and it scrambled to respond to the surprise demand. The action figures were proving tricky to design and manufacture. By Christmas 1977, the only toys that Kenner had ready to go were simple board games and puzzles. But children didn't want puzzles—they wanted action figures. In a brilliant and very optimistic sales move, the team at Kenner created the *Star Wars* Early Bird Certificate Package. This was an empty box with stickers and certificates that children could send in to get figures of Luke, Leia, Han Solo, and a Stormtrooper at a later date. With this packaging, Kenner sold the hope and idea of a toy—not the physical object. This scheme created a big demand for the action figures.

Children's dreams to attain the toys were finally fulfilled in early 1978 when Kenner released them. The toys flew off the shelves. Kenner's *Star Wars* toy line sold $100 million in the first year.[5] Sean O'Neal remembers his childhood in the late 1970s and early 1980s playing with "Kenner action figures and playsets, building model AT-ATs and X-wings."[6] Journalist Melissa Leon explains the cultural significance of the *Star Wars* toys: "They're the result of an intrinsically human impulse, one that seeks to turn abstract ideas (in this case, a movie set in a fictional galaxy, populated by larger-than-life figures) into something tangible."[7]

For children of the 1970s and 80s, *Star Wars* represented a break with the popular culture of their parents. As A. O. Scott of the *New York Times* reflects, their parents had the Beatles and Elvis, but his generation had something different. "It was *ours*—our own special tectonic shift, after which the landscape was forever altered."[8] The movie franchise appealed to a distinctive child-centered consumer culture that dramatically impacted childhood in the last two decades of the twentieth century. Gary Cross argues that this was a new era in which parents no longer served as the mediators between manufacturers and their children.[9] Now, toy companies appealed directly to children through media.

By the end of the twentieth century, typical boys' play had also shifted away from reenacting the Old West through toy guns and playing cowboys, as their fathers had done during the 1950s and 60s. According to John Pedesco, a psychologist at the Child Guidance Center in Des Moines, "When I was young, it was army men and cowboys and Indians. I think the format for fantasies has changed. It's become more space and surrealistic, but the nature of the play has not changed. . . . If you look at the media, it's not the Cisco Kid, it's not even the Lone Ranger, it's not even Gunsmoke. It's Star Wars."[10]

The *Star Wars* action figures allowed boys to play mock battles in a different setting than G.I. Joe and toy soldiers. Gary Cross remarks, "Science fiction figures from the late 1970s fought in a fantastic mini world of lasers and rocketry where a child could not fully identify with the creature or the violent acts he performed."[11] The *Star Wars* figures hit the market less than three years after the end of the Vietnam War. They defied the same anti-war rhetoric that had devastated the G.I. Joe market because when boys played with *Star Wars* figures they were not fighting other humans. Luke Skywalker was fighting an idea—*evil*.

As with almost all of the action figures released in the 1970s and 80s, they appealed heavily to boys. Some grown-ups noticed the lack of female representation in the toy lineup. In a letter to the editor of the Prescott *Courier* in 1983, a woman remarked, "Why is it that in all the mounds of Star Wars figures in all the stores in town there's not a single Princess Leia to be found? . . . Did Kenner only pretend to manufacture Princess Leias? Are they being snapped up as soon as they're stocked? Or is it bias on the part of the stores' buyers? The shelves are full of Strawberry Shortcake, Tinkerbell cosmetics, and Care Bears. How about moving them over a little and making room for Princess Leia?"[12]

Eventually, *Star Wars* toys expanded into all kinds of film-inspired products. There were remote controlled R2-D2s, play-sets like the *Star Wars* Creature Cantina, and the Death Star, which included a working trash compactor. The Millennium Falcon and Imperial TIE Fighters got their own models. When *The Return of the Jedi* came out in 1983, Kenner released the *Star Wars* Ewok Village.

These toys were often expensive and out of reach price-wise for some American families. But in the new child-centered consumer culture, kids begged their parents for the toys anyway. "My family was poor," recalls blogger Freeman McNeil. "Times were very, very tough. My brother and I, like many other kids, begged our parents to get us these wonderful 3 ¾ inch figures. We could only get one, maybe two if we were lucky, at a time. We just didn't have the extra money."[13]

Children who grew up with *Star Wars* toys in their homes continue to support the movie franchise by spending millions of dollars each year snatching up film-related products. With new films in the franchise in the 2010s, Hasbro releases new action figures and other toys for each new storyline. However, children of the early twenty-first century are not as excited about movie-related products as their predecessors. Sales of these toys have disappointed the toy company. According to market analyst Gerrick Johnson, "There is a new paradigm. Just because there is a movie with a toy tie-in doesn't necessarily mean it's going to work."[14]

35

Teenage Mutant Ninja Turtles

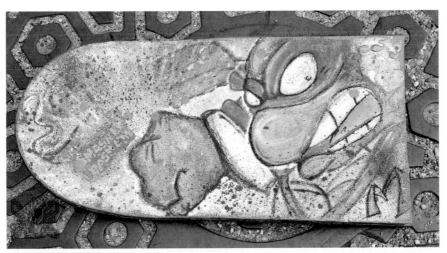

"Karate Chopin' Mike" by artist Tokka Oroku

Identifying Information:

Teenage Mutant Ninja Turtles

Maker: Mark Taylor and Playmates Toys Design Team

Manufacturer: Playmates Toys

Date: 1988

Credit: artist Tokka Oroku

A rtist Tokka Oroku first encountered Teenage Mutant Ninja Turtles (TMNT) when he saw them in a comic book in the late 1980s. As a kid, he saw a store clerk making a display of "some crazy little toys; some turtles and a pretty girl in a yellow jumpsuit."[1] The lady asked him if he thought the toys would take off. Neither one of them could have predicted that the Teenage Mutant Ninja Turtles would become a worldwide phenomenon within the year. The Turtles impacted boys growing up in the late 1980s and early 90s with their message of family and ecology. This passage explores specialized narratives behind children's toys, the role of action figures in solitary play, and the ways in which boys played with female action figures.

The Teenage Mutant Ninja Turtles first appeared in 1983. One day, comic designers Kevin Eastman and Peter Laird were joking around by drawing images of turtles in face masks wielding ninja weapons. They named the turtles after the Renaissance artists Michelangelo, Donatello, Raphael, and Leonardo.[2] After establishing Mirage Studios in their apartment, they drew a single-issue comic book for their Teenage Mutant Ninja Turtles characters. They bankrolled the project using money from a tax return and a loan from Kevin's uncle. They placed ads for their comic in industry publications and ended up selling all 3,000 copies in two months. They printed two more issues, and soon the turtles were starring in their own comic book line.[3]

Hollywood agent Mark Freedman contacted them and connected the pair with Playmates Toys. The company wanted to make TMNT action figures for the 4–8-years-old market. However, the turtle characters from the comic books were decidedly adult. If the company was going to sell the turtles to children, they needed to be reimagined. Part of this retooling involved creating the *Teenage Mutant Ninja Turtles* cartoon for kids. Playmates thought the cartoon would generate interest in the toys and sell more product.

The cartoon premiered in 1987. Playmates Toys produced 400 TMNT figures from 1988–1997 and sold $1.1 billion in the first four years.[4] Both the cartoon and the action figures were wildly successful. Pretty soon, little boys in the 1980s were chomping on pizzas and yelling "Cowabunga, Dude!" The turtles starred in a live-action movie in 1990, followed by two more shortly thereafter.

Because the turtles were fictional characters that existed in Eastman and Laird's imagination, the action figures hit the toy shelves with a complicated narrative already in place. If boys wanted to play properly with the toys, they needed in-depth knowledge of the mythos of the series. Although this was typical of other 1980s action figures, it was a new trend in the history of play. According to Howard Chudacoff, "While children playing time-honored forms of play such as jumping rope or building a snow fort needed only simple instructions on procedure, which they could learn directly from each other, playing with licensed commercial toys from the *Star Wars* films or the TV series about Teenage Ninja Turtles required special knowledge that only those exposed to these media phenomenon would understand."[5] Parents thought that this discouraged creative, imaginative play and forced their children's playtime to align with an existing narrative.

It was the complex storyline and rich characters that appealed to a boy named David growing up in Colorado Springs. The turtles had such a big impact on his life that he later renamed himself after two characters from the show: Tokka and Oroku Saki. Tokka was fascinated with the complex relationships among the Turtles and the Foot Clan. "One of the core dynamics with Turtles is about surrogate family, for both the Turtles and the bad guys. . . . Shredder is the surrogate father figure of the Foot Clan. Seeing that dynamic from a literary angle was interesting,"[6] he recalls. The narrative of TMNT spoke deeply to him in the midst of some difficult family situations when he was young.

Tokka also recalls that the *Teenage Mutant Ninja Turtles* cartoon and comic books promoted his interest in ecology. By the 1980s, environmental messaging made its way into children's television programming in an overt way. In one TMNT public service announcement, Leonardo goes for a swim in a lake, where he finds a fish stuck in a plastic six-pack holder. He warns, "This is what happens with a lot of these six-pack holders. When you throw them away, they can end up in lakes or oceans where fish and even birds can get tangled up in them. And because this kind of plastic never dissolves, they can be dangerous. Always cut these holders up before you throw them away!"[7] Although many children like Tokka responded positively to the message and started thinking about how they could help the planet, not everyone was pleased.

Environmentalism was a hotly contested political, moral, and religious issue during the 1980s (and still is in 2020). Many parents were not happy about the media teaching their children about environmental issues. In 1991, Stephen Chapman wrote a column for the *Chicago Tribune* in which he remarked, "These muscle-bound little reptiles, I regret to inform you, have a political agenda, which is the same color as their shells: green. Not content with entertaining children, the Turtles want to indoctrinate them in environmentalism dogma and put them to work spreading it."[8] Parents all over the country went to battle against children's television programming that promoted ecological messages.[9]

In addition to the broader themes of family and ecology that the Turtles taught, the ways in which boys played with the toys themselves reveal much about childhood at the end of the twentieth century. Although Tokka did play Turtles with his friends, he most often played with them alone. That corresponds well to the broader historical trend of children playing alone at the end of the twentieth century. Falling birth rates, shifting family dynamics, and a changing urban landscape often forced kids to play on their own. They weren't necessarily playing in groups of their peers or siblings as had been typical in the first half of the century, or with their entire family units as in the early 1800s.

Playing in groups seemed to reinforce the traditional narrative of the Turtles story and promoted violent play. "When I would play with people, we would have simple little battles,"[10] Tokka recalls. However, playing with the figures alone helped direct kids toward imaginative play when no others were present to pass judgment on the scenarios that they dreamed up. "When

I played on my own," Tokka recalls, "things got a little more complex."[11] He remembers a scenario in which Shredder kidnaps April in hopes of forcing her into a demonic wedding ceremony, with the Turtles arriving just in time to save the day.

April's presence in the 1980s action figure line reveals much about how little boys played with the girl characters in these toy lines. The first time that Tokka played with TMNT toys, he was babysitting some younger kids who were playing with the figures. They told him that he could play too . . . if he was the girl or the bad guy. "The girl or the bad guy . . . story of my life,"[12] he quips. For the younger boys in that story, being the girl was just as undesirable as being the villain. April existed merely as a damsel in distress that the bad guys could kidnap and the Turtles could rescue—she had no real agency of her own in the ways that boys played with her.

Savvy girls and women of the day were wise to what was going on with April's character, however. Carly Mallenbaum of *USA Today* recalls: "One particular episode really made me happy I never embodied April on the playground. . . . April investigates what is clearly a dangerous matter transporter . . . and idiotically steps right on it, thereby turning herself part-cat. Bad guy Shredder finds April, and forces her to obey his commands, which she does until the turtles save her, for the umpteenth time."[13]

Many of the kids who watched or played with TMNT bore the influence of the characters well into adulthood. For Tokka, the Turtles were influential in his future career as a designer and artist. His work was featured in the TMNT show in Los Angeles a few years ago, and he makes TMNT-inspired pieces among the other work that he does. Tokka also collects TMNT figures as a grown-up and actively participates in the global TMNT community. "There are people clear across the board who are fond of this stuff from little kids to grown-ups," he says. "For better or for worse, it's been overall good for me."[14]

Part VIII

PHYSICAL TOYS AND SPORTS

According to Quaker pastor William Forbush, "Play has the greatest value physically."[1] Thus far in this book, we've explored a variety of indoor toys and games. Now it is time to go outside. In this part, we'll explore changing ideas about the male and female body, as well as the changing landscape of play.

Throughout the nineteenth and twentieth centuries, experts praised the value of physical play because it promoted child development. According to Forbush, "The impulse to exercise or use the growing parts of the body furnishes the only explanation needed to account for the play activity."[2] Forbush thought that running and jumping developed the nervous system and muscles. He argued, "This ceaseless energy should be allowed free outlet daily and as far as possible without interference."[3]

Beginning in the 1850s, Muscular Christianity emphasized the importance of the male physical body. According to historian Steven Riess, "The idea that a man who was moral and devout could and should also be physically fit tied in very well with prevailing middle-class values."[4] There were four characteristics of the movement: manliness, morality, health, and patriotism. When a boy ran a race, for example, he built manly strength, learned self-restraint and hard work, strengthened his physical body, and in so doing, strengthened the nation. Thomas Wentworth Higginson emphasized that "America's development rested on a balance between spiritual and physical health . . . a strong mind and a strong body."[5]

During the latter half of the century, male physicality took on a more significant meaning for boys and the nation. According to historians Tony Ladd and James Mathisen, "Advocates of the sports creed not only believed that competitive sports engendered traits that were essential to middle-class success—self-discipline, self-denial, and even courage—but also that sedentary white-collar workers could utilize sports to demonstrate manliness."[6] Rough play made boys physically strong and mentally acute. "Sports redefined for them their sense of manliness and provided mechanisms to achieve it."[7]

Ideas about girls' physicality changed during the late nineteenth century too. Vigorous exercise for girls was gradually coming into acceptance. Authors Lina and Adelia Beard asserted that "Outdoor exercise is always to be preferred to in-door when one has a choice. Walking, tennis, archery, horseback, and swimming are some of the athletic sports for girls."[8] The Beard sisters liked physical play because it developed moral character. They reminded girls that "everyone *must* exercise to keep healthy and strong, for life is motion and activity. It is natural to be well and happy, and to keep so we must exercise all our muscles, as well as our moral and intellectual faculties, or they will dwindle and wither."[9] They encouraged girls to set aside an hour each day for "physical culture," which included bouncing balls against a wall, performing lunges, and balancing a broomstick on one finger.

By 1914, educators were beginning to realize that these gymnastic activities weren't entirely cutting it for girls. Forbush lamented that girls usually ceased physical play around the time team sports became popular for boys at ages 10–12. He remarked, "If play has value in human life, which we believe it has, it is certainly unfortunate that half the human race should lose the play and the play spirit."[10] He encouraged girls to participate in the new sports developing for their gender including volleyball and indoor baseball.[11]

The role of physical play and the amount of outdoor activity that children were getting changed dramatically in the twentieth century. The landscape of play had changed significantly. Urbanization took away forests and fields that children traditionally used for running or kite-flying. Now there were sidewalks and roads for children to negotiate during their play. Kids often co-opted these spaces by using them for jumping rope or Hula-Hooping.[12] Parents fretted over whether their children were getting enough outdoor activity.

This part explores five toys that children played with outdoors. First, kites tell the story of the changing landscape of play during the early twentieth century. Next, the passage on jump rope explores girls' physical culture in the nineteenth century, along with the sport's vital role in African American neighborhoods in the mid- to late twentieth century. Third, we'll look at football and its role in the development of male culture in the early twentieth century. Fourth, the Hula-Hoop tells the story of a fad toy that came to represent the 1950s to future generations. Finally, we'll look at the Nerf ball and how it brought outdoor play inside.

36

Kites

Illustration from *Sweetheart Travellers: A Child's Book for Children, for Women, and for Men* by S. R. Crockett; illustrated by Gordon Browne and W. H. C. Groome; published in London by Wells, Gardner, Darton & Co in 1896 (3rd edition).

CREDIT: WHITEMAY CREATIVE # 487047563 COLLECTION: DIGITAL VISION VECTORS

Identifying Information:

Kites

One of my neighbors likes to fly a giant parachute kite in the park across from my house. This grown man runs to the park like a gleeful little boy and prepares the kite for launch. On the days when we have strong Colorado Front Range winds, the kite lifts him off the ground. He floats in the air for a few glorious moments, and we neighbors watch him in breathless amusement and wonder. After he has had enough, the man packs everything up and walks home with a huge grin on his face. The park and kite have both done their magic. In this entry, we'll explore kites in relation to a changing urban landscape in the twentieth century, and how that affected playtime.

Kites are ancient objects, traditionally used as both tools and toys. They were likely invented in China and spread all over Asia along trade routes. People in Japan, Korea, India, and Micronesia used kites in war, for hunting, and recreation. Kites came to Europe sometime during the Middle Ages, where scientists and inventors used them in experiments. They came to North America with the colonists.[1]

The most famous early American kite-flyer was Benjamin Franklin. When he was ten years old, Franklin remembers that he "amused myself one day with flying a paper kite; and approaching the bank of a pond, which was near a mile broad, I tied the string to a stake and the kite ascended to a very considerable height above the pond while I was swimming."[2] He grabbed his kite and floated on his back in the pond. To his delight, the wind in the kite gently pulled him along the water's surface.

Franklin's boyhood play inspired his famous 1752 experiment involving a kite, a key, and a lightning storm. Franklin theorized that lightning was comprised of an electrical force. To prove this, he crafted an experiment using a kite made out of a silk handkerchief and attached a wire to act as a lightning rod. He tied two strings to the kite: one made of hemp and one of silk. To the hemp string, he tied a house key. He flew his kite during a thunderstorm and noticed that the key tied to the hemp rope carried an electrical charge when he touched it.[3]

Kites were very popular outdoor toys, particularly for boys, in the nineteenth century. In 1888, writer Daniel Beard included several chapters on kite-building in *The American Boy's Handy Book*. Beard wrote, "It is a pleasant sensation to sit in the first spring sunshine and feel the steady pull of a good kite upon the string, and watch its graceful movements as it sways from side to side, ever mounting higher and higher, as if impatient to free itself and soar away amid the clouds."[4]

When the country was young and rural, boys had plenty of open space to fly their kites without much concern for danger, save for rogue thunderstorms. By the turn of the twentieth century, however, growing cities and developing technology brought new threats to these kite-flyers. The landscape of play was changing. Open spaces disappeared in many areas. Busy roads were a danger to distracted kite-flyers. Even tall buildings could prove deadly. In 1940, ten-year-old Thomas Madden of Prescott, Arizona, died when he fell off a four-story building while flying his kite on the roof.[5]

The presence of electrical power lines was another big risk for kite-flyers. Little ones now ran the risk of getting their kites caught in these lines and accidentally electrocuting themselves. Suddenly, outdoor play became far less safe than it had been before. Humans have had eons to ingrain a fear of fires and other hazards into our brains. In the early twentieth century, however, power lines were something so new that children didn't quite know what to make of them.

So, electrical companies had to step in and educate these kids about how dangerous these wires could be. Power companies all over the country ran newspaper ads warning about the hazards of flying kites into lines. In 1923, the Duquesne Light Company warned about the double-edged threat of having a kite caught in a power line. There was the risk of short-circuiting the line, and an "element of danger to the boy himself exists when he climbs poles to extricate his kite from such lines, in that he may come into contact with wires and be severely burned or knocked to the ground. . . . If parents will impress upon their children, especially the boys, the dangers of such practices, they can save themselves much anxiety and worry and prevent interruption of electric service to their homes."[6]

In 1944, a policeman in Spokane, Washington, pled with the city's students, "If you must fly a kite, fly it in some other area free of power wires."[7] Another utility company ran an advertisement that said, "Hello boys and girls! Follow these kite-flying safety rules: NEVER fly your kite in busy streets or highways. Always fly your kite away from power lines or sub-stations. Always fly your kite in wide open spaces. Stay safe! Do the right thing!"[8]

Power lines and the growing American urban infrastructure forever changed the landscape of play. These changes forced kite-flyers to be newly cautious of their surroundings. In many other instances, however, children adapted to the new infrastructure and incorporated it into their play. We will explore this latter phenomenon next in the passage on jump rope.

37

Jump Rope

Girls jumping rope.
CREDIT: IMAGE SOURCE CREATIVE # 80410516 COLLECTION: PHOTODISC

Identifying Information:

Jump Rope

Growing up in the Texas Panhandle in the late 1940s and 50s, Glenna Brown recalls, "We played two-person jump rope a lot."[1] She and her sister weren't the only children playing with jump ropes in the mid-twentieth century. Far away in New York and Chicago, jump rope had become a very important social ritual for girls in the inner city. The game built community and communicated racial identity. This passage looks at the significance of jump rope in the physical culture of girls' play, the changing urban landscape, and the game's role in solidifying community in African American neighborhoods.

Jump rope is a longtime favorite activity in the United States. Dutch colonists brought the pastime to North America. According to historian Scott Eberle, most of the children who participated in skipping rope in the colonial era were boys.[2] However, girls took over the sport in the nineteenth century.

During the nineteenth century, jumping rope was one of the few socially sanctioned ways for girls to engage in physical activity. Rope-jumping could be a solitary or a communal activity for girls, which suited them no matter how many siblings or friends they had. Since girls were generally seen as being more delicate than boys, adults often warned them to be careful about their physical play. In 1833, Lydia Maria Child warned about jumping rope in *The Girl's Own Book*: "It is a healthy exercise and tends to make the form graceful but it should be used with moderation. I have known instances of blood vessels burst by young ladies, who, in a silly attempt to jump a certain number of hundred times, have persevered in jumping after their strength was exhausted."[3]

Jump ropes were popular in children's literature in the early twentieth centuries. Girls who read the British novel *The Secret Garden* encountered Mary

Lennox's first experience with a jump rope when the servant Martha gives the obstinate little girl a skipping rope.[4] Reading about the pastime made the sport a fashionable amusement for girls in the United States during this period.

In the 1950s, a jump rope craze hit the United States. It was a suitable pastime for girls of all economic circumstances because it required only an inexpensive jump rope and lots of energy. During the height of the craze, girls everywhere were jumping rope from the plains of Texas to the inner cities of Chicago and New York. Girls who lived in urban areas co-opted pavement and sidewalks for their play. The new urban landscape offered them level surfaces on which to jump, and the dense populations of inner cities also meant that there were always lots of playmates close by.

Double Dutch became an integral part of African American girlhood in the 1950s. Girls could play Double Dutch unsupervised in urban areas, giving them an outlet for independence and the formation of a strong network of female friends. Historian Patricia Hill Collins argues that jump rope is "an oral expression of collectivity, togetherness, and sisterhood forged through resistance to established norms and a drive to be recognized on individual merits."[5]

The singsong rhymes that black girls repeated as they jumped rope were evocative of the call-and-response chants of African American culture.[6] Ivory Ibuaka says, "The game, and use of chant, represents an activity capable of connecting Black girls of varying ages."[7] These jump rope chants built the foundation for the rhythms of hip-hop music. According to historian Kyra Gaunt, the black musical style transmitted through these jump rope rhythms "are *learned* through oral-kinetic practices that not only teach *an embodied discourse of black musical expression* but also teach *discourse about appropriate and transgressive gender and racial roles* (for both boys and girls) in African American communities."[8]

Double Dutch was held in high esteem in these neighborhoods, and adults relied on the game to keep kids out of trouble. In 1973, New York City policemen Ulysses Williams and David Walker formed a Double Dutch youth outreach program called Rope Not Dope for the girls in their community. They started Double Dutch tournaments, which became hugely popular. In the 1980s, New York had fifteen Double Dutch teams—and supporters claimed that these teams were responsible for a decrease in drug use and crime.[9] According to teacher Maria Williams, "When I taught in Brooklyn (2001–2003),

Double Dutch was still a big deal. I have some great memories of watching my students in the schoolyard! They were incredible."[10]

Jump rope remains a favorite activity for little girls in the twenty-first century and is still a vital part of the African American community in many American cities. It is an art form, musical outlet, pastime, and community builder. According to feminist writer Julianna Lee Marino, the game "acts as a means to combat the controlling images and assert agency against a world that erases black girls' and women's existence."[11]

38

Football

Football is an iconic part of American childhood.
CREDIT: JOHNNYMAD CREATIVE # 172808944 COLLECTION: STOCK/GETTY IMAGES

Identifying Information:

Football

Americans were obsessed with college football games in the 1890s. The game originated as a cross between rugby and soccer, both imports from England in the 1860s. American football became a popular sport in the 1880s when Walter Camp established the game's rules.[1] Camp believed that football was "the means of satisfying the instinct innate in every youth for a contest to demonstrate physical supremacy."[2] The popularity of football coincided with a reinvention of boyhood and manhood that took place in the late nineteenth and early twentieth centuries.

Football was symbolic of the tension between savagery and civilization in the 1890s and early 1900s. G. Stanley Hall and other advocates of recapitulation theory argued that boys reenacted the evolutionary stages of mankind as they grew up, starting out life as little more than senseless savages and slowly evolving into modern civilized men.[3] Hall thought that in order to create a powerful, manly civilization, all males must have free access to the primitive. Hall's "new man" joined fraternal orders, opposed excessive femininity, and "appropriated activities which had been deemed working-class."[4] Even the ideal male body was different at the end of the century than it had been a few decades earlier. In the 1860s, the ideal middle-class man was tall, lean, and self-restrained. By the 1890s, however, the ideal man was virile and muscular. Camping, hunting, and fishing became very popular for boys and men because they helped them get in touch with their primitive nature.[5]

These changing definitions of manhood impacted boys' leisure time. Hall told parents and educators that they must "encourage boys to relive the evolutionary progress of the race—to be savages and barbarians as boys so that they would develop the strength to be both virile and civilized as men."[6] Rough play among boys and young men emphasized the primitive nature of sports.

Playing football gave boys the chance to act out primitivism and turned them into virile specimens.

Organized sports for young men flourished toward the end of the nineteenth century. Muscular Christianity promoted rough sport by telling parents that it helped produce "the hardier and sterner virtues in and for an age of luxury."[7] Boys of this era enjoyed boxing, hunting, and shooting. However, they seemed to prefer team sports, "which were sociable, entertaining, sufficiently hazardous . . . and highly congruent with their future work options."[8]

Advocates of recapitulation theory thought football was a solution to a boy's need for social recreation and physical play. In 1914, Carl Guise explained the new popularity of football by connecting the sport with a boy's need to belong to a tribe and to have a physical outlet:

> Among the games that are most commonly indulged in by adolescents, games of contest far outnumber all the others. . . . Football has gained its prestige because of the opportunity that it offers for personal encounter, and it is claimed by many that it has its charm in the opportunity that it gives for secret rough playing.[9]

People liked the sport because it prepared boys for their future careers and built character. The game prepared them for leadership roles and promoted teamwork, cooperation, and ambition.[10] According to William Forbush in 1912, "It is not necessary to describe those two great field games, football and baseball, in which boys began to take an active interest as early an age as 10 and which engross young men as long as they continue to be athletic. As examples of physical agility, grace and endurance they match any sport, ancient or modern, while they are no doubt the two greatest team games ever invented."[11]

Despite the glorification of football as one of the "greatest team games ever invented," the sport was brutal during this period (and one could argue that it still is). The savagery that boys were supposedly reenacting could be deadly. Players suffered fractured spines, broken ribs and collarbones, and concussions. In 1894, a football match that became known as the "Hampden Park Blood Bath" resulted in so many injuries to the Harvard and Yale football teams that the game was suspended at Yale for two years.[12]

The carnage continued into the twentieth century. In 1902 alone, there were twelve football-related deaths.[13] In 1905, there were nineteen fatalities during football games, with 137 injuries. That year, an article in the *Chicago Tribune* stated, "Of those slaughtered to make a touchdown eleven were high school players and ten of the killed were immature boys of 17 and under."[14] One of these players was Carl Osborn, a high school football player who died when a broken rib pierced his heart.[15] Theodore Roosevelt's son was also injured during the 1905 football season at a freshman game of Harvard versus Yale. Roosevelt, a supporter of the game, called for a revision of rules to help curb these fatalities. These rule changes included legalizing the forward pass, getting rid of mass formations, and extending the first-down to ten yards.

Women and girls played a tangential role in the manly world of football during this time. They obliged the men in their lives by watching them as spectators. In 1914, Dean Hodges encouraged mothers to take up an interest in football as a way to support their children. "For privileged children, their mother is the heart of all the joy of life. She knows a thousand games, and is deeply interested in several others in which she does not personally play, such as baseball and football, she wants to know what the score is, often sits in the sun on the benches among the spectators."[16] In 1914, William Forbush lamented, "It is, unfortunate, physically and morally, that girls come into these games only as spectators and that they have no sports that are similarly magnificent and engrossing."[17]

Football continued to be a key aspect of boyhood throughout the twentieth century and continues to be so today. Just like grown-ups used Double Dutch to keep girls out of trouble, adults turned to football to keep boys in line. In 1929, factory owners in northeast Philadelphia were victims of juvenile delinquents who liked to throw rocks at their windows. One owner asked his friend Joseph J. Tomlin to figure out a way to give these kids something useful to do. Tomlin was an athlete himself, and he set up a four-team Junior Football Conference for the 1929 football season. The conference was named after legendary football coach Glenn Scobie "Pop" Warner in 1934. Twenty-five years later, Pop Warner became a national organization.[18]

In the early twenty-first century, concern over the risk of traumatic brain injuries during tackle football games has led to a decline in the popularity of the sport. From 2009–2019, the number of youth tackle football players in Fort Collins, Colorado, dropped from 795 to 213.[19] Nationwide, participation in Pop Warner tackle football declined 30 percent in the same time period.[20] The panic over the safety of football in the 1880s seems to have returned as we understand more about brain injuries.

39

Hula-Hoop

A little girl enjoys the iconic 1950s pastime of Hula-Hooping.
CREDIT: GRADYREESE CREATIVE # 1001435068 COLLECTION: E+

Identifying Information:

Hula-Hoop

Maker: Alex Tolmer, Arthur "Spud" Melin, Dick Kerr

Manufacturer: Wham-O

Date: 1958

In 1967, a British news agency broadcasted a Hula-Hoop competition in New York's Central Park. A dozen children Hula-Hooped in the bandshell under a large American flag, symbolizing the revival of the worldwide fad. The boys and girls on the stage were of all ages and diverse racial backgrounds. Each of them demonstrated their hula prowess for the judges and the eager crowd. The narrator of the broadcast stated, "These kids know all the tricks of a pastime that most people thought went out with rock and roll . . . the 1967 technique is something to marvel at. The lads and lasses of the new Hula-Hoop age certainly sure know a thing or two about ring craft. It was quite a happy hula happening."[1] The Hula-Hoop symbolizes the fad culture of the 1950s and a continuing nostalgia for that time period.

Hoops in various forms have entertained children since ancient Egypt, Greece, and Rome. Children made hoops out of reeds and vines and then rolled them around on the ground. In the fourteenth century, a hooping craze swept through England until doctors started blaming the craze for a rise in heart attacks and back injuries. In nineteenth-century America, girls enjoyed rolling hoops along the ground and running after them.[2] In 1901, play expert Lina Beard wrote an article in *The Delineator* about a hoop dance, in which girls rolled their hoops from one quadrant to another, performing a graceful dance.[3]

Hoop toys lost much of their popularity in the first few decades of the twentieth century, and by the 1930s few children were still rolling them around, except in passing curiosity. That all changed at mid-century. In the 1950s, a gym teacher in Australia taught her students how to swing large bamboo hoops around their hips. This activity caught the attention of a toy buyer from Coles Department stores. The store contacted Australian toy maker Alex Tolmer to develop these hoops into mass-produced toys. Tolmer's company Toltoys had developed a type of plastic that could be molded into rings, which could be used to make plastic hoops. Tolmer sold these plastic hoops in Australia, and he sent his invention to the American International Toy Fair.[4]

These Hula Hoops caught the attention of Wham O, an American toy company that partnered with Toltoys. Arthur "Spud" Melin and Richard Kerr acquired the rights to make these plastic hoops in the United States. They improved on the design, and 1958 they began selling Hula-Hoops for $1.98 a piece.[5] A Hula-Hooping craze swept America along with the rest of the world. In the first year, Wham-O sold nearly $100 million.

The Hula-Hoop craze happened, in part, because it appealed to both boys and girls, as well as grown-ups of all ages. Parents could spend summer evenings bonding with their children over the game. The Hula-Hoop also encouraged girls to be physically active in an era when girls weren't always allowed to be athletic. Journalist Dan Webster wrote a story about his childhood neighbor Penny, who was a Hula-Hoop champion. He recalled, "In those days, girls didn't play sports. . . . When the boys ran through the neighborhood playing guns, Penny practiced twirling her Hula-Hoop."[6] Penny twirled thirteen Hula-Hoops at the same time for almost two hours straight, which impressed her rough-and-tumble boy neighbors.

Although the Hula-Hoop was fun and brought families together, it also caused physical injuries. Grown-ups tore muscles and strained their backs. There were severe injuries around the world when the hooping craze went global. In 1958, a teenager in Japan twirled a Hula-Hoop five hundred times and later reported a headache. He died of a cerebral hemorrhage, which his doctors attributed to "too much Hula-Hooping."[7] The Tokyo police responded by banning Hula-Hoops on the streets.

The Hula-Hoop craze passed quickly, and by 1959 it was over. However, Hula-Hoops somehow remained embedded in the American psyche. Hula-Hoops make a reappearance about every ten years. Each time they do, they remind a new generation of the exuberant 1950s. In the late 60s, Wham-O reintroduced the toy, adding metal bearings to make it spin faster. To kick off this revival, Wham-O sponsored a nationwide contest and offered a $1,000 savings bond for the first prize national winner. In Manhattan, thirty-two contestants ranging from three years old to fifteen entered their local bracket, where they hooped for nearly four hours. Twelve-year-old Cathy Flood took first place and advanced to the national competition.[8]

A second Hula-Hoop revival a decade later harkened back to the hoop's origins as an Australian gym prop. In the mid-1970s, physical fitness became very popular in the United States, and educators rethought how they taught gym class. Old military-style rope climbs and chin-ups were exchanged for child-friendly activity. In Long Beach, New York, a school district started a program that used Hula-Hoops to get reluctant exercisers interested in free movement. Teacher Edward Canner said, "I want to get every child to come here to play, to get achievement out of doing something and feel good about themselves at the same time."[9]

Unfortunately, Hula-Hoops just didn't have the same fad-appeal to children of the early 1970s as they did to their parents who grew up in the late 50s. By this time, play was moving indoors, the streets were increasingly unsafe, and many of the fields and empty spaces that their parents had Hula-Hooped in were developed in urban areas. The trendy toys of the 1970s were Nerf balls, G.I. Joes and Barbies, and the new electronic toys, all of which were inside toys.

By the late 1980s and early 90s, adults who had grown up during the 50s and 60s were increasingly concerned about the state of modern childhood. Their kids appeared to be staying inside all day playing video games. What happened to the outdoor fun that they had enjoyed during their own youth? One newspaper columnist lamented, "While modern computer and electronic games are mental stimulation, old-fashioned games encourage camaraderie, friendship, physical activity, coordination and social interaction. Kids don't get that now."[10]

The revival of Hula-Hoops in the late 1980s placated these concerned parents. In 1988, Wham-O's sales of the toys doubled from the previous year, selling $2 million. It was nowhere near the $25 million per year that Hula-Hoops sold during the height of their popularity in the late 50s, but it was still good news for the company. In trying to explain the hoop revival, *New York Times* columnist Richard Stevenson pondered, "The sociological significance of the Hula-Hoop in 1988 remains open to question. Perhaps the rediscovery of the hoop among my members of the aging baby-boomer generation is an expression of yearning for lost youth."[11]

40

Nerf

Original Nerf Ball
COURTESY OF THE STRONG, ROCHESTER, NEW YORK

Identifying Information:

Nerf Ball

Maker: Reyn Guyer and Will Krause

Manufacturer: Parker Brothers, Hasbro

Date: 1969

If you were a kid growing up in the 1970s–1990s, chances are pretty high that you played with at least one Nerf product. In my neighborhood, most of the boys had Nerf Super Soakers. When the girls would run through the sprinklers on hot summer days, the boys liked to ambush us with their water guns. We also played with Nerf footballs and basketballs. This passage is about the development of the Nerf ball, and how it symbolizes the changing landscape of play in the late twentieth century.

Nerf inventor Reynolds Guyer graduated from Dartmouth with a degree in journalism, but instead of going into that field, he worked for his father. His family owned a toy and game business, which was famous for its game *Twister*. In 1968, the company was in the process of developing a caveman game, and they needed some fake rocks. So Guyer cut a small piece of polyurethane foam that looked more like a ball than a rock.

Polyurethanes were a thirty-year-old technology that had revolutionized all kinds of industries, from the automotive sector to mattresses. Dr. Otto Bayer discovered the basic chemistry of polyurethanes in 1937, and they became widely used in WWII as a substitute for rubber. By the 1950s, they were used in everyday consumer products including shoes, cushions, and even spandex.[1] This material would soon revolutionize the toy industry too.

During the product-testing phase, Guyer and his teammates threw the fake polyurethane rocks at one another. One of Guyer's teammates started bouncing the chunk of foam up and down, and they decided to use it as an indoor ball.[2] The discovery was significant because up until that time if a child wanted to play ball, that had to be done outdoors lest they break everything in the house. The team decided to name their indoor ball Nerf. According to historian Tim Walsh, the term had been used in the hot-rod circuit as a reference to bumping other cars out of the way. The product's box advertised, "SAFE! The Nerf Ball is made of incredibly soft and spongy synthetic foam. Throw it around indoors; you can't damage lamps or break windows. You can't hurt babies or old people."[3]

In the last few decades of the twentieth century, play moved increasingly indoors. According to historian Howard Chudacoff, "Parental anxieties over real and imagined dangers have expanded indoor playtime."[4] The Nerf ball facilitated these changes. These toys were revolutionary for children's play because they allowed activities customarily reserved for the outdoors to come inside. "There's a whole new classification of action toys which allow rough and tumble play *safely*, indoors. . . . Nerf can take it, but they *can't* give it out because they're made of soft, squeezable foam. . . . Their soft qualities will just about eliminate the need for Mom to have to say 'No' every five minutes when youngsters are romping 'round the room."[5]

Nerf soon started selling more than balls, and soon all kinds of activities usually reserved for the outdoors could come inside. Nerf fencing, soccer, golf, and badminton were released shortly after the original product. The company wanted to make a football, but the polyurethane foam wasn't sturdy enough for kicking, so they invented a new way of pouring liquid foam into a mold rather than simply cutting out foam from more substantial pieces.[6] Historian Bob Beatty owned one of these footballs when he was growing up and recalls, "[It] was fun to throw around. I could play with my younger brother and not hurt him if he missed the catch."[7]

Part IX

PLAYING GROWN-UP

Much of children's play involves mimicking what they see happening in the grown-up world. Kids play house, teacher, and detective, reenacting all sorts of professions and activities that they see the grown-ups in their lives doing. Throughout the nineteenth and twentieth century, the toys that children played with helped them imitate grown-up life. As children gained increasing amounts of leisure time throughout this period, adults began to see play as a child's work. It prepared them for what lay ahead. This part will explore the concept of play as a rehearsal for the future by looking at five toys that educated children on proper gender roles and specific professions.

According to historian Howard Chudacoff, during the nineteenth and early twentieth centuries, "in the minds of experts, play was not the opposite of work; rather, it should be a productive activity through which a child rehearsed for modern adulthood by following the guidance of wise, rational adults."[1] William Forbush's ideas in his 1914 book *The Manual of Play* are good examples of this philosophy. "Play seems to have two great meanings—it prepares for life and it enhances life. . . . It develops the senses, reveals capacities, satisfies and stimulates curiosity, trains the higher mental powers, helps courage to overcome difficulties and broadens the social nature. This is the unconscious side of play."[2] Parents who were anxious about the moral legitimacy of their children's increasing amounts of leisure time in the late nineteenth century felt better when they saw their kids playing with things that helped them learn to be grown-ups.

Play as preparation for the future often entailed socializing boys and girls into specific gender roles. According to historian Paula Fass, when paid work moved outside of the household in the early nineteenth century, women were left with the sole care of the household and the children. According to Fass, "This encouraged what historians have called the 'cult of domesticity,' in which the spheres of male and female influence were radically divided, and a woman's home duties were elevated and came to define her sphere."[3] During the nineteenth and the majority of the twentieth century, much of girls' play involved rehearsal for future roles as wives and mothers. Parents and child experts encouraged girls to play with dolls, dollhouses, tea sets, toy ovens, and other artifacts that promoted domesticity. In 1891, Dr. Julia Holmes Smith described the ideal playroom in a middle-class household: "In one corner was a real little kitchen, with oilcloth on the floor, a toy stove and its paraphernalia, tubs, clothes horse, etc., that the little girls might taste in advance the delights of housework."[4]

Similarly, boys' play prepared them to become men. Gary Cross notes that "boys imitated men in their use of playthings. . . . They were self-consciously embedded with messages about gender roles, technology, and business, they were designed to teach expectations about the future."[5] In the late nineteenth and early twentieth centuries, useful play for boys involved activities that would help them learn all kinds of valuable career skills, from construction and engineering (see part 5) to science and medicine. In an era of rapid technological advancement, parents were happy to let their boys play with chemistry sets, toy airplanes, trains, and other objects that celebrated American ingenuity. Child-rearing experts also encouraged fathers to spend more time playing with their children. Toy companies responded by marketing chemistry sets and toy trains as a way to help fathers and sons bond over scientific inquiry.[6]

For both boys and girls, dramatic, imaginative play is an integral part of their psychological development. Karl Groos explored this idea in the early twentieth century as he developed his pre-exercise theory of play. According to historians Olivia Saracho and Bernard Spodek, "Because play encourages children to imitate and practice adult roles, Groos considered it to be an essential need of childhood, one that reinforces the instincts that allow children to prepare for their roles."[7] Play theorists who favor a Freudian psychoanalytic model argue that children use dramatic play to mimic adult roles so they can gain control over situations that would otherwise overwhelm them. Even contemporary play theorists encourage parents and teachers to supply children with materials that will help them mimic what they see in the grown-up world.

This part explores five toys that encouraged children to imitate the adult world, preparing them for the future. Dollhouses promoted useful domesticity. Tea sets allowed girls to rehearse their future roles as hostesses. Chemistry sets prepared boys for future careers as scientists. The Easy Bake Oven prepared girls to be cooks by enabling them to bake food in a real oven. Last, toy medical kits took away some of the trauma of going to doctor's appointments for both boys and girls and prepared them for careers in medicine.

Dollhouse

John Everett Millais British (1829–1896) *The Doll House*, etching on chine applique

Identifying Information:

The Doll House, John Everett Millais

Date: c. 1872

National Gallery of Art Object ID 1983.36.1

In 1974, writer Nicole Cooley's mother built a Victorian dollhouse for her daughter. It was a Victorian home, furnished with handmade curtains and rugs, and even had real electric lights. "The dollhouse was the best toy I would ever own," Cooley recalled. "When I arranged tiny brass beds or slid a plastic roast chicken in the oven, I entered another universe. And yet, at the same time, I also ventured more deeply inside myself."[1] Dollhouses allowed girls to build a world of their own, prepared them for a useful future, and gave them room for freedom and imagination.

Although we usually think of dollhouses as children's toys, grown-ups owned the first miniature houses. In 1558, Duke Albrecht V of Bavaria had a "baby house" built for himself. It was an art piece that depicted his worldly possessions. According to journalist Charles Siebert, "Soon a fad among the nobility and rich, such distillate minidwellings were intended not for play but for study, as working models of how to properly design and manage a home."[2] In the seventeenth and eighteenth century, wealthy families in Denmark and Germany commissioned miniature replicas of their homes.[3] In the 1700s, Duchess Augusta Dorothea had several doll cabinets made to show off her wealth.[4]

Miniature houses became children's playthings toward the end of the eighteenth century in Central Europe and were designed to teach girls about domestic arts.[5] In the nineteenth century, dollhouses educated American girls on the practical skills of homemaking and taught them problem-solving skills. Furnishing a dollhouse was preparation for a future when a young woman would need to set up her own home. According to Catharine Beecher, the dollhouse served as a "miniature domestic establishment"[6] in which girls could prepare for their future roles as the mistress of a home. Dollhouses gave girls control over a domestic situation and allowed them to enact the various trials and joys that they would experience as adults. Dollhouses positioned play as "an exercise in adapting to adult responsibilities."[7]

These toys that girls played with ranged from simple, homemade structures to elaborate art pieces. In the 1880s, Nettie Wells was growing up in Kansas City. Her middle-class father built her a small wooden house with a pretty starburst on the front. Nettie's granddaughter later donated the house to the National Museum of Toys/Miniatures. According to museum staff, "Nettie's dollhouse was a teaching tool for her adult life. Sadly, Nettie had to assume that role at the age of just twelve when her mother fell ill."[8] When the doll-house came to the museum, curators looked inside the little house and found a hand-sewn crazy quilt that Nettie had made for her dolls.

Other dollhouses were elaborate creations that wealthy parents commissioned for their children. The Coleman family of Lebanon, Pennsylvania, had a nine-foot tall, eight-foot wide giant dollhouse built for their children in the 1880s.[9]

Dollhouses turned girls into both producers and consumers. They often furnished their dollhouses with handmade creations, making curtains out of bits of lace and even sewing their own dolls. Mothers and daughters bonded with one another spending the afternoon "searching through the advertising pages of old magazines and the catalogs of furniture houses and department stores, for suitable articles for the different rooms."[10]

In the late 1800s, a rise of consumer goods and changes to manufacturing technology "brought more children to the upper-class traditions of doll-houses and tea sets."[11] Lithographed dollhouses were portable and cheaper to produce, which put them in the hands of girls whose families couldn't have afforded them before or manufactured them on their own. Toy companies also started making miniature versions of domestic objects, reflecting the changing technology of domesticity. Just as their mothers were purchasing the newest household appliances, girls could furnish their tiny houses with the latest fads in home goods including electric irons and, much later in the twentieth century, refrigerators.

Girls spent many of their free hours decorating their parents' houses once they had gotten the hang of decorating their dollhouses. And making a home lovely fell into the realm of feminine usefulness, so parents encouraged this spirit of enterprise. *The American Girls Handy Book* gave instructions on how to paint china, prepare make-shift bookshelves, sew curtains, and make screens, small tables, lanterns, and other decorative ornaments. It also advised decorating a fireplace mantle, creating a canopy above the bed, and sewing cushions for a rocking chair.[12] In this way, older girls took the skills they learned furnishing their dollhouses and applied them to real domestic situations.

By the early twentieth century, the number of consumer goods available to Americans had skyrocketed. This allowed girls to expand their dollhouse play into the realm of pure economic fantasy. Girls could either purchase specialized miniature pieces or cut out pictures of items from magazines to paste up in their little houses. According to *American Motherhood* in 1914, "When every possible room has been added to the house, the stable may be furnished with horses and carriages, and automobile house filled with a variety of touring cars and runabouts, and even a boathouse equipped with rowboats, motor launches, and sailing yachts. A conservatory may be added, in which plants cut from the florist's catalogs flourish in long rows."[13]

By the twentieth century, the purpose of dollhouses changed. No longer strictly objects for teaching useful domesticity, dollhouses became widely accepted as vehicles for imaginative play. Often the imaginative stories girls told in their dollhouses were more important than the objects adorning the room. "Creating scenes and acting out dialogue helps children to develop emotionally, socially, and intellectually,"[14] according to the Fractus Learning company.

For Cooley, the girl in the opening story, "The social history of dollhouses is at odds with the idea that dollhouses are spaces of emotion, freedom, and imagination."[15] When Cooley grew up, she gave her old dollhouse furnishings to her daughters, who continue their mother's playtime traditions.

42

Tea Set

Augusta Brown's tea set
CREDIT: SUSAN A. FLETCHER

Identifying Information:

Miniature Tea Set

Collection of Ruth Brown Fletcher

When we were little, my best friend Tanya hosted a teddy bear tea party. Her mother had constructed an impressive Barbie Doll cake complete with edible skirt. We enjoyed dressing up for the party and acting like proper grown-up ladies. We practiced what we thought adult life would be like. Tea parties are a common girlhood tradition in the United States, dating to the nineteenth century. For girls in the late 1880s, tea parties were common rituals in the imitation of their mothers and aunts. According to Gary Cross, "girls learned their play scripts through imitating pictures of tea parties and other social rituals—often from trade cards or stereograph images."[1]

Miniature dishes had become popular in the seventeenth and eighteenth centuries as furnishings for decorative dollhouses. These dishes became children's playthings in the nineteenth century. They often matched the china that a girl's mother was using. The tea sets often came with many different pieces including sugar bowls, plates, and cups. According to decorative arts historian Nina Ranalli, "That each part is intended for a specific purpose was likely not lost on the children who played with these sets; social rules are implicit in the objects, and it seems clear that children began to enter into adult society by playing with them."[2]

Part of the adult responsibilities that nineteenth-century parents wanted their daughters to know was how to entertain guests by holding tea parties. "Tea-drinking has become very fashionable among us of late years,"[3] according to an article in *Youth's Companion* in 1898. The article reminded girls that their grandmothers had enjoyed the ritual of tea and that they needed to learn how to carry on the tradition. Articles in *Youth's Companion* and *St. Nicholas* gave instructions on holding doll tea parties, including how many guests to invite, what kind of food to serve, and how to be a hostess.

Girls sometimes acquired their own tea sets by selling subscriptions to ladies magazines. In 1886, *The Ladies Home Journal* offered a china set as a premium for gathering six subscriptions.[4] Selling these subscriptions was a form of feminine usefulness by increasing social contacts. An enterprising girl could craft her own future.

Tea parties socialized girls into feminine usefulness in four different ways. Girls learned domesticity by playing with their tea dishes and preparing small treats for their friends. They learned social usefulness by practicing conversation with friends and mimicking adult behavior. Girls also learned how to be consumers as they played with manufactured tea sets and cajoled their parents into buying food for the parties. Lastly, girls learned the usefulness of aesthetics in pouring the tea properly and having beautiful dishes. By having tea parties with their dolls and friends, girls could mimic the behavior that they saw their mothers engaging in, learning how to navigate the female world of ritual.

43

Chemistry Set

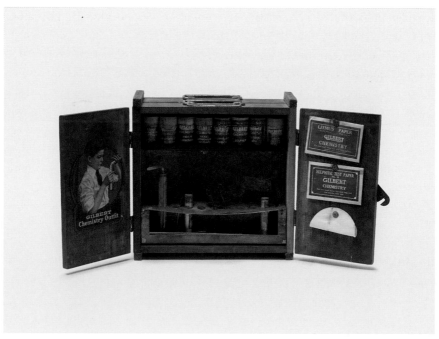

Gilbert Chemistry Outfit 1930–1939
COURTESY OF SCIENCE HISTORY INSTITUTE, PUBLIC DOMAIN

Identifying Information:

Gilbert Chemistry Outfit

Manufacturer: A. C. Gilbert Company

Date: 1930s

Courtesy of Science History Institute

In 1962, young Billy O'Brien got a chemistry set for his birthday. One day, he accidentally spilled a chemistry experiment he was working on. His father wiped up the spilt chemicals with a handkerchief. According to a newspaper article, the dad "then later mopped his nude pate with the handkerchief. Later, lo! And behold, hair sprouted. Two friends tried it. They, too, got results. O'Brien has been bald for 21 years. If Billy's formula is the cause, he's really made it. If he can remember it."[1] Despite the serious role that chemistry sets had in preparing children for the future, they sometimes caused happy accidents.

Chemistry sets were some of the most important toys in the early twentieth century. As scientific discovery advanced rapidly this era, children's toys imitated the lives of professional scientists. The same desire to prepare boys for a stable career in engineering and architecture that sparked the nation's obsession with construction toys (see part 5) during this time period was also behind the popularity of chemistry sets. Parents of the early twentieth century hoped their boys would grow up to be scientists, and chemistry sets were vehicles for these wishes. Companies like Chemcraft and the A. C. Gilbert Company sold kits that contained *real* chemicals so boys could start their scientific discoveries early.

Scientific education through play is a time-honored tradition in America. During the nineteenth century, a variety of playtime activities educated children on the scientific method and the importance of experiments. We've already discussed optical science toys in part 3. In the 1880s, children also played with science kits, which contained a variety of natural specimens. One of these kits came with a wooden chest containing 125 different specimens including gum Arabic, quicksilver, seeds, insects, and ores.[2] These kits gave children hands-on education about the world around them.

Experiential learning found a welcome place in middle-class homes. Children created "parlor magic" by using their expertise on chemistry, physics, optics, and mechanics. Prescriptive literature taught chemistry lessons that doubled as magic tricks. *The American Boy's Book of Sports and Games* taught children how to make sympathetic (invisible) ink, magic milk, and incombustible paper. Boys astounded their audiences by creating "paper oracles" that had answers to questions written in "nitro-muriate of gold," which was invisible until the magician exposed it to heat.[3] They restored faded roses by pouring sulfur into a dish of hot coals and holding the flower over the fumes, dipping it in water, and placing it in a drawer for four hours. In performing such tricks, children learned the basic properties of chemicals and used their showmanship to explore the tensions between scientific logic and magic, learning and fun.

In the twentieth century, these childhood experiments prepared boys for careers in science. Many of the chemical sets that were available to American children prior to 1914 were imported from Europe. With the start of World War I, however, the chemicals that European manufacturers had previously supplied to children were diverted for wartime use. So, Americans started producing their own chemistry sets.

In 1914, American chemist John J. Porter formed Chemcraft. Each of his kits came with chemicals, equipment, and instruction booklets, and sold for $5 to $10.[4] The packaging made the link between scientific education and leisure time overt: "the fundamentals of Chemistry, and its application to the things we use every day, are made clear by a series of experiments which teach and amuse." Soon, these chemistry sets were one of the hottest toys for middle-class boys.

A few years later, A. C. Gilbert of Erector Set fame started making his own chemistry sets in 1920. The Gilbert Chemistry set that you see in the photograph at the beginning of this chapter contained litmus paper, test tubes, and a variety of chemicals including nickel ammonium sulfate, tartaric acid, and sodium carbonate. A label warned that the product was for older boys: "This set is not intended for children who cannot read and understand the accompanying instruction book."[5]

Parents liked chemistry sets because they hoped their boys would become scientists. According to curator Rosie Cook of the Chemical Heritage Foundation, "Coming out of the Depression, that was a message that would resonate with a lot of parents who wanted their children to not only have a job that would make them money but to have a career that was stable."[6]

In 1941, a newspaper columnist named Ruth Peck McLeod wrote an article masquerading as a teenage boy. She linked the value of educational play to a boy's future career path:

> Sometimes I work with my chemistry set for hours. I did that after a great chemist lectured here at the High School. Dad's a chemist, so he had him come to our house to dinner, and then Dad told him about my chemistry set, and that great scientist went down into our old basement to see what I'd been doing. And he complimented my mother and father on letting me have this 'means of developing my talents,' as he called it. . . . He said that often hobbies prepare boys for their life work.[7]

Sometimes, chemistry sets really did inspire children to go into scientific careers. Astronomy professor Dr. Henry T. Harvey credited his career choice to educational toys. His parents gave him a telescope and a chemistry set when he was little.[8] Although chemistry sets were initially intended for boys' use only in the early twentieth century, in 1958 the A. C. Gilbert company produced a Lab Technician set for girls. In 1972, sixteen-year-old Nina Felice Tabachnik won the grand prize in the Westinghouse Science Talent Search. She was the first girl to win the top prize in the thirty-one-year history of the contest. Tabachnik credited her win to a childhood spent playing with science toys. Her parents bought her a chemistry set and microscope, which inspired her dream of becoming a neurosurgeon.[9]

Chemistry sets were very popular in the 1950s. The Gilbert Company manufactured an Atomic Energy Lab that came with *radioactive* ore and a Geiger counter.[10] In the atomic age, scientific inquiry was patriotic. Chemcraft changed the tagline on its products to "Porter Science Prepares Young America for World Leadership."[11]

Chemistry sets gradually fell out of favor in the 1960s and 70s. In the 60s, parents questioned the wisdom of letting their children play with real—potentially very dangerous—chemicals. A new series of laws regulated both the chemical and toy industries in the late 1960s, including the Toy Safety Act of 1969. Instead of being starry-eyed over how well chemistry sets prepared their kids for the future, suddenly parents decided that chemistry sets posed unacceptable risks for their offspring and were thus banned in many households. The decline in chemistry set sales was devastating for their manufacturers; The Gilbert Company went out of business in 1967 and Porter closed in 1984.

However, as Cook notes, in the 1980s interest in scientific toys reemerged. In 1986, Katherine Wollard of the *Los Angeles Times* presented the benefits of science toys to girls, "mixing chemicals in the basement or lugging her very own telescope out at night—away from boys who often act as if they own the school lab equipment—can be an ideal, unpressured way for a girl to discover her own innate joy in discovery."[12]

44

Easy Bake Oven

1970s Easy Bake Oven

Identifying Information:

Easy Bake Oven

Maker: Ronald Howes and James O. Kuhn

Manufacturer: Kenner

Date: 1968

The Easy Bake Oven prepared young Alton Brown for his future life as a chef and television personality. Inspired by his 1960s boyhood obsession with the Easy Bake Oven, Brown brought his grown-up version of the oven to Colorado Springs on his "Edible Inevitable Tour" in 2014. He calls it The Mega Bake. Forget the dinky 100-watt lightbulb from the original Easy Bake Oven; the Mega Bake is comprised of fifty-four 1,000-watt lightbulbs, generating 1,026,000 lumens of light. The oven produced temperatures over 600 degrees.[1] His audience watched in amazement as Brown sent an uncooked pizza and pan of raw brownie batter along the conveyor belt. After both passed under the lights, the pizza came out perfectly cooked, followed by a pan of hot brownies.

Brown later explained, "When I was a very little kid I wanted one of these, really, really badly. And my parents wouldn't let me have one because they were for girls, and back in those days that was a line you didn't want to cross."[2] So he traded some G.I. Joes to a cousin in exchange for his first Easy Bake Oven. "It was very empowering. However, by the time I was five, this was just not cutting it for me. But the memories stayed with me."[3] Celebrity chefs Bobby Flay and Rick Bayless have also confessed to owning Easy Bake Ovens in their youth.[4]

The Easy Bake Oven came out in 1963 as part of a long tradition of toy stoves. These toys were usually intended to prepare girls for their future roles as cooks. During the nineteenth and early twentieth century, helping in the kitchen was often a household necessity for many girls, especially those with large families. Girls of the lower classes sometimes worked in the kitchens of wealthy families. For them, being in the kitchen was work, not play. However, children of the middle and upper classes who *did* have leisure time often played with toy stoves anyway as part of their gender role socialization.

Toy kitchens remained popular into the 1950s and 60s. Most of them were just for "pretend cooking." However, for imaginative kids who did use them for "real cooking," disaster loomed. In 1956, four-year-old Peggy Clark "fired up her toy stove with some honest-to-goodness fuel."[5] The blaze caught her room on fire before her parents could put the flames out. Fortunately, no one was hurt. There was a clear need for a toy oven that could bake things without burning the house down.

In 1963, Ronald Howes and Kenner Products created the Safety Bake Oven to fill this need. They modeled their toy after hot dog and pretzel stands, with James O. Kuhn overseeing product development. The heat from two 100-watt lightbulbs powered the oven. The National Association of Broadcasters did not agree that the product was as "safe" as its name implied, so Kenner added a protective grate and renamed it the Easy Bake Oven.[6] Kenner sold 500,000 units the first year for $15.95 a piece.[7] It came with mixes for cakes, biscuits, and other baked treats.

In 1967, General Mills acquired Kenner and all of its products, including the Easy Bake Oven. General Mills also owned Betty Crocker, and soon the Easy Bake Oven was sold with Betty Crocker cake mixes including Devil's food cake, white cake, brownies, and chocolate fudge.

A television commercial for the Easy Bake Oven made the link between playtime and helping in a real kitchen. "Remember when you were little and had fun making mud pies? And then you grew up and helped mommy bake a Betty Crocker Cake. Now that you're older, guess what? There's an Easy Bake Oven just for you."[8]

The marketing campaign also turned girls into consumers. The commercial emphasized that when girls ran out of the mixes that were provided in the original kit, they could buy more Betty Crocker mixes at the grocery store using the coupons included in the box. It was the razor/razor blade marketing approach at work again, just like Barbie and all of her accessories.

The oven claimed that it taught its users all kinds of useful skills. Girls learned math as they discovered how to measure ingredients. They did chemistry experiments by seeing how certain ingredients react with one another.

An advertisement for the toy in a 1967 newspaper stated that the oven was "a real fun-time toy that lets youngsters learn how to cook."[9]

Nevertheless, as with almost all mass-produced toys, children played with it in ways that often subverted the intentions of the manufacturer and the expectations of grown-ups. Some children used the Easy Bake Oven to destroy their other toys. Diette Ward recalls, "It occurred to me that I could use the oven for other things, like testing the melting point of things like LEGOs and Barbies. For me it became more of a science thing—my mom was just afraid I'd start a fire."[10] Diette's mother eventually took the Easy Bake Oven away from her inquisitive daughter.

45

Medical Kits

Mickey Mouse Medical Kit

Identifying Information:

Mickey Mouse Medical Kit

Manufacturer: Empire Toys

Date: 1977

Strong Museum of Play Object ID 112.6549

Alexis Puyleart, a senior physics and pre-med major at St. Norbert College, recalls, "For as long as I can remember, I have wanted to be a medical doctor. Some of my earliest memories include playing with toy medical kits or reading anatomy books."[1] Toy medical kits inspired generations of children to pursue careers in medicine.

During the 1940s and 50s, toy medical kits were very popular, and several models existed. The wartime-inspired Army Doctor/Nurse Kit advertised that "every little boy can play a doctor and every little girl can play a nurse."[2] In 1952, the Sears Roebuck in Tuscaloosa, Alabama, sold toy doctor kits featuring a diploma and a stethoscope for $1.59.[3] All of these kits fell under the category of play as preparation for the future, just like dollhouses, tea sets, and chemistry sets.

There was another purpose for toy medical kits too, though: they helped children prepare for doctor appointments. In 1956, Lynn Pressman Raymond created a "Doctor Bag" to ease children's anxieties when they visited their physicians.[4] Kids could use toy stethoscopes and reflex hammers to rehearse how a real-life medical appointment might go. Freudian psychoanalytic play theory argues that this type of dramatic play helped children feel in control of situations that might be scary for them.

Kids of the 1950s had plenty of reasons to feel nervous about being at the doctor's office. Adequate medical care for children was a relatively recent innovation for American children at mid-century. Their grandparents growing up only forty years before likely would not have had regular check-ups, especially if they had grown up in rural areas. So, the doctor's office was a somewhat strange place to be in the history of childhood. That wasn't a bad thing, however. Access to medical care meant that kids were much more likely to survive infancy during this time period than they ever had been before. The infant mortality rate plummeted from 100 deaths per 1,000 live births in 1915 to 29.2 deaths per 1,000 in 1950.[5]

Despite the decline in infant mortality rates in the first half of the century, the 1950s were also a time of profound medical anxiety for American parents and their kids. Disease epidemics swept the country including diphtheria, measles, and of course, polio (see the chapter on *Candyland* in part 1). In 1952, 57,568 polio cases were reported in the United States.

Science writer Dr. Ricki Lewis recalls her own experience with childhood epidemics: "When I was 3 I had the measles for a full month."[6] Her physician warned her parents that Ricki could lose her hearing or go blind, but Ricki eventually recovered. A few years later, the measles vaccine came out and her younger sister Edith was lucky enough to get one. "I watched several people hold down a screaming Edith as she got the new measles vaccine, two shots back then. But we both had mumps, chickenpox, and German measles, their vaccines not yet perfected."[7]

"Doctors loomed large for the baby-boom generation—powerful figures only too willing to inflict pain."[8] Medical personnel were often the first authority figures that young children encountered apart from their family members. They were notorious for prescribing total rest for sick children, which hampered kids' ability to play and have fun. Young Peter Stockley was diagnosed with a rheumatic fever in the 1950s, which caused a heart murmur. Stockley's doctor told him, "Listen, Peter, you are ill . . . you cannot exert yourself *at all*! That means no running, swimming, riding your bike, climbing or exercising in any way."[9] Upon hearing this news, Peter yelled out a curse word, flung a bottle of pills across the room, and fled the hospital.[10] No wonder mid-century children were nervous about their doctor appointments!

These toys eventually intersected with children's popular culture. Fictional characters and iconic toy brands hawked their own versions of doctor kits. Pressman Toys came out with Nurse Barbie Kit in 1962, which featured a toy stethoscope, needles, glasses, and a nurse hat. The company later produced a Ken Doctor Kit, offering gender-specific career advice. In 1977, the Mickey

Mouse Medical Kit came with twenty-five pieces, including a blood pressure cuff, scissors, reflex hammer, head lamp, stethoscope, and play microscope. The box of the Mickey Mouse kit stated that the toy was for "boys and girls," with the cartoon packaging depicting Mickey as the enthusiastic doctor while Minnie was the nurse who takes chart notes.[11]

The gender-specific messaging on toy medical kits reflected the realities of the gender breakdown of the medical profession. In 1949, women comprised only 6 percent of the physician workforce and 5.5 percent of med school students. With the passage of Title IX of the Education Amendments, however, medical schools began to open opportunities for equal education to women. By 1990, women comprised 17 percent of the physician workforce.[12] In 2015, this number had jumped to 36 percent. Many of these female physicians played with toy medical kits when they were kids, which inspired their career choice.

One of these medical students was Rachel Giordano, the woman that you met in the section on LEGOs. She's the girl who was featured in the famous 1981 LEGO advertisement targeting the product to girls. Giordano is a naturopathic doctor now. She recalls, "How I played as a girl shaped who I am today. It contributed to me becoming a physician . . . I now co-own two medical centers in Seattle. Doctor kits used to be for all children but now they are on the boys' aisle. I simply believe that they should be marketed to all children again."[13]

Part X

ELECTRONIC GAMES

If you grew up in the last few decades of the twentieth century, you likely played with some type of electronic games. You may have gone to the arcade, used a video-gaming system, used your family's personal computer, or squinted at a handheld device. Electronic toys increasingly defined the playtime of Generation X and Millennials. According to electronic gaming expert Jane McGonigal, these "games make us happy because they are hard work that we choose for ourselves."[1] They have made children and teenagers happy for decades, at the same time causing anxiety for parents and child-development experts. This part explores five electronic toys, examining the impact of moral panics upon play, the universality of many video game themes, and the changing landscape of play.

Electronic components found their way into toys starting in the early 1900s. Erector Set and other construction toys had motorized pieces that propelled a child's imagination. Pinball games gradually added electronic flippers and lights, making the games extra-appealing and easier to play. In the mid-twentieth century, advances in technology helped electronics evolve into a category unto themselves. In 1958, physicist William Higinbotham created one of the earliest video games. He worked at the Brookhaven National Laboratory's instrument lab, where he was in charge of making an exhibit that would help visitors understand the laboratory's mission. He thought the other exhibits were boring and decided to make things more exciting by creating a video game for visitors to play. So he designed one of the first electronic games: *Tennis for Two* in which players could hit a ball back and forth.[2] The game was a hit, and pretty soon video games left the physics lab and entered the arcade.

Video game design took off in the late 1960s. Sega produced many of the early games including *Missile* and *Duck Hunt*. In the early 1970s, Nolan Bushnell and Ted Dabney formed the Atari company and produced an electronic arcade game called PONG, which was the first of its kind to have widespread success. Electronic games made the leap from the arcade to home gaming systems and personal computers in the 1980s and quickly became an integral part of American childhood and play.[3]

For better or worse, these games dramatically impacted imaginative play in the last two decades of the twentieth century. As historian Howard Chudacoff notes, video games forced children into a scripted play in ways that had never been seen before. When children play war or house, for example, they make up the script for how things should go. According to educator Eugene Provenzo, however, "This simply cannot happen in the physically impoverished and tightly rule-bound universe of video games. . . . Players must follow a complex series of instructions according to a very carefully defined set of rules."[4]

Electronic games are also notorious for creating parental anxieties. According to Dr. Benjamin Spock, "The best that can be said of them is they may help promote eye-hand coordination in children. The worst that can be said is that they sanction, and even promote, aggression and violent responses to conflict. But what can be said with much greater certainty is this: most computer games are a colossal waste of time."[5]

Colossal waste of time or not, children of the late twentieth century found themselves hypnotized by pixilated characters and landscapes. Many of these games became pop culture phenomena, taking on a life of their own in the form of merchandise, cartoons, and music. They created toy crazes rivaling Cabbage Patch Dolls and teddy bears. They wormed their way into the subconscious minds of children all over America; the familiar theme song to *Super Mario Brothers* stays with one well into adulthood.

In this part, we'll explore five electronic toys and games, starting with the moral panic over electronic pinball. Did you know that people used to *hate* pinball, to the point where the machines were banned in New York City for decades? Second, the computer game *The Oregon Trail* highlights children's changing relationships to technology at the end of the twentieth century. Third, we'll look at *Pac-Man* as another example of a toy craze in the 1980s. Next, we'll look at *Tetris* and its creation story in the context of the Cold War. Last, *Super Mario Brothers* tells the story of panic over children's health.

Electronic Pinball

Electronic pinball games at Arcade Amusements in Manitou Springs, Colorado.

Identifying Information:

Electronic Pinball

Collection of Arcade Amusements

On summer afternoons, vintage arcade games keep visitors of all ages entertained for hours at Arcade Amusements in Manitou Springs, Colorado. In one wing of the complex are the oldest games dating to the early twentieth century, including an impressive collection of pinball machines. Players insert nickels and dimes into *Jumpin' Jack Flash*, *The Smart Set*, and *Honey*, and soon the familiar ring of bells and flapping bumpers rings out across the arcade. For budget-conscious and nostalgic visitors, these pinball games are an affordable and fun way to entertain oneself. However, these pinball games weren't always so innocent; they were once the cause of moral panic in America over the machines' potential ties to gambling and the corruption of youth.

The American arcade is more than a century old. Indoor spaces for entertaining youth and grown-ups arose during the late nineteenth century. According to Jeremy Saucier of the Strong Museum of Play, "At the end of that century, parlor owners filled their establishments with such new novelties of the Industrial age as phonographs, kinetoscopes, and mutoscopes. . . . However, by the turn of the century, as the novelty of those inventions wore off, many amusement parlors transformed into penny arcades."[1]

Soon, pinball games joined the peep shows, penny soccer games, and fake shooting ranges in these arcades. The concept of pinball originated several centuries ago, having roots in an eighteenth-century French game called bagatelle. In 1931, David Gottlieb developed *Baffleball*, followed by Raymond Moloney's *Ballyhoo* in 1932, the first coin-operated pinball game.[2] The earliest pinball games developed in the United States didn't have flippers to control the ball's movement, so winning a game was left to luck. Guardians of American morality didn't like games that left winning to luck. They called them "games of chance" and said they smacked of gambling. We'll get back to this concept soon.

Pinball flippers weren't invented until 1947. That year, Dr. Gottlieb and Company developed the game *Humpty Dumpty*, which was the first game to feature the electromechanical "flipper bumpers" that we are familiar with today. Players could press buttons to make the flippers spin the ball around the playing field, enabling them to manipulate the ball's trajectory. With more interaction from the players and the ability to control what happened in the pinball game, there was less strength to the argument that these were mere games of chance.[3]

Despite these changes, however, parents were still suspicious of pinball games. The early Bally and Williams pinball games had a cash payout at the end. Moral advocates were alarmed that players were winning money for doing absolutely nothing other than putting a coin in a slot. These suspicions did have some merit: according to entertainment historian Daniel Reynolds, "In the 1930s and 40s, the pinball industry had strong ties to organized crime; from an industrial standpoint (and, in many ways, from a law-enforcement standpoint), the pinball industry was very much a successor to the 'slot machine racket.'"[4] Historian Laura June remarks that "Cash payouts were quickly abandoned as it became clear that pinball and gambling weren't a comfortable (or legal) match."[5]

Because pinball games were associated with gambling, adults thought they were a gateway to hell for their children. If teenage boys started playing pinball, surely it was an open door for them to begin playing pool, poker, wasting all sorts of time, and turning to a life of crime. According to Benjamin M. Day, President of the Society for the Prevention of Crime in 1942, "The pinball is step-brother to the slot machine and has always been a heavy contributor to youthful delinquency. The schoolboy who uses his lunch money on a pinball machine frequently steals to make up the deficit."[6] In the words of the musical *Music Man,* parents thought they had trouble with a capital T, that rhymes with P, that stands for . . . pinball.

So, officials all over the country began a crusade against pinball machines. In 1941, several pinball machines were confiscated in New Jersey, and the State Supreme Court decided to weigh in on the morality of the devices. An article in the *New York Times* declared the case would determine "the mission of pinball machines in American civilization."[7] The police hauled the confiscated pinball machines into the courtroom, which irritated the judges. Justice Joseph L. Bodine declared, "You don't have to argue that this is a gambling device. . . . Men and boys are not going to stand around sticking nickels in a wall without getting money back. In this day and generation, it may be that youth has so deteriorated that it has become a practice, but if so, some doctor should place them in an insane asylum and have their heads examined."[8]

In January 1942, pinball machines were banned in the states of New York and New Jersey on the basis that they were games of chance. Justice Joseph Perskie declared, "The pinball machines involved are nothing but ingeniously designed and purposefully constructed mechanical gambling devices to appeal to, induce, lure and encourage the gaming instinct in the public generally and in children particularly."[9] As evidence of how the machines corrupted American youth, a sixteen-year-old schoolboy testified that he had skipped school to play pinball machines with his lunch money. [10]

In the early 40s, pinball games faced their greatest enemy: New York City Mayor Fiorello La Guardia. During the chaos of World War II, La Guardia banned pinball machines in the city, suggesting that the metal "in these evil contraptions [should] be manufactured into arms and bullets which can be used to destroy our foreign enemies."[11] La Guardia ordered a raid on all pinball machines. He rounded up the confiscated games and held a press conference, where he smashed the offending machines with a sledgehammer.

Even if a pinball machine didn't have a cash payout, the concept of getting what we would now call "free lives" was problematic. In 1949, circuit judge Warren L. White of Springfield, Missouri, ruled that pinball machines that gave out free games were gambling devices. The judge wrote, "If the first game is worth five cents, is not the second game worth as much? And if the player be so favored by fortune to win a free game, has he not gained something which, but for his good fortune, would cost him another five cents?"[12] Even fifteen years later, these free lives were a problem. In Klickitat County, Washington, prosecuting attorney Alf M. Jacobsen required pinball owners put up signs declaring, "Amusement Device Only. No Payoff for Free Games."[13]

As late as the 1970s, pinball was still associated with gambling. A Washington, DC lawyer on a crusade against the game wrote, "These machines wherever they go involve corruption, and they involve corruption for money."[14]

An article in the *New York Times* in 1975 declared that pinball was "still the devil's game."[15]

New York City finally legalized pinball in 1976 after pinball champion Roger Sharpe played a demonstration game before the New York City Council, proving that pinball was a game of skill, not chance. The council voted unanimously to repeal the ban, and other communities across the country followed.[16] With the rise of other electronic games in arcades and homes in the 1970s and 80s, however, adults still found much to get upset over, as we'll find out in the rest of the chapters in this part.

The Oregon Trail

The Oregon Trail handheld game

Identifying Information:

The Oregon Trail

Maker: Don Rawitsch, Bill Heinemann, and Paul Dillenberger

Manufacturer: Minnesota Educational Computing Consortium

Date: 1974

Collection of James Case

Ask a child of the 80s about *The Oregon Trail* and you are likely to get a big grin and happy, wistful sigh. Oh, the nostalgia of making a journey westward in a pixilated covered wagon, hunting bears, and hoping your family wouldn't die of dysentery. The beloved computer game defines a microgeneration of American children. Kids born in the late 1970s and early 80s grew up using computers at school and home, and *The Oregon Trail* was often one of the first computer games that they played. The game highlights this generation's changing relationship to technology.

By the 1970s, children in America were very far removed from their pioneer past. Whereas their migrant ancestors traveling on the real Oregon Trail from 1843 to the 1880s faced innumerable perils, most kids growing up in the United States one hundred years later had tame lives in comparison. They lived in homes with central heat and electricity. Most had plenty of food to eat. Childhood vaccines and clean water prevented scary diseases. The westward journeys they made happened in cars on family road trips. Nevertheless, the allure of the westward migration continued to be strong in the American imagination. In 1971, a trio of student teachers created the game *The Oregon Trail* to teach this generation of children about the past.

In 1971, Carleton College seniors Don Rawitsch, Bill Heinemann, and Paul Dillenberger moved to Minnesota to student teach at local elementary schools. They rented an apartment together to save money, and being roommates would soon prove fortuitous in gaming history. Don's teaching assignment was an eighth-grade US History class, and he had a lesson coming up on the history of the westward movement. Rawitsch later recalled, "I thought of ways to make it more interesting than the usual approach. I started experimenting with what a board game might look like, with a massive map of the western United States."[1]

He created cards representing various scenarios that might happen on the journey westward. He showed his prototype to his roommates. Bill suggested they put the game on the computer, which was a relatively new possibility in 1971.[2] Bill and Paul knew how to do programming, so the pair turned the card game into a computer game using a teletype machine and their school's computer mainframe. They included all kinds of scenarios that the real westward migrants may have encountered in the 1880s: a child getting lost, hailstorms, and broken wagon wheels. A player could go hunting by typing out "BANG." Don's students loved the game, vying to see who could reach Oregon most successfully.[3]

After the roommates ended their student teaching roles, Don kept a copy of the game's code. He got a job in 1974 with the Minnesota Educational Computing Consortium (MECC), which was a state-funded initiative that distributed educational software. He uploaded *The Oregon Trail* to MECC's mainframe, and soon Minnesota school children were playing the game. From there, the consortium made the game available for Apple II computers, which made it available in classrooms across the country.[4]

Here is where my story intersects with *The Oregon Trail*. When I was in elementary school in the mid-1980s, personal computers were a new technology, and quite rare and expensive. Schools had computer labs that allowed children to learn the basics of computing on Apple machines. We were allowed to play *The Oregon Trail*, probably before I had learned what the real Oregon Trail was all about in the classroom. My friends and I spent hours watching the little wagon bumping along the screen, hunting lumbering bears, and fording rivers. We loved the game and wanted to play it all the time. Eventually, my father purchased our first home computer, an IBM PC DOS machine, and *The Oregon Trail* was the first computer game that he bought for me. Since we were the first family on our street with a computer, my friends came over to play the game with me, and it entertained us for hours.

It taught us all sorts of lessons. In addition to teaching about life on the Oregon Trail and the geography of the west, it offered practical life lessons. We learned about the intense planning involved in a long journey, and it taught us math as we gauged how far it was from one landmark to another. The game was a lesson on class and economics too. When given a choice among being a banker from Boston, a carpenter from Ohio, or a farmer from Illinois, I always chose the first option. There was just too much stuff to buy, and starting with the right equipment helped a player win the game.

Of course, playing *The Oregon Trail* was far different from actually *being on* the Oregon Trail. The game allowed children of the late twentieth century to reenact the perils of the Western settlement experience in a 100 percent safe environment. If the computerized wagon party ran out of food, the player wouldn't starve in real life. Fording the river took place only onscreen while the player sat safely in a computer chair in a climate-controlled environment. And having a screenshot with the dreaded message "Betty Jo has died of dysentery" was indeed a bummer, but nowhere near comparable to the tragedy of death and disease on the real Oregon Trail.

Playing the game was such a standard, communal experience in this era that the micro-generation of children born in the late 1970s and early 1980s has been nicknamed "The Oregon Trail Generation." *The Oregon Trail* game represents a tipping point in how children relate to technology. According to Anna Garvey of Social Media Week, "When we first placed our sticky little fingers on a primitive Mac, we were elementary school kids whose brains were curious sponges. . . . This made us the first children to grow up figuring it out, as opposed to having an innate understanding of new technology the way Millennials did, or feeling slightly alienated from it the way Gen X did."[5]

In 2018, History Colorado created an interactive experience called "The Oregon Trail: IRL." (IRL stands for "in real life"—an important distinction from digital life in the early twenty-first century.) The institution invited adults who had grown up playing *The Oregon Trail* into their building to navigate obstacles, solve puzzles, and have a drink. An event listing invited grown-ups to "relive your childhood, as the vintage The Oregon Trail® video game becomes a live-action experience set throughout the museum. Test your pioneering skills as you hunt for food, ford a river, play the original game in our '90s throwback library computer lab, plus so much more."[6] *The Oregon Trail* experience had left the computer and returned to real life, where it continued to educate participants on the perils of the real Oregon Trail.

48

Pac-Man

Pac-Man
CREDIT: ABBY LABADIE

Identifying Information:

Pac-Man

Maker: Toru Iwatani

Manufacturer: Namco, Midway

Date: 1980

Joanne Friedman was part of the first wave of girls playing *Pac-Man* when it first appeared in the 1980s. She recalls, "I loved a rousing game of *Pac-Man* on the big machine at the roller rink during intermission!"[1] *Pac-Man* fever hit American youth hard. It was the first time that an electronic game caused the same level of toy-craze that teddy bears did in the early 1900s and that Hula-Hoops did in the 50s. In this chapter, we will explore the ways in which the game welcomed girls into arcade culture, and the impact that the game had on pop culture.

In 1978, twenty-four-year-old game designer Toru Iwatani was working at Namco, a Japanese video game company. He had been thinking about how to create video games that appealed to a broad base of players, including women and girls. Up until that time, most of the video games in arcades had some type of violent or warlike aspect, appealing heavily to males. Iwatani was looking for something different: universal themes that could transcend gender and nations. As it turned out, a meal inspired his most beloved creation. One day, Iwatani ate a pizza. As he ate a few slices, he pondered the empty space left behind in the pie. He thought that the joy of eating was universal, so he based a video game on this pizza-shaped character who devours fruit, dots, and ghosts.[2] He named this main character *Puck man*. The game enjoyed instant popularity in Japan.

Soon, *Puck man* came to the United States. Bally-Midway licensed the game for distribution in this country. The company was famous for its electronic pinball games, which by the 1980s had finally become legal most places in the United States. Bally-Midway made some important changes to the game, most notably giving it a new name. They knew there was a chance juvenile delinquents would deface the name *Puck man* by scratching out part of the letter "P," thus turning it into . . . well, you get the idea.[3] So, *Pac-Man* it was. The newly renamed game was an instant hit, selling 350,000 arcade machines in the first eighteen months on the US market. By 1982, there were 30 million American players.[4]

Until this point, most of the arcades in the United States attracted only young men and teenage boys. As Iwatani explains, "In the late 1970s, there were a lot of games in arcades which featured killing aliens or other enemies that mostly appealed to boys to play. The images of arcades was that they were darkly lit and their restrooms were dirty."[5] Although some females went to arcades and enjoyed playing the games, these were largely spaces for teenage males to congregate. However, when *Pac-Man* came to the arcade, things changed. It was a simple chase game—not violent or war-based. According to game expert Chris Melissinos, "What it really wound up doing was it changed the social dialogue around arcades. Now, for the first time, you had women in arcades, and you had kids—both boys and girls—in these arcades that were typically full of older teens and adult males. . . . It made it more permissible for everyone to be included in arcade culture."[6]

Thus, boys and girls, teenagers, and young adults succumbed to *Pac-Man* fever in the early 1980s. Pac-Man and his pursuing ghosts Blinky, Inky, Pinky, and Clyde were just as recognizable to Gen-X children as Disney characters were to their parents. In 1982, Stanley Jarocki, vice president of marketing for Midway, proclaimed, "Pac-Man is to today's youth what Mickey Mouse was to the children of the 1950s."[7] Jerry Buckner and Gary (no, not Jerry) Garcia wrote a song about the game called *Pac-Man Fever*. The artists were in awe of the craze that the game had sparked. *Pac-Man Fever* sold 1.2 million copies by 1982. The single was part of the *Pac-Man Fever* album, which had eight songs, each inspired by video games including *Frogger*, *Donkey Kong*, and *Asteroids*.[8]

For Christmas 1982, *Pac-Man* merchandise were among the most frequently requested toys from Santa. "Dear Santa Claus," wrote young Kelly Davis, "I want a pair of chic jeans, roller skates, a Pac-Man game. . . . Santa, please tell mom and dad I hate dolls."[9] The Christmas letters to Santa in newspapers across the country are indicative of the big win that *Pac-Man* had in attracting female fans. Dolls were out—*Pac-Man* was in. Soon, other video games would follow in *Pac-Man*'s footsteps, influencing culture and creating a high demand for game-related merchandise.

Pac-Man continues to be a source of joy and comfort to children who grew up during this time. Although technology has far outpaced the simple arcade games of 1982, there is still something endearing about watching Pac-Man munch his way through the playing field, avoiding his pursuing ghosts. In 2005, the game won the Guinness World Record for being the "Most Successful Coin-Operated Game."[10]

49

Tetris

Tetris

CREDIT: SUSAN A. FLETCHER

Identifying Information:

Tetris

Maker: Alexey Pajitnov

Manufacturer: Spectrum Holobyte/Nintendo

Date: 1984

Collection of Susan A. Fletcher

In the late 1980s and early 1990s, children across America sat transfixed in front of their televisions as they tried to fit falling blocks into tidy stacks. Math teacher Paul Lilley recalls, "I used to play hours and hours of *Tetris*."[1] The addicting game taught mathematical principles and spatial awareness, which contributed to his ultimate career choice. According to designer Tom Cadwell, "You always feel like you are learning as you play it, because you are, and because there are multiple layers on which one can improve at the game. This is intrinsically motivating to humans."[2] In addition to teaching kids math, *Tetris* tells a larger story of American childhood at the end of the Cold War.

In 1980, the United States and the USSR were still embroiled in Cold War tensions. The inauguration of Ronald Reagan in 1980 ramped up friction between the two superpowers. In 1980, the United States and sixty-three other countries boycotted the 1980 Olympics in Moscow, and in turn, the USSR boycotted the 1984 Los Angeles Olympics. With Gorbachev's rise to power in 1985, however, relations with the United States changed drastically. Reagan and Gorbachev had a summit in Geneva in 1985 to discuss a 50 percent reduction in intercontinental ballistic missiles and a ban on space weapons. Suddenly, it looked like things might have a chance to get better.

In this time of heightened global tension, a Soviet game designer created a video game that would end up uniting the two countries through play. Computer scientist Alexey Pajitnov was the son of disaffected intellectuals in the

Soviet Union. Growing up in the USSR, he enjoyed math, logic, and puzzles. He particularly enjoyed pentominoes: ancient tiling puzzles popularized in the 1950s by American professor Samuel Golomb. When he grew up, he became a software engineer for the Dorodnitsyn Computing Center at the Soviet Academy of Sciences. One day, he passed by a toy shop and saw a pentomino puzzle in the window, and he decided to translate the physical game into a video game.[3]

He built blocks using tetrominoes—four squares connected. The blocks fall down from the top of the screen and players rotate them to fit together at the bottom. He combined the words "tetromino" and "tennis" to create the name for the game—*Tetris*.[4] His co-workers were instantly addicted to the game, and it was a big success. The game was translated into many programming languages and was extraordinarily popular in the Eastern Bloc.

Tetris came to the United States in 1987 as a home-PC game. For the US version, game company Spectrum Holobyte added "colorful graphics that evoke images of the Soviet Union, including an opening scene of a Cessna aircraft buzzing past Red Square"[5] to make sure Americans knew it was a Soviet import. The *New York Times* reported that "it is believed to be the first Soviet-developed computer software to be sold in this country. . . . The introduction of Soviet software in the United States is an indication of the growing availability of relatively advanced personal computers in the Soviet Union."[6] *Tetris* sold one hundred thousand copies in the first year.

Tetris symbolized adolescence at the end of the Cold War. In the late 1970s and early 1980s, teenagers in the United States were acutely aware of the political situation and how it affected them and their future. A 1984 Gallup survey polled 514 teenagers about their attitudes toward nuclear war. Fifty-one percent thought it was likely that a nuclear war would be started in their lifetime, and 49 percent indicated that the possibility of atomic war impacted their future plans.[7] In 1983, a survey of California junior high and high school students indicated that nuclear war was third on a list of things they were afraid of, after the death of a parent and getting bad grades.[8]

Teenagers had mixed opinions on America's role in the Cold War. In another Gallup youth survey, a fifteen-year-old girl wrote, "The freedom I have here I would not give up for all the money in the world. Living under a communist rule would be like a living hell!"[9] However, an eighteen-year-old girl from Minnesota felt differently: "I'd rather live in a country that's neutral, anti-war, and has a very small chance of getting involved in any war—for instance, Australia."[10]

Things changed dramatically within just a few years, however. With Gorbachev's policies of Perestroika and Glasnost, Western leaders began to see him as someone with whom they could work. *Tetris* came to the United States during the very last few years of the Soviet Union's existence. By the time Americans first played *Tetris* in 1988, they were feeling reasonably confident that they were about to win the Cold War. Spectrum Holobyte's advertising for *Tetris* took advantage of this national spirit. "The Cold War Is Over . . . Almost," declared the provocative advertisement. "Just when East/West tensions are beginning to ease, the Soviets have scored a direct hit on the U.S. TETRIS. . . . The Soviet game of quick thinking and fast reflexes."[11]

The game was appealing on numerous levels. As with *Pac-Man*, the game was based on universal themes, in this case square shapes and a desire for everything to fit together. Writer Tom Stafford argues that the game fills a "deep-seated psychological drive to tidy up."[12] He says that the game creates unfinished tasks that hold our attention. Lilley remembers his childhood addiction to the game, recalling, "I would have Tetris dreams and play the game in my sleep."[13] There's an official term for this phenomenon: the *Tetris* Effect, "a phrased coined by psychologists to explain what occurs when individuals devote so much attention to something that it begins to affect their thought patterns and invade their dreams."[14] We'll explore parental fears about video game addiction in the next entry on *Super Mario Brothers.*

Super Mario Brothers

Mario is one of the most recognizeable Nintendo characters.
CREDIT: SUSAN A. FLETCHER

Identifying Information:

Super Mario Brothers

Maker: Shigeru Miyamoto

Manufacturer: Nintendo

Date: 1985

Super Mario Brothers was my first introduction to the world of video games. My best friend's family had a Nintendo NES. After school, we went to her house to play *Super Mario* and *Duck Hunt*. With the iconic theme music bopping in the background, plumbers Mario and Luigi ran, jumped, and floated across their magical 8-bit world. *Super Mario Brothers* is a window into the changing landscape of play at the end of the twentieth century and parental fears about children's health.

Mario started life as a character in the arcade game *Donkey Kong*. His designer Shigeru Miyamoto created him to fight Donkey Kong in an attempt to rescue his girlfriend. Mario wasn't a plumber back then, and he didn't really have a name—he was a carpenter who was simply called "Jumpman." The staff at Nintendo's Washington warehouse thought the character looked like their landlord Mario Segale, and the name stuck.[1]

In 1983, Nintendo released an arcade game entitled *Super Mario Bros.* They changed Mario's profession from carpenter to plumber and introduced a new member of the family named Luigi. Miyamoto's childhood inspired the game design. He grew up in rural Japan, where he loved drawing comics. This hobby gave him a strong foundation in art and storytelling. He loved playing outdoors, hiking, and climbing mountains. The landscape where he had his outside adventures inspired the scenery in the *Legend of Zelda* and *Super Mario Bros.* Miyamoto thinks that the elements of *Super Mario Bros.* appealed to a broad range of cultures because it had universal aspects of running and jumping, just like the theme of eating in *Pac-Man*.[2]

Ironically, for children growing up in late twentieth-century America, *Super Mario Bros.* and other video games sometimes became a substitute for running, jumping, and playing outside. This was partially a function of their parents' concerns over how dangerous the world had become. In some ways, playing video games was a safer alternative to many common childhood activities of the day. According to Howard Chudacoff, "Among all classes, many of today's parents tolerate extensive television viewing and video game playing as alternatives to unsupervised activity on the city streets where, if the media could be believed, perils of abuse, abduction, and assault stalk every corner."[3]

Playing video games inside wasn't exactly a safe alternative to outdoor play, however. The games had their own hazards. In 1990, a thirteen-year-old girl suffered an epileptic seizure after playing *Super Mario Brothers*. According to a newspaper article, she was playing a "marathon stint" with only a short ten-minute break when she suffered the seizure, brought on by "flickering patterns, exploding lights, and rapid movements on the video screen."[4] Doctors called this phenomenon "Nintendo epilepsy" and cautioned parents against such games. Children using video game controllers also suffered from "Nintenditis" of the fingers after spending hours doing repetitive motions.[5]

Parents were also concerned about the addictive qualities of games like *Super Mario* and *Tetris*. Writer A. Craig Purcell of the *New York Times* recalled how the game entered his household and changed how he interacted with his son. He bought the game for his seven-year-old son, and the two of them spent many hours happily battling each other in the game.[6] Soon, however, his son had rapidly advanced beyond Purcell's gaming prowess, which defeated his hoped-for father-son bonding moments. Soon, his son was spending all of his spare time playing video games. At first, Purcell and his wife rationalized this behavior, because all of the son's friends were doing it too. "It kept them busy and out of trouble (and out of our hair) for hours at a time, and it certainly seemed innocent enough."[7]

Soon, however, the son began ignoring all of his other toys and spending hours in the basement with his friends playing the game. Purcell was initially worried that the boy's little sister would start displaying this addictive behavior, but he changed his mind when he realized that the two siblings were actually playing peacefully together whenever *Mario* was on the screen. "Maybe something really good can come of this yet," Purcell opined, "if we buy them just one or two more games, perhaps we can promote the kind of peace and harmony heretofore lacking in our home."[8]

Despite its criticisms, *Mario* was a massive success. According to *A History of Video Games in 64 Objects*, "One cannot understate the importance of *Super Mario Bro.* to Nintendo and the history of video games."[9] Mario continues to be recognizable and well-loved today due to the characters' continued presence in Nintendo's game empire.

Afterword

Go Play

As we enter the third decade of the twenty-first century, playtime remains vitally important for American children and families. According to parenting expert Jessica Joelle Alexander, "Playing together is a fundamental cornerstone for children and parents alike. . . . Given the positive effects it has on our wellbeing and happiness levels, family play should be the most important 'homework' of all."[1] Let's explore the state of early twenty-first century playtime by examining it in regard to three major themes that we have discussed in this book.

THE AMOUNT OF PLAYTIME AVAILABLE TO CHILDREN

From 1840–2000, children gained increasing amounts of free time to play. As historian Howard Chudacoff reminds us, in the nineteenth century a romantic view of childhood made parents willing to "grant their offspring more time for toys, game, and hobbies, as long as time was not spent 'idling.'"[2] By the early twenty-first century, middle- and upper-class children had gained a significant amount of free time to play. This trend continued until the late twentieth century when it started reversing itself. According to a study by the American Academy of Pediatrics, children's playtime decreased 25 percent from 1981 to 1997.[3]

In the early twenty-first century, "educational activities" have supplanted much of the unstructured free time that children had even a few decades ago. Anxieties over America's place in the global economy have placed increased pressure on our children to be high achievers. So, we put them in after-school programs that teach STEM, foreign languages, and sports. These anxieties harken back to early nineteenth-century parenting styles, which dictated that almost all play have some educational purpose. We're in a time of regress after nearly two centuries of progress in the area of free playtime. Although there is undoubtedly a place for these enrichment activities, cutting down on the time that children have to play on their own has negative consequences. "The more we over-schedule children's lives, the less likely they are to de-stress and process what they have experienced in their day," says Alexander. "Play isn't about accomplishing something or creating an adult-led activity that leads to measurable 'learning.' Play is learning."[4]

THE NUMBER OF CONSUMER GOODS AVAILABLE FOR CHILDREN'S PLAYTIME

The number of toys available to children increased dramatically over the nineteenth and twentieth centuries. According to Chudacoff, "Evolving from a society that once considered toys as insignificant baubles or ornamental objects . . . to a society in which manufacturers flood the market with several thousand new toys each year, American culture has linked toys so closely with childhood that in the minds of many people toys define play itself."[5]

As we learned in the entry on the SoWee Sunbabe Doll, it was common for most American children of the middle and lower classes to own only a few toys at a time before the 1950s. After the 50s, however, a child-centered consumer culture combined with a rise in media influence and the cheapening of raw materials to produce an explosion in the number of manufactured toys.

Toy companies used television and film to appeal straight to children in an attempt to sell these products, skipping their gatekeeping parents. In the latter half of the twentieth century, children who earned allowances or held small jobs outside the home had money of their own to spend on whatever they wanted. Often what they wanted were *Star Wars* characters or Teenage Mutant Ninja Turtles because they had seen those products advertised on TV.

In the twenty-first century, experts are rethinking these trends. The American Academy of Pediatrics (AAP) considers the number of consumer goods available to children a barrier to effective play. For one thing, these toys can be expensive and unattainable for many families. According to a 2018 AAP report, parents who can afford to buy their children mass-produced toys "may think that allowing their children unfettered access to these objects is healthy and promotes learning. The reality is that children's creativity and play is enhanced by many inexpensive toys (e.g., wooden spoons, blocks, balls, puzzles, crayons, boxes, and simple available household objects) and by parents who engage with their children by reading, watching, and playing alongside their children."[6]

In the early twenty-first century, we live in an era of excessive consumption and mindless spending. There are more commercially manufactured toys available to children right now than at any other point in human history. Although I am a huge fan of toys and games (after all, I wrote an entire book about them), I think it would be helpful to take a step back and ask ourselves some hard questions about the motivations behind our buying choices. Here are some questions that you may want to keep in mind the next time you are thinking of buying the child in your life yet another new toy:

1. Is this product something that your child wants because she saw it on television, online, or in another form of media? How do you feel about toy companies directly appealing to kids through these advertisements? Are there steps you could take to decrease this influence in your own household?
2. Is the product an "accessory" for a toy such as a Barbie Doll or My Little Pony? Would you even be buying this item at all if your child didn't already own something in that play system? Consider the razor/razor blade marketing scheme of Barbie that we learned about in chapter 29 and be aware of how easy it is to keep spending money on accessory products.
3. What sort of play does this toy promote? Is it educational, pure fun, or a mixture of both?
4. Why do you think the product is available at this point in American history? What are some of the cultural, social, religious, technological, and political forces that are behind it? Do you think this toy would have been popular in another era, or does it really only make sense right now? Do you think it will continue to be popular in the future? Do you think it is of high enough quality to last into the future?
5. What is the life span of the technology that you want to buy? Will that video game system still be the *must-have* thing in five years? Will you have to upgrade it and buy all new games in a few short years?

6. Are you buying this product because you feel guilty about something, or feel like you don't spend enough time with your kids? Are you purchasing the product as a substitution for love, or as a show of love?

THE LANDSCAPE OF PLAY HAS CHANGED

The landscape of play has changed dramatically over the last three centuries. American society has moved increasingly from rural life to urban life. Some childhood activities like jump rope adapted to these urban settings and took on a life of their own. This change, however, diminished other activities like kite flying and free exploration of the outdoors.

In the late twentieth century, playtime had moved largely indoors. Panics over kidnapping, gangs, and other modern perils have caused many parents to fear outside playtime. This trend continues into the twenty-first century. According to the 2018 AAP report, "Neighborhood threats such as violence, guns, drugs, and traffic, pose safety concerns in many neighborhoods, particularly low-income areas."[7] According to Chudacoff, "There are powerful indictors that youngsters at present spend far more time indoors—mostly occupied by TV, the computer, and formal activity—than their predecessors did."[8]

Health experts mourn this loss of outdoor time and are trying to do what they can to revive this crucial part of childhood. According to a report by Harvard Medical School, outdoor play gives children access to sunshine, Vitamin D, and exercise, and it helps them learn to appreciate nature and take risks. Echoing the sentiments of Daniel Beard and other child-play experts of the late nineteenth century, Dr. Claire McCarthy states, "Yes, you can break an arm from climbing a tree, and yes, you can be humiliated when you make a friend and get rejected. But that doesn't mean you shouldn't try; the lessons we learn from failure are just as important as those we learn from success."[9]

GO PLAY

In closing, thank you for reading this book. I hope that our exploration of these fifty toys, games, and objects of material culture has inspired you to take a closer look at your favorite toys. The toys and games you played with and the things your children are playing with now all have historical contexts of their own. If you are curious to know more, you can start by investigating the object's micro-history, tracing how it came to be and why. Then you can dive into its historical context by exploring the cultural, religious, technological, and political themes happening at the time of its development.

Before you launch into your research, though, it's time to close this book and do something else. Whatever grown-up tasks you have in front of you, please keep in mind that play is important for adults too. It helps us deal with stress, keeps our brains and bodies healthy, connects families, and helps us make friends. You have my permission to take the rest of the day off to do something fun.

Go play.

Notes

PREFACE

1. Fred Rogers, Mr. Rogers' Neighborhood, https://www.misterrogers.org/the-messages/.

2. Ruth Brown Fletcher, interview with author, May 2, 2018.

3. Ibid.

PART I

1. "Games Children Can Play to Cure Rainy Day Blues," *The Nevada Daily Mail,* October 6, 1976, 3A.

2. Ibid.

3. Howard Chudacoff, *Children at Play: An American History* (New York: New York University Press, 2007), 32–33.

4. "Traveller's Tour through the United States," Board Game Geek, https://boardgamegeek.com/boardgame/3184/travellers-tour-through-united-states.

5. "American Board and Card Game History," The Strong National Museum of Play online exhibit, https://artsandculture.google.com/exhibit/9wJiZCrQ9FmHJw.

CHAPTER 1

1. *The Mansion of Happiness* (New York: W. & S. B. Ives, 1864) in Margaret Hofer, *The Games We Played* (New York: Princeton Architectural Press, 2003), 78–79.

2. "Board Games: Five Centuries of Board Games," BibliOdyssey, November 19, 2008, http://bibliodyssey.blogspot.com/2008/11/board-games.html.

3. Ellis Lewis, "The Principle of Parental Authority and Filial Obedience," 1842, in Robert Bremner, ed. *Children and Youth in America: A Documentary History, Volume I, 1600–1865* (Cambridge: Harvard University Press, 1970), 365.

4. "Mansion of Happiness Game Instructions," 1 (Parker Brothers, 1926), LeRoy Howard Papers, Box 3, Folder 31, ID 114.3440, Strong Museum of Play.

5. Ibid.

6. William C. Ketchum Jr., *Toys and Games,* The Smithsonian Illustrated Library of Antiques from the Cooper-Hewitt Museum (Washington, DC: Smithsonian Institution, 1981), 105.

7. Hofer, *The Games We Played*, 78.

CHAPTER 2

1. Tim Walsh, *Timeless Toys: Classic Toys and the Playmakers Who Created Them* (New York: Andrews McMeel Publishing, 2005), 182.

2. Grace Bedell, letter to Abraham Lincoln, October 15, 1860, in George Dondero, "Why Abraham Lincoln Wore a Beard," *Journal of the Illinois State Historical Society* 24, no. 2 (July 1931): 323.

3. Walsh, *Timeless Toys*, 183.

4. "The Checkered Game of Life Rules," Milton Bradley Company, 1970, https://www.hasbro.com/common/documents/5b96f7161d3711ddbd0b0800200c9a66/858C69C319B9F3691003C63AB0E8078A.pdf.

5. James Shea, *It's All in the Game*, quoted in Walsh, *Timeless Toys*, 183.

6. Margaret Hofer, *The Games We Played* (New York: Princeton Architectural Press, 2003), 78.

7. http://www.museumofplay.org/online-collections/3/48/104.804.

8. "Checkered Game of Life," in the Checkered Game of Life Rulebook, 1970, https://www.hasbro.com/common/documents/5b96f7161d3711ddbd0b0800200c9a66/858C69C319B9F3691003C63AB0E8078A.pdf.

9. Walsh, *Timeless Toys*, 184.

10. "The Game of Life Commercials—1960s, 1980s, 1990s," CJ Douangchak YouTube Channel, August 9, 2017, https://www.youtube.com/watch?v=ixwA9CYPdV8.

CHAPTER 3

1. *The American Boy's Book of Sports and Games* (New York: Dick and Fitzgerald, 1864; reprint, New York: Lyons Press, 2000), 223 (page citations are to the reprint edition).

2. Jean Ferguson Carr, "Nineteenth-Century Girls and Literacy," in *Girls and Literacy in America: Historical Perspectives to the Present Moment*, ed. Jane Greer (New York: ABC CLIO, 2002), 52.

3. William Thayer, quoted in Jane Hunter *How Young Ladies Became Girls: The Victorian Origins of American Girlhood* (New Haven/London: Yale University Press, 2002), 38.

4. "Authorized Entertainment," in *Country Home*, August 1995, 48.

5. "Authors Games," accessed November 4, 2018, http://www.indiana.edu/~liblilly/games/authors.html.

6. Kevin J. Hayes, "Playing with American Literature," *Oxford University Press Blog*, May 24, 2012, accessed November 4, 2018, https://blog.oup.com/2012/05/playing-with-american-literature-authors-card-game/.

7. Don Webb, comment on Hayes, "Playing with American Literature."

CHAPTER 4

1. Scott Eberle, *Classic Toys of the National Toy Hall of Fame: Celebrating the Greatest Toys of All Time!* (New York: Running Press Book Publishers, 2009), 57.

2. Calvin Trillin, "Monopoly and History," *The New Yorker*, February 13, 1978, 90. Quoted in Mary Pilon, "The Secret History of Monopoly: The Capitalist Board Game's Leftwing Origins," *The Guardian*, April 11, 2015, https://www.theguardian.com/lifeandstyle/2015/apr/11/secret-history-monopoly-capitalist-game-leftwing-origins.

3. US Patent *The Landlord's Game*, September 23, 1924, no. 1,509,312. LeRoy Howard Papers, Box 1, Folder 4, Strong Museum of Play.

4. Ibid.

5. Tim Walsh, *Timeless Toys: Classic Toys and the Playmakers Who Created Them* (New York: Andrews McMeel Publishing, 2005), 45.

6. Ibid., 48.

7. Ibid.

8. "Children and the Great Depression," Digital History.uh.edu, February 2019, http://www.digitalhistory.uh.edu/active_learning/explorations/children_depression/depression_children_menu.cfm.

9. Unknown girl, Letter to Mrs. Roosevelt, October 14, 1936, http://www.digitalhistory.uh.edu/active_learning/explorations/children_depression/child_georgia.cfm.

10. M. K., Letter to Eleanor Roosevelt, April 27, 1938, http://www.digitalhistory.uh.edu/active_learning/explorations/children_depression/9yearold.cfm.

11. *Monopoly Rule Book* (Hasbro, 2005), 1, accessed November 11, 2018, https://www.hasbro.com/common/instruct/Monopoly_Vintage.pdf.

12. Rachel Doepker and Ellen Terrell, "Monopoly Patented," Business Reference Section, Library of Congress, February 2009, accessed November 11, 2018, https://www.loc.gov/rr/business/businesshistory/December/monopoly.html#1.

CHAPTER 5

1. Jason Beaubien, "Wiping Out Polio: How the US Snuffed Out a Killer," All Things Considered, NPR, October 15, 2012, https://www.npr.org/sections/health-shots/2012/10/16/162670836/wiping-out-polio-how-the-u-s-snuffed-out-a-killer.

2. Samira Kawash, "Polio Comes Home: Pleasure and Paralysis in Candy Land," *American Journal of Play* (Fall 2010): 195.

3. "Whatever Happened to Polio?" https://amhistory.si.edu/polio/americanepi/communities.htm.

4. Scott Eberle, *Classic Toys of the National Toy Hall of Fame: Celebrating the Greatest Toys of All Time!* (New York: Running Press Book Publishers, 2009), 198.

5. Alexander B. Joy, "Candy Land Was Invented for Polio Wards," *The Atlantic*, July 28, 2019, accessed July 29, 2019, https://www.theatlantic.com/technology/archive/2019/07/how-polio-inspired-the-creation-of-candy-land/594424/.

6. Eberle, *Classic Toys*, 198.

7. Kawash, "Polio Comes Home," 194.

8. Kawash, "Polio Comes Home," 188.

9. Walsh, *Timeless Toys*, 83.

PART II

1. Lucy Larcom, *A New England Girlhood Outlined from Memory* (Cambridge: Riverside Press, 1889), 157.

2. Ibid.

3. Ibid, 159.

4. Jesse Raber, "The Arts in the Public Schools: An Intellectual History," *Process: A Blog for American History*, March 28, 2017, accessed January 11, 2019, http://www.processhistory.org/raber-arts-public-schools/.

5. Katharine Morrison McClinton, *Antiques of American Childhood* (New York: Bramhall House, 1970), 95.

6. Peter Smith, "The Ecology of Picture Study," *Art Education* 39, no. 5 (1986): 48–54, doi:10.2307/3192927.

7. Margaret Hofer, *The Games We Played: The Golden Age of Board and Table Games* (New York: Princeton Architectural Press, 2003), 66–68.

CHAPTER 6

1. Barbara Wittmann and Christopher Barber, "A Neolithic Childhood: Children's Drawings as Prehistoric Sources," RES: Anthropology and Aesthetics, no. 63/64 (2013): 125–42, http://www.jstor.org/stable/23647759.

2. Elizabeth Stewart Dunford, "The Prang Textbooks of Art Education and the Emergence of a Transcendental Voice in Art Education Curricula," Harvard University Master's Thesis, May 2017, 10, https://dash.harvard.edu/bitstream/handle/1/33826220/DUNFORD-DOCUMENT-2017.pdf.

3. Horace Mann, *The Common School Journal for the Year 1844* (Boston: William B. Fowle and N. Capen, 1844), 134.

4. "Louis Prang, 1834–1909," Dixon, http://www.dixonusa.com/history/prang.cfm.

5. Ibid.

6. Ibid.

7. Lucy Larcom, *A New England Girlhood Outlined from Memory* (Cambridge: Riverside Press, 1889), 128.

8. Little Folks Color Kit, Milton Bradley, 1890, New-York Historical Society object ID 2004.494, https://www.nyhistory.org/exhibit/little-folks-color-kit.

9. Tara Winner, "Color Me Happy," Playstuff Blog, Strong Museum of Play, January 13, 2014, http://www.museumofplay.org/blog/play-stuff/2013/01/color-me-happy.

10. Wittmann and Barber, "A Neolithic Childhood," 126.

CHAPTER 7

1. Franz Lidz, "The Artist Who Made Coloring Books Cool for Adults Returns with a New Masterpiece," *Smithsonian Magazine,* October 2018, accessed November 29, 2018, https://www.smithsonianmag.com/arts-culture/johanna-basford-coloring-books-180970305/.

2. NPR Staff, "Artist Goes Outside the Lines with Coloring Books for Grown-Ups," NPR, April 1, 2015, accessed November 29, 2018, https://www.npr.org/2015/04/01/396634471/artist-goes-outside-the-lines-with-coloring-books-for-grown-ups.

3. Helen Nieuwenhuis, NPR All Things Considered Facebook Page, March 26, 2015, accessed November 29, 2018, https://www.facebook.com/npratc/photos/a.320446011440244/463419287142915/?type=1&theater.

4. Scott Eberle, *Classic Toys of the National Toy Hall of Fame: Celebrating the Greatest Toys of All Time* (New York: Running Press, 2009), 20.

5. Tim Walsh, *Timeless Toys: Classic Toys and the Playmakers Who Created Them* (New York: Andrews McMeel, 2005), 21.

6. Walsh, *Timeless Toys*, 21.

7. Eberle, *Classic Toys*, 20.

8. Crayola Crayon Box, 1903.

9. Paul Cracroft, "Man of Many Faces," *Continuum* (Spring 1996): 20–21.

10. Eberle, *Classic Toys*, 24.

11. Henry Wolff Jr., "Dirt Crayon Will Give Some Children an Inside Track to Dirt," *The Victoria Advocate*, November 21, 1995, 3A.

12. "The Upper Room," *The Daily News*, August 9, 1983, 2, accessed January 12, 2019, https://news.google.com/newspapers?nid=1241&dat=19830809&id=3W5TAAAAIBAJ&sjid=A4YDAAAAIBAJ&pg=7164,1239156.

13. Rubens' Crayola Crayons Box, Strong Museum of Play object ID 116.16.19, accessed January 12, 2019, https://artsandculture.google.com/asset/crayon-crayola-drawing-crayon-rubens-crayola-crayon/uAFPlQLamI8ckg.

14. "Grant Wood. Part 1 of The American Regional Painter," accessed November 29, 2018, https://mydailyartdisplay.wordpress.com/2018/06/17/grant-wood-part-1-the-early-years-of-the-american-regionalist-painter/.

15. Walsh, *Timeless Toys*, 21.

16. Ibid., 22.

17. Kathryn DeVan, "Crayola Colors Children's Memories in 64 Shades and More," Pennsylvania Center for the Book Blog, Fall 2008, accessed November 29, 2018, https://pabook.libraries.psu.edu/literary-cultural-heritage-map-pa/feature-articles/crayola-colors-childrens-memories-64-shades-and.

18. Dorothy Palmer, quoted in Cracroft, "Man of Many Faces," 21.

19. Ibid.

CHAPTER 8

1. Alexa Westerfeld, "Play-Doh Memories," The Swell Designer Blog, August 27, 2009, http://www.theswelldesigner.com/2009/08/play-doh-memories.html.

2. Tim Walsh, *Timeless Toys: Classic Toys and the Playmakers Who Created Them* (New York: Andrews McMeel Publishing, 2005), 119.

3. Clean Wall Paper Cleaner Advertisement, *The Massillon Evening Independent*, April 25, 1946, 16.

4. Walsh, *Timeless Toys*, 115.

5. Ibid., 116.

6. Ibid.

7. Ibid., 117.

8. "Hasbro Toys Playdo [*sic*] Modeling Clay," TVDays YouTube channel, accessed January 13, 2019, https://www.youtube.com/watch?v=n8y69FYSlT8.

9. "Play-Doh 1970," Deftmahatma YouTube channel, accessed January 13, 2019, https://www.youtube.com/watch?v=9-63fxXY0Jk.

10. "Get Bent Out of Shape: Fun Facts for National Play-Doh Day," *USA TODAY,* September 16, 2016.

CHAPTER 9

1. "Etched in Memory," Planet Retro, https://blog.retroplanet.com/etched-memories-etch-a-sketch/.

2. Etch A Sketch Advertisement, Ohio Art, 1973, "Classic Toys—Ohio Art Etch-A-Sketch—1973," YouTube, https://www.youtube.com/watch?v=jqa9dON2Dpk.

3. "Andre Cassagnes," *The Economist,* February 16, 2013, https://www.economist.com/news/obituary/21571846-andré-cassagnes-inventor-died-january-16th-aged-86-andré-cassagnes.

4. Margalit Fox, "Andre Cassagnes, Etch A Sketch Inventor, Is Dead at 86," *New York Times,* February 3, 2013.

5. Tim Walsh, *Timeless Toys: Classic Toys and the Playmakers Who Created Them* (New York: Andrews McMeel Publishing, 2005), 179.

6. Ibid.

7. Fox, "Andre Cassagnes."

8. Etch A Sketch advertisement, https://clickamericana.com/eras/1960s/etch-a-sketch-ohio-arts-toy-ads-1967.

9. Ibid.

10. Ibid.

11. Scott Eberle, *Classic Toys of the National Toy Hall of Fame: Celebrating the Greatest Toys of All Time!* (New York: Running Press Book Publishers, 2009), 36.

12. Heesun Wee, "Etch A Sketch's Incredible Toy Legacy—And Burden," CNBC, February 22, 2013, https://www.cnbc.com/id/100471234.

13. Martin Killgallon, quoted in Laura Rosenfeld, "A Brief History of the Etch A Sketch: Why We're Still Fascinated by the Toy after 55 Years," *Tech Times,* July 10, 2015, https://www.techtimes.com/articles/67257/20150710/etch-a-sketch-history.htm.

CHAPTER 10

1. "Kinematic Models," National Museum of American History, http://americanhistory.si.edu/collections/object-groups/kinematic-models.

2. The Marvelous Wondergraph advertisement, *Sears Catalog,* 1908.

3. Tim Walsh, *Timeless Toys: Classic Toys and the Playmakers Who Created Them* (New York: Andrews McMeel Publishing, 2005), 21.

4. Ibid., 207.

5. Original Spirograph set, 1965, in Walsh, *Timeless Toys*, 208.

6. Chuck Miller, "Remembering Spirograph: The Toy That Made Artists of Us All," *Albany Times Union*, February 22, 2010, https://blog.timesunion.com/chuckmiller/ remembering-spirograph-the-toy-that-made-artists-of-us-all/1067/.

7. John Bowers, "A Lesson from Spirograph," *Design Observer*, May 8, 2008, accessed January 23, 2019, https://designobserver.com/feature/a-lesson-from-spirograph/6847.

8. 1973 Spirograph Commercial, Robert Zimmermann YouTube channel, https://www. youtube.com/watch?v=LbvmKzf_wr4.

9. Martin Venezky, comment on "A Lesson from Spirograph," John Bowers, *Design Observer*, May 8, 2008, https://designobserver.com/feature/a-lesson-from-spirograph/6847.

10. Dennis Ippolito, "The Mathematics of the Spirograph," *Mathematics Teacher* 92, no. 4 (April 1999): 354–58, https://eric.ed.gov/?id=EJ584655.

11. Ben Freed, "Classic Toy Spirograph Makes a Comeback Thanks to Ann Arbor-Based Company," *The Ann Arbor News*, December 25, 2012, http://www.annarbor.com/ business-review/classic-toy-spirograph-makes-a-comeback-thanks-to-ann-arbor-based-company/.

PART III

1. William Clarke, *The Boy's Own Book: A Complete Encyclopedia of All the Diversions, Athletic, Scientific, and Recreative, of Boyhood and Youth* (Boston: Monroe and Francis, 1829; Reprint, Bedford, MA: Applewood Books, n.d.), 109.

2. Ibid., 116.

3. D. C. Beard, *The American Boy's Handy Book: What to Do and How to Do It* (New York: Charles Scribner's Sons, 1882), 367.

CHAPTER 11

1. Jack Anderson, "Dance Review: Using the Magic of Lights, Projections and Fairy Tales," *New York Times*, November 15, 2000, https://www.nytimes.com/2000/11/15/arts/ dance-review-using-the-magic-of-lights-projections-and-fairy-tales.html.

2. T. H. McAllister, *Catalogue of Stereopticons, Dissolving-View Apparatus, and Magic Lanterns* (New York, 1897), 4, http://www.archive.org/stream/cataloguepriceli00thmc #page/n23/mode/2up.

3. Koen Vermeir, "The Magic of the Magic Lantern (1660–1700): On Analogical Demonstration and the Visualization of the Invisible," *British Journal for the History of Science* 38, no. 2 (2005): 127–59, http://www.jstor.org/stable/4028694.

4. McAllister, *Catalogue of Stereopticons*.

5. "Magic Lantern!" *Ladies Home Journal*, December 1886.

6. Ibid.

7. "A Profitable Business for the Man with Small Capital," *Journal of Education* 60, no. 23 (1507) (1904): 396, http://www.jstor.org/stable/44066003.

8. Meredith A. Bak, "'Ten Dollars' Worth of Fun': The Obscured History of the Toy Magic Lantern and Early Children's Media Spectatorship," *Film History* 27, no. 1 (2015): 111–34, doi:10.2979/filmhistory.27.1.111.

9. "Barnard Receives Gift," *New York Times,* February 2, 1930, 2N, https://timesmachine.nytimes.com/timesmachine/1930/02/02/96018514.html.

CHAPTER 12

1. "Charles Wheatstone," King's College Alumni website, https://www.kcl.ac.uk/aboutkings/history/famouspeople/charleswheatstone.aspx.

2. "Brewster Stereoscope Collections Website," Yale Center for British Art, https://collections.britishart.yale.edu/vufind/Record/3417989.

3. Oliver Wendell Holmes, quoted in Clive Thompson, "Stereographs were the Original Virtual Reality," *Smithsonian Magazine,* October 2017, https://www.smithsonianmag.com/innovation/sterographs-original-virtual-reality-180964771/.

4. Thompson, "Stereographs."

5. Oliver Wendell Holmes, quoted in Scott Eberle, *Classic Toys of the National Toy Hall of Fame: Celebrating the Greatest Toys of All Time!* (New York: Running Press Book Publishers, 2009), 113.

6. "Stereoscopes and Views Specially Priced," *The Brooklyn Daily Eagle,* February 15, 1909.

7. T. H. McAllister, *Catalogue of Stereopticons, Dissolving-View Apparatus, and Magic Lanterns* (New York, 1897), 3, http://www.archive.org/stream/cataloguepriceli00thmc#page/n23/mode/2up.

8. Frank Murray McMorton, *The World Visualized for the Classroom: 1000 Travel Studies through the Stereoscope and in Lantern Slides, Classified and Cross-Referenced for 25 Different School Subjects: Teachers' Manual* (New York: Underwood and Underwood, 1915), iv.

9. "Balancing Rocks, Garden of the Gods Stereoscope card," (New York: Underwood and Underwood).

10. "Stereoscope Gives Children Pleasure at Local Library," *Brooklyn Eagle,* September 16, 1945, 18, https://bklyn.newspapers.com/image/52834970/?terms=stereoscope%2Bchildren.

11. Ibid.

CHAPTER 13

1. Tim Walsh, *Timeless Toys: Classic Toys and the Playmakers Who Created Them* (New York: Andrews McMeel Publishing, 2005), 57–58.

2. "Sawyer's View-Master: Natural Color Stereoscopes Product Manual," July 1942.

3. Scott Eberle, *Classic Toys of the National Toy Hall of Fame: Celebrating the Greatest Toys of All Time!* (New York: Running Press Book Publishers, 2009), 116.

4. Ibid., 117.

5. Enid Nemy, "Mrs. Reagan Gets a Chance to Unwind among Alaskans," *New York Times*, May 3, 1984, A8.

6. http://www.view-master.com/en-us.

CHAPTER 14

1. Clive Thompson, "The Invention of the 'Snapshot' Changed the Way We Viewed the World," *Smithsonian Magazine*, September 2014, https://www.smithsonianmag.com/innovation/invention-snapshot-changed-way-we-viewed-world-180952435/.

2. Palmer Cox, *The Brownies: Their Book* (New York: Apple-Century-Crofts Inc., 1887), iii.

3. Chuck Baker, "The First Brownie Camera," *The Brownie Camera Guy's Blog*.

4. Eric Schewe, "How the Brownie Camera Made Everyone a Photographer," *JSTOR Daily*, December 26, 2018, https://daily.jstor.org/how-the-brownie-camera-made-everyone-a-photographer/.

5. Thompson, "The Invention of the 'Snapshot.'"

6. "Eastman Kodak Co's Brownie Cameras," *The Youth's Companion*, October 18, 1900.

7. "Hints for Christmas Presents," *Brooklyn Daily Eagle*, December 8, 1904.

8. "A Brownie at the Seaside" c. 1905, Science Museum Group collection, https://blog.scienceandmediamuseum.org.uk/a-z-photography-collection-b-is-for-brownie/.

9. "A Vacation Contest," *Brooklyn Daily Eagle*, June 10, 1906, 39.

10. Marc Olivier, "George Eastman's Modern Stone-Age Family: Snapshot Photography and the Brownie," *Technology and Culture* 48, no. 1 (2007): 1–19, http://www.jstor.org/stable/40061221.

11. Thompson, "The Invention of the 'Snapshot.'"

12. Ibid.

13. Colin Harding, "B is for . . . Brownie," *Science and Media Museum Blog*, October 2012, https://blog.scienceandmediamuseum.org.uk/a-z-photography-collection-b-is-for-brownie/.

CHAPTER 15

1. "Movie Camera," Wikipedia, accessed April 15, 2019.

2. Rick Prelinger, "Personalizing the Past: History through Home Movies," American Experience website, August 9, 2017, https://www.pbs.org/wgbh/americanexperience/features/personalizing-past-interview-rick-prelinger/.

3. Ibid.

4. Jacqueline Stewart, "University of Chicago Research Projects: South Side Home Movie Project," University of Chicago, 2004, http://blackfilm.uchicago.edu/research_projects/south_side_project.shtml.

5. Ibid.

6. Maxwell family film reel, 1963, Philip Maxwell Sr. Collection, South Side Home Movie Project, University of Chicago, Identifier SSHMP.2008.MAXWELL.00001.

7. Jacqueline Stewart, quoted in Nicole Cardos, "South Side Home Movie Project Aims to Fill in Historical Gaps," April 4, 2019, WTTW.

PART IV

1. Antonia Fraser, *A History of Toys* (New York: Delacorte Press, 1966), 26.

2. Ibid.

3. John R. Nelson Jr., "Folk Toys," *Encyclopedia of the Great Plains*, 2011, University of Nebraska Lincoln, http://plainshumanities.unl.edu/encyclopedia/doc/egp.fol.018.

4. G. Stanley Hall, quoted in Steven Mintz, *Moralists and Modernizers: America's Pre–Civil War Reformers* (Baltimore: Johns Hopkins University Press, 1995), 71.

CHAPTER 16

1. "'Floating Zoo' Here Welcomed by Boys," *New York Times*, March 5, 1921, 10.

2. Janet M. Davis, "America's Big Circus Spectacular Has a Long and Cherished History," *Smithsonian.com,* March 22, 2017, https://www.smithsonianmag.com/history/americas-big-circus-spectacular-has-long-and-cherished-history-180962621/.

3. Dan Rich's Great Show poster, August 1868, Harry Ransom Center, University of Texas at Austin, https://slate.com/technology/2014/02/circus-posters-some-bygone-animal-acts.html.

4. The Great Adam Forepaugh and Sells Bros Circus poster, c. 1906. Library of Congress POS - CIRCUS - Fore. & Sells 1906, no. 1 (C size) [P&P].

5. Gary Cross, *Kids' Stuff: Toys and the Changing World of American Childhood* (Cambridge: Harvard University Press, 1997), 40.

6. "52 for 150: What's So Special about Your Library's Schoenhut Collection?" Topeka Library YouTube Channel, December 21, 2011, https://www.youtube.com/watch?v=eOble7PdebA.

7. "Donation of the Month, Object: Schoenhut Circus Toys," Rogers Arkansas Historical Museum, https://rogersar.gov/DocumentCenter/View/683/Schoenhut-Circus-Toys-PDF.

8. "At Schoenhut's Toy Humpty Dumpty Circus," under the title "Schoenhut's Humpty Dumpty Circus Toys," Schoenhut Company, 1928, 3. Quoted in Patricia Simpson, "Albert Frederick Schoenhut (1840–1912)," August 31, 2015, ImmigrantEntreprenuership.org.

9. Ibid.

CHAPTER 17

1. "The History of Steiff Teddy Bears," Bel Air Presents Steiff website, accessed January 5, 2019, https://www.steiffteddybears.co.uk/more-things-steiff/history-of-steiff-bears.php.

2. "Unzerbrechlch Filzspeilwaren Felt-Toys," Steiff Catalog, 1901, accessed January 5, 2019, http://www.teddybaer-antik.de/steiffkatbis20.html.

3. "Steiff: The Story," Steiff USA website, accessed January 5, 2019, http://www.steiffusa.com/steiff-the-story/.

4. Dorothy Comyns Carr diary, January 5, 1903, Colorado Springs Pioneers Museum, Tim Nicholson Collection, Box 4, (V) A:5.

5. Charles Emery, "Glen Eyrie Boasted Finest of Everything, and General William Jackson Palmer Was Master," *Free Press*, June 3, 1959.

CHAPTER 18

1. Theodore Roosevelt, *Theodore Roosevelt: An Autobiography by Theodore Roosevelt, 1923* (Project Gutenberg ebook, December 17, 2012), http://www.gutenberg.org/files/3335/3335-h/3335-h.htm.

2. Ibid.

3. Ibid.

4. "Theodore Roosevelt Timeline," NPS.gov, https://www.nps.gov/thro/learn/historyculture/theodore-roosevelt-timeline.htm.

5. Gail Bederman, *Manliness and Civilization* (Chicago: University of Chicago Press, 1995), 173.

6. "Real Teddy Bear Story," Theodore Roosevelt Association, accessed January 7, 2019, http://www.theodoreroosevelt.org/site/c.elKSIdOWIiJ8H/b.8684621/k.6632/Real_Teddy_Bear_Story.htm.

7. Gilbert King, "The History of the Teddy Bear: From Wet and Angry to Soft and Cuddly," *Smithsonian Magazine*, December 21, 2012, accessed January 7, 2019, https://www.smithsonianmag.com/history/the-history-of-the-teddy-bear-from-wet-and-angry-to-soft-and-cuddly-170275899/.

8. Minor Ferris Buchanan, "Holt Collier: Guiding Roosevelt through the Mississippi Canebreaks," accessed January 7, 2019, https://www.fws.gov/southeast/pdf/brochure/holt-collier-national-wildlife-refuge-guiding-roosevelt.pdf.

9. Tim Walsh, *Timeless Toys: Classic Toys and the Playmakers Who Created Them* (New York: Andrews McMeel Publishing, 2005), 16.

10. Ibid.

11. Gary Cross, *Kids' Stuff: Toys and the Changing World of American Childhood* (Cambridge: Harvard University Press, 1997), 95.

12. "Teddy Roosevelt Bears Advertisement" *Pittsburgh Press,* December 10, 1907.

13. Cross, *Kids' Stuff,* 95.

14. Ibid., 97.

15. "Dolls and Teddy Bears," *New York Times,* July 9, 1907, 6.

CHAPTER 19

1. Uri Berliner, "A Toy Monkey That Escaped Nazi Germany and Reunited a Family," *NPR,* November 14, 2018, https://www.npr.org/2018/11/14/663059048/a-toy-monkey-that-escaped-nazi-germany-and-reunited-a-family.

2. Ibid.

3. Bat-Ami Zucker, "France Perkins and the German-Jewish Refugees, 1933–1940," http://francesperkinscenter.org/wp-content/uploads/2014/01/Frances-Perkins-and-the-German-Jewish-Refugees-1933-1940.pdf.

4. "The Immigration of Refugee Children to the United States," *Holocaust Encyclopedia,* https://encyclopedia.ushmm.org/content/en/article/the-immigration-of-refugee-children-to-the-united-states.

5. John Lang, "From Kristallnacht to the Kindertransport to, Finally, America," *Wall Street Journal,* November 8, 2015, accessed January 6, 2019, https://www.wsj.com/articles/from-kristallnacht-to-the-kindertransport-to-finally-america-1447019141.

6. Zucker, "France Perkins."

7. Thea Lindauer, "'Kindertransport' to America," *Washington Post,* October 10, 2000, accessed January 6, 2019, https://www.washingtonpost.com/archive/opinions/2000/10/10/kindertransport-to-america/69418ac7-5c5c-41d2-ac2b-509121495c72/.

8. Lindauer, "Kindertransport."

9. Edith Schumer, quoted in Veronica Gonzalez, "Children Who Escaped Holocaust Celebrate Life," *Chicago Tribune,* 2002, https://onethousandchildren.yivo.org/cimages/children_who_escaped_holocaust_celebrate_life.pdf.

10. Kurt Rothschild, quoted in "Finding Young Survivors of the Holocaust," Barbara Nachman, *The Journal News* August 1, 2002, https://onethousandchildren.yivo.org/cimages/finding_young_survivors_of_the_holocaust.pdf.

11. Berliner, "A Toy Monkey."

12. Ibid.

CHAPTER 20

1. "A History of the Care Bears," July 31, 2009, Care Bear Toys website, https://www.carebeartoys.com/article/a-history-of-the-care-bears/.

2. "Care Bears," Wikipedia, https://en.wikipedia.org/wiki/Care_Bears.

3. Sherryl Connelly, "High 'aaah' factor has meant millions," *Boca Raton News,* April 2, 1985, 48.

4. Kenyth Mogan, "The Care Bears: 35 Years of Caring," *Huffington Post,* September 1, 2017, https://www.huffingtonpost.com/entry/the-care-bears-35-years-of-caring_us_5978de82e4b06b305561cd87.

5. Connelly, "High 'aaah' factor."

6. "Jogging Around," *Beaver County Times,* November 23, 1984, A6.

7. "80s Care Bears Toy Commercial," Spacecraft YouTube channel, October 16, 2008, accessed January 6, 2019, https://www.youtube.com/watch?v=bYm3TFZ3B-w.

8. Television Bureau of Advertising, "Target Selling the Children's Market," quoted in Howard Chudacoff, *Children at Play: An American History* (New York: New York University Press, 2007), 167.

9. "Care Bears Ad, Australia, 1984," Panalouis channel, YouTube, May 22, 2007, accessed January 6, 2019, https://www.youtube.com/watch?v=5M3LqSDWWHo.

10. Chudacoff, *Children at Play,* 168.

11. Natalie Coulter, "The Consumption Chronicles: Tales from Suburban Canadian Tweens in the 1980s," *Counterpoints* 245 (2005): 330–46, http://www.jstor.org/stable/42978708.

12. Gary Cross, *Kids' Stuff: Toys and the Changing World of American Childhood* (Cambridge: Harvard University Press, 1997), 210.

13. "The Care Bears Movie," *Boca Raton News,* April 2, 1985, 48.

14. Joanna Rempel Knighten, comment on the author's Facebook page, January 2, 2019.

PART V

1. "60's Ads: 1963 Erector Set and Chemistry Set by Gilbert," PhakeNam YouTube channel, February 2, 2014, https://www.youtube.com/watch?v=GfTFCQh9vKM.

2. Gary Cross, *Kids' Stuff: Toys and the Changing World of American Childhood* (Cambridge: Harvard University Press, 1997), 60.

3. Susan Blackley and Jennifer Howell, "A STEM Narrative: 15 Years in the Making," *Australian Journal of Teacher Education* 40, no. 7 (July 2015).

4. Gwen Dewar, "Can Lego Bricks and Other Construction Toys Boost Your Child's STEM Skills?" Parentingscience.com, accessed January 19, 2019, https://www.parentingscience.com/Lego-bricks-construction-toys-and-STEM-skills.html.

5. Ibid.

CHAPTER 21

1. Lisa Hammel, "For Children, It Really Is a Discovery Center," *New York Times,* January 3, 1970, 28.

2. John Locke, quoted in "Alphabet Blocks," Strong National Museum of Play, https://www.toyhalloffame.org/toys/alphabet-blocks.

3. Witold Rybczynski, "Architecture View: The Pleasures of Playing Architect," *New York Times,* February 17, 1991, 28.

4. Ibid.

5. Inez and Marshall McClintock, *Toys in America* (Washington, DC: Public Affairs Press, 1961), 156.

6. "Crandall's Blocks for Children," *American Agriculturalist,* August 1877, 318.

7. Scott Eberle, *Classic Toys of the National Toy Hall of Fame* (Philadelphia: Running Press Books, 2009), 168.

8. Frank Lloyd Wright, quoted in "The Froebel Gift Takes Form Again," *New York Times,* October 13, 1985, 87.

CHAPTER 22

1. Bill Beutel, correspondence with the author, January 19, 2019.

2. Museum visitor, quoted in Ashley P. Taylor, "Winning Fame and Fortune at Play," Yale School of Medicine website, Spring 2014.

3. John A. Lucas, "A. C. Gilbert," *Journal of Olympic History,* September 2000, 12.

4. Ibid.

5. Steven D. Goldberg, "A. C. Gilbert: The Demise of the A. C. Gilbert Company," Eli Whitney Museum website, accessed January 14, 2019, https://www.eliwhitney.org/7/museum/-gilbert-project/-man/a-c-gilbert-scientific-toymaker-essays-arts-and-sciences-october-6.

6. Erector Set advertisement, 1913, Library of Congress.

7. Ibid.

8. Ibid.

9. Erector Set advertisement, c. 1922, Wikimedia Commons.

10. Ibid.

11. Gilbert Catalog Archive, Eli Whitney Museum and Workshop, https://www.eliwhitney.org/catalog7/products?page=5.

12. Ellen Terrell, "A. C. Gilbert's Successful Quest to Save Christmas," December 14, 2016, Library of Congress Blog, https://blogs.loc.gov/inside_adams/2016/12/a-c-gilberts-successful-quest-to-save-christmas/.

13. A. C. Gilbert, October 25, 1918. Quoted in Terrell, "A.C. Gilbert's Successful Quest."

14. Ibid.

CHAPTER 23

1. Trotman family photographs, Dawson Trotman Collection, Navigators Archives, Box 10, M 0002.

2. Patricia Hogan, "100 Years of Tinkering," Play Stuff Blog, February 9, 2015, accessed January 8, 2019, http://www.museumofplay.org/blog/play-stuff/2015/02/100-years-of-tinkering.

3. Ibid.

4. Ibid.

5. Ibid.

6. D. M. Christian Company advertisement, *The Owosso Daily Argus,* December 18, 1916, 7, https://news.google.com/newspapers?nid=2447&dat=19161218&id=A541AAAA IBAJ&sjid=eKwFAAAAIBAJ&pg=3411,2995005.

7. Tinkertoys advertisement, *Child Life,* 1927, Strong Museum of Play object Tinker Toys advertisement, *Child Life,* 1927. Strong Museum of Play object ID 114.7547.

8. "Tinker Toys and Christmas," advertisement, *Junior Home,* 1928, Strong Museum of Play object ID 114.7554.

9. Ibid.

10. Waldemar Kaempffert, "A New 'Tinkertoy' Speeds Production," *New York Times,* September 20, 1953, 46.

11. "Monsters to Cavort under the Yule Tree," *Reading Eagle,* December 18, 1964, 1, accessed January 8, 2019, https://news.google.com/newspapers?nid=1955&dat=19641218 &id=U4gtAAAAIBAJ&sjid=dpwFAAAAIBAJ&pg=1928,2014608.

CHAPTER 24

1. John Lloyd Wright, *My Father Who Is on Earth* (New York: GP Putnam's Sons, 1946), 16.

2. Ibid.

3. Ibid, 53.

4. Andrew Clayman, "Lincoln Logs Company, est. 1916," Made in Chicago Museum website, https://www.madeinchicagomuseum.com/single-post/lincoln-logs.

5. Taylor Horst, "From Lincoln Logs to Blueprints," History Colorado website, October 23, 2015, https://www.historycolorado.org/story/collections-library/2015/10/23/lincoln-logs-blueprints.

6. Lincoln Logs advertisement, in Tim Walsh, *Timeless Toys: Classic Toys and the Playmakers Who Created Them* (New York: Andrews McMeel Publishing, 2005, 32.

7. Horst, "From Lincoln Logs to Blueprints."

8. Lincoln Logs advertisement, in Clayman, "Lincoln Logs Company, est. 1916."

9. John Coats, correspondence with the author, March 13, 2019.

CHAPTER 25

1. Sam Rowland, quoted in Tom Smeaton, "Celebrate the LEGO 60th Anniversary with our Childhood Memories," Jet Blog, February 1, 2018, https://blog.jet.com/article/lego-60th-anniversary/.

2. Ole Kirk Kristiansen, 1932, quoted in "A New Reality," Lego.com, https://www.lego.com/en-us/themes/lego-history/articles/a-new-reality-df3385c635ef42a486602960cabbe0f7.

3. Erin Blakemore, "The Disastrous Backstory behind the Invention of LEGO Bricks," History.com, September 21, 2017, https://www.history.com/news/the-disastrous-backstory-behind-the-invention-of-lego-bricks.

4. Tim Walsh, *Timeless Toys: Classic Toys and the Playmakers Who Created Them* (New York: Andrews McMeel Publishing, 2005), 191.

5. "The Beginning of the LEGO Group," Lego.com, https://www.lego.com/en-us/themes/lego-history/articles/the-beginning-of-the-lego-group-a148d3b09fb045c5a52ea65f9257f085.

6. Walsh, *Timeless Toys*.

7. "LEGO from Samsonite (1955)," Toy Tales YouTube Channel, October 20, 2015, https://www.youtube.com/watch?v=iqat-GCr7uQ.

8. "Vintage Lego Commercial," Vintage Fanatic YouTube Channel, July 29, 2013, accessed January 19, 2019, https://www.youtube.com/watch?v=ihsLhHcF_t0.

9. LEGO advertisement, 1981, https://womenyoushouldknow.net/little-girl-1981-lego-ad-grown-shes-got-something-say/.

10. Ibid.

11. Gary Cross, *Kids' Stuff: Toys and the Changing World of American Childhood* (Cambridge: Harvard University Press, 1997), 220.

12. Ibid.

13. Paul Lilley, interview with author, Feburary 25, 2019.

14. Gwen Dewar, "Can Lego Bricks and Other Construction Toys Boost Your Child's STEM Skills?" Parentingscience.com, accessed January 19, 2019, https://www.parentingscience.com/Lego-bricks-construction-toys-and-STEM-skills.html.

PART VI

1. Antonia Fraser, *A History of Toys* (London: Weidenfelt and Nicholson, 1966), 33.

2. Ibid.

3. "History of Hopi Kachina Dolls," History of Dolls, http://www.historyofdolls.com/doll-history/history-of-hopi-kachina-dolls/.

4. "Primary Source of the Month," Colonial Williamsburg Foundation, https://www.history.org/history/teaching/enewsletter/volume10/jun12/primsource.cfm.

5. Ibid, 181.

6. Karin Calvert, *Children in the House: The Material Culture of Early Childhood, 1600–1900* (Boston: Northeastern University Press, 1992), 117.

7. Catharine Beecher and Harriet Beecher Stowe, *American Woman's Home* (New York: J. B. Ford and Company, 1869; reprint, Watkins Glen, NY: American Life Foundation, 1975), 293.

8. Calvert, *Children in the House*, 107.

9. Priscilla Ferguson Clement, *Growing Pains: Children in the Industrial Age, 1850–1890* (New York: Twayne Publishers, 1997), 118.

10. Gary Cross, *Kids' Stuff: Toys and the Changing World of American Childhood* (Cambridge: Harvard Univerity Press, 1997), 70.

CHAPTER 26

1. "Antique Kestner Dolls," *Collector's Weekly*, accessed January 30, 2019, https://www.collectorsweekly.com/dolls/kestner.

2. Ibid.

3. Margaret Woodbury's The Baby's Journal, Brian Sutton-Smith Library and Archives, ID 117.8003, Box 1, Folder 1.

4. Margaret Woodbury Strong Photographs, Brian Sutton-Smith Library and Archives, ID 117.8003, Box 52, Folder 4 MWS 161.

5. Margaret Woodbury Strong Photographs, Brian Sutton-Smith Library and Archives, ID 117.8003, Box 52, Folder 2 MWS98a.

6. Margaret Woodbury Strong Photographs, Brian Sutton-Smith Library and Archives, ID 117.8003, Box 52, Folder 4 MWS 160.

7. Margaret Woodbury Strong Photographs, Brian Sutton-Smith Library and Archives, ID 117.8003, Box 53, Folder 1.

8. Katie Hackett, "Margaret Woodbury Strong: Collector and Philanthropist," Play Stuff Blog Strong National Museum of Play, January 29, 2016, https://www.museumofplay.org/blog/play-stuff/2016/01/margaret-woodbury-strong-collector-and-philanthropist.

9. Ibid.

10. Ibid.

11. Margaret Woodbury Strong, quoted in Genevieve Angione, *All Dolls Are Collectible* quoted in Carol Sandler, "Strong Connections," Play Stuff Blog Strong Museum of Play, June 21, 2011, accessed January 30, 2019, https://www.museumofplay.org/blog/play-stuff/2011/06/strong-connections.

CHAPTER 27

1. Ruth Brown Fletcher, interview with author, April 4, 2018.

2. "The Sun Rubber Company," Barberton Historical Society Facebook page, August 16, 2004, https://www.facebook.com/Barberton.Historical.Society/posts/the-sun-rubber-companygiven-our-propensity-for-saving-name-stones-in-barberton-j/10154527528910437/.

3. Fletcher.

4. Gary Cross, *Kids' Stuff: Toys and the Changing World of American Childhood* (Cambridge: Harvard University Press, 1997), 70.

5. Glenna Brown, interview with author, May 19, 2018.

6. Fletcher.

7. Brown.

8. Ibid.

CHAPTER 28

1. Debbie Behan Garrett, "Collecting the Dolls I Never Had," *New York Times*, December 30, 2011, accessed February 4, 2019, https://www.nytimes.com/roomfordebate/2011/12/29/why-we-collect-stuff/collecting-the-dolls-i-never-had.

2. Myla Perkins, *Black Dolls: An Identification and Value Guide, Book II* (Paducah, KY: Collector Books, 1995), 25.

3. Ibid.

4. Reginald Stuart, "Black Dolls Are Biggest Feature in Woman's Collection," *The Day*, January 9, 1978, 19, https://news.google.com/newspapers?nid=1915&dat=19780109&id=Qi0iAAAAIBAJ&sjid=B3MFAAAAIBAJ&pg=1359,1223652.

5. Perkins, *Black Dolls*, 26.

6. Kenneth B. Clark and Mamie P. Clark, "Racial Identification and Preference in Negro Children," 169, https://i2.cdn.turner.com/cnn/2010/images/05/13/doll.study.1947.pdf.

7. Ibid.

8. Ibid.

9. "Interview with Dr. Kenneth Clark," November 4, 1985, Washington University Digital Gateway Texts.

10. "Doll for Negro Children: New Toy Which Is Anthropologically Correct Fills an Old Need," *Life Magazine*, December 17, 1951, 61–62.

11. Gordon Patterson, "Color Matters: The Creation of the Sara Lee Doll," *The Florida Historical Quarterly* 73, no. 2 (1994): 147–65. http://www.jstor.org/stable/30148757.

12. "Doll for Negro Children."

13. Ibid.

14. Emily Temple, "How Zora Neale Hurston Helped Create the First Realistic Black Baby Doll," Literary Hub, January 7, 2019, https://lithub.com/how-zora-neale-hurston-helped-create-the-first-realistic-black-baby-doll/.

15. "Doll for Negro Children."

16. Stuart, "Black Dolls Are Biggest Feature in Woman's Collection," 19.

17. Debbie Behan Garrett, quoted in Lisa Hicks, "Black Is Beautiful: Why Black Dolls Matter," *Collector's Weekly*, February 21, 2013.

CHAPTER 29

1. Gary Cross, *Kids' Stuff: Toys and the Changing World of American Childhood* (Cambridge: Harvard University Press, 1997), 172.

2. Howard Chudacoff, *Children at Play: An American History* (New York and London: New York University Press, 2007), 156.

3. Ibid.

4. If you're interested in knowing more about the intricacies of Barbie's history, I suggest that you read one of the many excellent histories of Barbie and Mattel. If I were to cover all of the iterations of Barbie and all of the drama surrounding the Handlers, this entry would go on forever. For the purposes of this book, I'm much more interested in the broader impacts that Barbie has had on childhood, concentrating on Barbie's role in turning children into consumers and the controversial role that she's had in defining American girlhood and sexuality.

5. Miriam Forman-Brunell, "What Barbie Dolls Have to Say about Postwar American Culture," Smithsonian Artifact and Analysis, http://www.smithsonianeducation.org/idealabs/ap/essays/barbie.htm.

6. Ibid.

7. Chudacoff, *Children at Play*, 170.

8. Chudacoff, *Children at Play*, 171.

9. "Feminists Protest 'Sexist' Toys in Fair," *New York Times,* February 29, 1972, 20.

10. Sharon Schuster, quoted in Bob Greene "Barbie! Say It Isn't So!" *Chicago Tribune*, October 13, 1992, https://www.chicagotribune.com/news/ct-xpm-1992-10-13-9204020848-story.html.

11. Barbie Liberation Organization Flyer, 1993. Barbie Liberation Organization Collection, Strong Museum of Play, 94.86.

12. Barbie Liberation Organization Video, 1993. Barbie Liberation Organization Collection, Strong Museum of Play, 94.86.

13. Zak Zelen, *NBC Nightly News Report*, December 1993, Barbie Liberation Organization Collection, Strong Museum of Play, 94.86.

14. Hannah Henze, *NBC Nightly News Report*, December 1993. Barbie Liberation Organization Collection, Strong Museum of Play, 94.86.

CHAPTER 30

1. Tim Walsh, *Timeless Toys: Classic Toys and the Playmakers Who Created Them* (New York: Andrews McMeel Publishing, 2005), 251.

2. Ibid.

3. Fay S. Joyce, "Cabbage Patch Kids Spur a Battle over Parentage," *New York Times*, December 6, 1983, 22.

4. Walsh, *Timeless Toys*, 251.

5. Fred Ferretti, "Cabbage Patch Kids: Born for 'Adoption' at a Price," *New York Times* January 16, 1984.

6. Howard Chudacoff, *Children at Play: An American History* (New York: New York University Press, 2007), 170.

7. Gary Cross, *Kids' Stuff: Toys and the Changing World of American Childhood* (Cambridge: Harvard University Press, 1997), 211.

8. JCPenny advertisement, *Ludington Daily News*, December 22, 1984, 5.

9. "From 1983: Demand for Cabbage Patch Kids Causes Chaos in Stores across America," PIX11 News YouTube Channel, August 20, 2014, https://www.youtube.com/watch?v=VaQuxCWWTaI.

10. Debra Brookhart, comment on the author's Facebook page, January 3, 2019.

11. Cross, *Kids' Stuff*, 211.

12. Ferretti, "Cabbage Patch Kids."

13. Ibid.

14. Official Adoption Papers, Aggie Grazie Cabbage Patch Kid, 1984, http://yello80s.com/80s-toys/girls-toys/dolls/cabbage-patch-kids/cabbage-patch-kid-collector-info/.

15. John Tepper Marlin, "About Adoption, Real and Make-Believe," *New York Times*, December 20, 1983, 30.

16. "Coleco Hits Cabbage Patch Slump," *Wilmington Morning Star*, January 10, 1987, 5B.

PART VII

1. "Christmas Toy Memories—The Year I Got Kenner Real Ghostbusters Action Figures," Pixel Dan YouTube Channel, December 25, 2017, https://www.youtube.com/watch?v=4OdMrA1FOFk.

2. "Action Figure," *Cambridge Dictionary*, https://dictionary.cambridge.org/us/dictionary/english/action-figure.

3. Lawrence Kilman, "Aggressive Fantasies Still Fuel Type of Toys That Boys Prefer," *The Day*, February 19, 1985, https://news.google.com/newspapers?nid=1915&dat=19850219&id=jCVSAAAAIBAJ&sjid=DDYNAAAAIBAJ&pg=3864,4180567.

4. Joseph Cassius, quoted in Kilman, "Aggressive Fantasies."

CHAPTER 31

1. "A Brief History of Toy Soldiers," The Toy Soldier Company, https://www.toysoldierco.com/resources/toysoldierhistory.htm.

2. Kenneth D. Brown, "Modelling for War? Toy Soldiers in Late Victorian and Edwardian Britain," *Journal of Social History* 24, no. 2 (1990): 237–54, http://www.jstor.org/stable/3787497.

3. "Stocking Fillers: GA Holland and Sons advertisement," *The Westmount News*, November 20, 1914.

4. E. Parson, "The Toy Soldier," *Educational Review* (June 1915): 92, quoted in Brown, "Modelling for War?"

5. Pablo Casals, "Casals Found God Everywhere," *Virgin Islands Daily News,* October 30, 1973, 19, https://news.google.com/newspapers?nid=757&dat=19731030&id=mjMwAAAAIBAJ&sjid=zEQDAAAAIBAJ&pg=2529,6425169.

6. John Coats, email to author, March 13, 2019.

7. Marc Blacburn, email to author, February 15, 2019.

8. Coats.

9. "Toy Soldiers Invade Washington," *The Gadsden Times,* November 18, 1982, 16.

10. Malcolm Forbes quoted in "Toy Soldiers Invade Washington."

CHAPTER 32

1. Allie Townsend, "Army Men," *Time Magazine*, February 16, 2011, accessed February 16, 2019, http://content.time.com/time/specials/packages/article/0,28804,2049243_2048649_2049009,00.html.

2. Cam Clark, "Little Green Army Men: Origins," 4LN Blog, September 10, 2017, accessed February 15, 2019, http://fourletternerd.com/tag/plastic-army-men/.

3. Charles Garcia, *I'll Be a Good Boy Forever*, https://books.google.com/books/about/I_ll_Be_A_Good_Boy_Forever.html?id=hPFmDwAAQBAJ&printsec=frontcover&source=kp_read_button#v=onepage&q&f=false.

4. Peter Hartlaub, "The Five Worst Army Men of All Time," *SFGate*, April 28, 2010, accessed February 15, 2019, https://blog.sfgate.com/parenting/2010/04/28/the-five-worst-army-men-of-all-time/.

5. Ibid.

6. Clark, "Little Green Army Men."

7. Paul Lilley, interview with the author, February 15, 2019.

8. Patricia Hogan, "Little Green Army Men Join Forces with the National Toy Hall of Fame," Play Stuff Blog Strong Museum of Play, November 7, 2014, https://www.museumofplay.org/blog/play-stuff/2014/11/little-green-army-men-join-forces-with-the-national-toy-hall-of-fame.

9. Bob Beatty, email to author, February 8, 2019.

10. Ibid.

11. Ibid.

CHAPTER 33

1. Tim Walsh, *Timeless Toys: Classic Toys and the Playmakers Who Created Them* (New York: Andrews McMeel Publishing, 2005), 197–98.

2. Don Levine, quoted in "Now You Know the History of G.I. Joe. And Knowing Is Half the Battle," Jimmy Stamp, *Smithsonian.com*, March 29, 2013, accessed January 22, 2019, https://www.smithsonianmag.com/arts-culture/now-you-know-the-history-of-gi-joe-and-knowing-is-half-the-battle-11506463/.

3. Walsh, *Timeless Toys*, 197–98.

4. "1963 G I Joe Toy Fair Presentation Video," Wario7793 YouTube Channel, accessed January 21, 2019, https://www.youtube.com/watch?time_continue=159&v=oUHW5zri2Io.

5. Ibid.

6. Gary Cross, *Kids' Stuff: Toys and the Changing World of American Childhood* (Cambridge: Harvard University Press, 1997), 176.

7. "G.I. JOE (1964) Debut TV Commercial!," Tommy Retro's Blast from the Past! YouTube Channel, February 6, 2014. https://www.youtube.com/watch?v=9X382bCvVvo

8. Sally Ryan, "Militant Mothers Are Protesting War Toys," *Gettysburg Times*, December 22, 1966.

9. Ibid.

10. "GI Joe Adventure Team, Search for the Stolen Idol TV Commercial Retro Toys," Marksebiz YouTube channel, July 16, 2011, accessed January 21, 2019, https://www.youtube.com/watch?v=aQUGY1vPqos.

11. Rob Lammle, "A History of G.I. Joe: A Real American Hero," Mentalfloss, July 4, 2015, accessed January 21, 2019, http://mentalfloss.com/article/62636/history-gi-joe-real-american-hero.

12. Cross, *Kids' Stuff*, 203.

13. "GIJoe Original Theme Song!!" Cool ToysHD YouTube Channel, June 22, 2015.

14. Stamp, "Now You Know the History of G.I. Joe."

15. Steven Mintz, *Huck's Raft: A History of American Childhood* (Cambridge: Belknap Press of Harvard University, 2004), 345.

16. Lammle, "A History of G.I. Joe."

17. "Public Service Announcement List," G.I. Joe Wiki, accessed January 21, 2019, http://gijoe.wikia.com/wiki/Public_Service_Announcement.

18. "Diversity in Action (Figures)," Action Insider Blog, June 14, 2009, accessed January 22, 2019, http://www.actionfigureinsider.com/diversity-in-action-figures/.

CHAPTER 34

1. Josh Modell, comment on "What's Your Earliest *Star Wars* Memory?" AV Club.com, March 25, 2017, https://film.avclub.com/what-s-your-earliest-star-wars-memory-1798288252.

2. George Lucas, interview in *Chicago Tribune* 2005, quoted in Christopher Klein, "The Real History That Inspired 'Star Wars,'" History.com, December 17, 2015, https://www.history.com/news/the-real-history-that-inspired-star-wars.

3. Klein, "The Real History That Inspired 'Star Wars.'"

4. Gwen Ihnat, comment on "What's Your Earliest *Star Wars* Memory?," AV Club.com.

5. James Whitbrook, "The Groundbreaking History of *Star Wars* Toys," Gizmodo, May 22, 2015, https://io9.gizmodo.com/the-groundbreaking-history-of-star-wars-toys-1706298670.

6. Sean O'Neal comment on "What's Your Earliest *Star Wars* Memory?," AV Club.com.

7. Melissa Leon, "How 'Star Wars' Revolutionized the Toy Industry," The Daily Beast, January 6, 2018.

8. A. O. Scott, "How 'Star Wars' Defined My Generation," *New York Times,* October 25, 2015, https://www.nytimes.com/2015/11/01/movies/star-wars-elvis-and-me.html?searchResultPosition=1.

9. Gary Cross, *Kids' Stuff: Toys and the Changing World of American Childhood* (Cambridge: Harvard University Press, 1997), 219.

10. John Pedesco, quoted in Lawrence Kilman, "Aggressive Fantasies Still Fuel Type of Toys That Boys Prefer," *The Day*, February 19, 1985, https://news.google.com/newspapers?nid=1915&dat=19850219&id=jCVSAAAAIBAJ&sjid=DDYNAAAAIBAJ&pg=3864,4180567.

11. Cross, *Kids' Stuff*, 191.

12. Susan Mills, Letter to Editor, *The Courier*, December 9, 1983, 5A.

13. Freeman McNeil, "How Star Wars Shaped My Childhood," Sidespin, May 25, 2017, https://sidespin.kinja.com/how-star-wars-shaped-my-childhood-1795539115.

14. Gerrick Johnson, quoted in "With 'Star Wars' Toys, the Force May Be Strong but Retail Sales Aren't," Bloomberg, *Fortune*, January 18, 2018.

CHAPTER 35

1. Tokka Oroku, interview with author, March 23, 2019.

2. Rob Lammle, "The Complete History of Teenage Mutant Ninja Turtles," Mentalfloss, June 27, 2015, http://mentalfloss.com/article/30862/complete-history-teenage-mutant-ninja-turtles.

3. Ibid.

4. Ibid.

5. Howard Chudacoff, *Children at Play: An American History* (New York and London: New York University Press, 2007), 171.

6. Oroku.

7. "Teenage Mutant Ninja Turtle Environmental Message," Wilinerd 37 YouTube Channel, June 18, 2009, accessed March 25, 2019, https://www.youtube.com/watch?v=EgUn_ewgF58.

8. Stephen Chapman, "The Environment according to the Ninja Turtles," *Chicago Tribune,* October 27, 1991, accessed March 25, 2019, https://www.chicagotribune.com/news/ct-xpm-1991-10-27-9104060778-story.html.

9. Asawin Suebsaeng, "A Political History of the 'Teenage Mutant Ninja Turtles,'" The Daily Beast, August 6, 2014, https://www.thedailybeast.com/a-political-history-of-the-teenage-mutant-ninja-turtles.

10. Oroku.

11. Ibid.

12. Carly Mallenbaum, "April is (still) the worst part about 'Teenage Mutant Ninja Turtles.'" *USA Today*, June 8, 2016. https://www.usatoday.com/story/life/entertainthis/2016/06/08/april-still-worst-part-teenage-mutant-ninja-turtles/85461328/

13. Ibid.

14. Oroku.

PART VIII

1. William Byron Forbush, *Manual of Play; with a Graded and Annotated List of Playthings, Toys and Occupations* (Philadelphia: Jacobs, 1914), 276.

2. Ibid, 276.

3. Ibid, 78.

4. Steven A. Riess, "Sport and the Redefinition of American Middle-Class Masculinity," *The International Journal of the History of Sport* 8, no. 1 (1991): 11.

5. Tony Ladd and James A. Mathisen, *Muscular Christianity: Evangelical Protestants and the Development of American Sport* (Grand Rapids: Baker Book House, 1999), 26.

6. Ibid., 10.

7. Ibid., 5.

8. Lina and Adelia Beard, *The American Girl's Handy Book* (New York: Charles Scribner's Sons, 1887; reprint, New Hampshire: David R. Godine, Publisher, Inc., 1987), 353.

9. Ibid., 353.

10. Forbush, *Manual of Play*, 192.

11. Forbush, *Manual of Play*, 194.

12. Howard Chudacoff, *Children at Play: An American History* (New York and London: New York University Press, 2007), 129.

CHAPTER 36

1. "Kite History," National Kite Month, no date, http://www.nationalkitemonth.org/kite-history-overview/kite-history/.

2. Benjamin Franklin, quoted in M. Robinson, "Kites in the Age of Reason," Kiteshistory.com, http://kitehistory.com/Miscellaneous/Ben_Franklin.htm.

3. "Benjamin Franklin and the Kite Experiment," The Franklin Institute, https://www.fi.edu/benjamin-franklin/kite-key-experiment.

4. Daniel Carter Beard, *The American Boy's Handy Book* (New York: Charles Scribner's Sons, 1907), 3.

5. "Youth Flying Kite Killed by Tumble," *Prescott Evening Courier,* August 24, 1940, 4.

6. "Kite Season," *Pittsburgh Gazette Times*, April 9, 1923, 3.

7. "Warns Kite Flyers about Power Lines," *The Spokesman-Review*, March 6, 1944, 6.

8. "Kite Flying Safety Rules," *Stabroek News*, April 18, 1992.

CHAPTER 37

1. Glenna Brown, interview with the author, May 2018.

2. Scott Eberle, *Classic Toys of the National Toy Hall of Fame: Celebrating the Greatest Toys of All Time!* (New York: Running Press Book Publishers, 2009), 128.

3. Lydia Maria Child, *The Girl's Own Book* (New York: Clark and Austin Co, 1833), 103.

4. Frances Hodgson Burnett, *The Secret Garden* (New York: F.A. Stokes, 1911), http://www.authorama.com/secret-garden-8.html.

5. Patricia Hill Collins, *Black Feminist Thought: Knowledge, Consciousness, and the Politics of Empowerment* (New York and London: Routledge, 2002), 201.

6. Howard Chudacoff, *Children at Play: An American History* (New York: New York University Press, 2007), 132.

7. Ivory Ibuaka, "Jumping Rope, Pushing Back," The Silences and Sounds of Black Girlhood, The Albert and Shirley Small Special Collections Library, University of Virginia, January 2017, https://pages.shanti.virginia.edu/The_Silences_and_Sounds_of_Black_Girlhood/2017/01/07/jumping-rope-pushing-back/.

8. Kyra Gaunt, *The Games Black Girls Play: Learning the Ropes from Double-Dutch to Hip-Hop* (New York: New York University Press, 2006), 19.

9. Gia Kourlas, "The Art and Artistry of Double Dutch," *New York Times,* July 25, 2017.

10. Maria Dunn Williams, comment on the author's Facebook page, February 20, 2019.

11. Julianna Lee Marino, "Double Dutch: A Classic for Whom?" Medium.com, May 8, 2018, https://medium.com/africana-feminisms/double-dutch-a-classic-for-whom-ee47acf3531c.

CHAPTER 38

1. "Birth of Pro Football," Pro Football Hall of Fame, https://www.profootballhof.com/football-history/birth-of-pro-football/.

2. Walter Camp, quoted in Carla Killough McClafferty, *Fourth Down and Inches: Concussions and Football's Make-or-Break Moment* (Minneapolis: Carolrhoda Books, 2013), 10.

3. Amy Susan Green, "Savage Childhood: The Scientific Construction of Girlhood and Boyhood in the Progressive Era," PhD dissertation, University of Michigan, 1995, 75.

4. Gail Bederman, *Manliness and Civilization: A Cultural History of Gender and Race in the United States 1880–1917* (Chicago: University of Chicago Press, 1995), 17.

5. Ibid., 23.

6. Ibid.

7. Charles F. Thwing, quoted in Michael Oriard, *How the Popular Press Created An American Spectacle* (Chapel Hill: University of North Carolina Press, 1998), 208.

8. Steven A. Riess, "Sport and the Redefinition of American Middle-Class Masculinity," *The International Journal of the History of Sport* 8, no. 1 (1991): 19.

9. Carl Conrad Guise, "The Theory of Recapitulation in Child Development," master's thesis, May 15, 1914, University of Kansas.

10. Ibid., 191.

11. William Byron Forbush, *Manual of Play; with a Graded and Annotated List of Playthings, Toys and Occupations* (Philadelphia: Jacobs, 1914), 89.

12. Jacqueline Sahlberg, "Memorable Games in Harvard-Yale History," *Yale Daily News*, November 18, 2011.

13. Riess, "Sport and the Redefinition of American Middle-Class Masculinity," 18.

14. "Football Year's Death Harvest," *Chicago Tribune*, November 26, 1905.

15. Ibid.

16. Dean Hodges, quoted in Forbush, *Manual of Play*, 29.

17. Forbush, *Manual of Play*, 89.

18. "History of Pop Warner Little Scholars, Inc.," Pop Warner Little Scholars website, https://tshq.bluesombrero.com/Default.aspx?tabid=1579750.

19. Kelly Lyell, "Safety Concerns Prompt Sharp Drop in Youth Football Participation," *Fort Collins Coloradoan,* September 3, 2018, https://www.coloradoan.com/story/sports/2018/09/03/safety-concerns-drop-youth-football-participation-us-colorado/1134593002/.

20. Ibid.

CHAPTER 39

1. "Hula Hoop Hula Hoop (1967)," British Pathe YouTube channel, April 13, 2014, https://www.youtube.com/watch?v=pjJgMuCwHlM.

2. Tim Walsh, *Timeless Toys: Classic Toys and the Playmakers Who Created Them* (New York: Andrews McMeel Publishing, 2005), 142.

3. Lina Beard, "Hoop Dance," *The Delineator*, lvvi, no. 1 (January 1901): 457.

4. Walsh, *Timeless Toys*, 143.

5. Ibid.

6. Dan Webster, "Hula Hoop Turns 30 but Some Things Will Always Be Ageless," *The Spokesman-Review,* April 6, 1988. https://news.google.com/newspapers?nid=1314&dat=19880406&id=j1pWAAAAIBAJ&sjid=mu8DAAAAIBAJ&pg=7236,2938681.

7. "Death Laid to Hula Hooping," *New York Times,* November 23, 1958, 32.

8. Leslie Maitland, "Manhattan Hula-Hoop Contest Recalls All the Hoopla of 1958," *New York Times,* July 17, 1975, 33.

9. Colleen Sullivan, "Uncoordinated Children Are Putting It All Together," *New York Times,* March 2, 1975, 6.

10. "Final Preparations Made for Alive at 65," *Cherokee County Herald,* August 7, 2002, 3A.

11. Richard Stevenson, "Hula-Hoop Is Coming Around Again," *New York Times,* March 5, 1988, 35.

CHAPTER 40

1. "Polyurethanes Timeline," Polyurathanes.org, http://polyurethanes.org/en/what-is-it/timeline.

2. Matt Nelson, "Happy Birthday, Nerf," *Gainesville Sun*, May 8, 1995, 6G, https://news.google.com/newspapers?nid=1320&dat=19950508&id=JkRWAAAAIBAJ&sjid=reoDAAA AIBAJ&pg=3658,1595798.

3. Tim Walsh, *Timeless Toys: Classic Toys and the Playmakers Who Created Them* (New York: Andrews McMeel Publishing, 2005), 220.

4. Howard Chudacoff, *Children at Play: An American History* (New York: New York University Press, 2007), 222.

5. "Games Children Can Play to Cure Rainy-Day Blues," *Nevada Daily Mail*, October 5, 1976, https://news.google.com/newspapers?nid=1908&dat=19761005&id=q5MfAAAAIB AJ&sjid=VNQEAAAAIBAJ&pg=2254,480963.

6. Walsh, *Timeless Toys*, 221.

7. Bob Beatty, Facebook post on author's page, February 9, 2019.

PART IX

1. Howard Chudacoff, *Children at Play: An American History* (New York: New York University Press, 2007), 98.

2. William Forbush, *Manual of Play* (Philadelphia: George W. Jacobs & Co, 1914), 275.

3. Paula Fass, *The End of American Childhood: A History of Parenting from Life on the Frontier to the Managed Child* (Princeton: Princeton University Press, 2016), 33–34.

4. "A Child's Play Room," *The Day*, January 9, 1891, 3.

5. Gary Cross, *Kids' Stuff: Toys and the Changing World of American Childhood* (Cambridge: Harvard University Press, 1997), 52.

6. Ibid, 53.

7. Olivia N. Saracho and Bernard Spodek, "Children's Play and Early Chidhood Education and Theory," *Journal of Education*, vol. 177, no. 3, 1995, 138.

CHAPTER 41

1. Nicole Cooley, "Dollhouses Weren't Invented for Play," *The Atlantic*, July 22, 2016, https://www.theatlantic.com/technology/archive/2016/07/dollhouses-werent-invented-for-play/492581/.

2. Charles Siebert, "Letter of Recommendation: The Thorne Miniature Rooms," *New York Times Magazine*, September 17, 2015, https://www.nytimes.com/2015/09/20/magazine/letter-of-recommendationthe-thorne-miniature-rooms.html.

3. "History of the Doll's House," Antik Toy Store, https://www.antiktoystore.de/en/dolls-houses.

4. Gary Cross, *Kids' Stuff: Toys and the Changing World of American Childhood* (Cambridge: Harvard University Press, 1997), 16.

5. Ibid.

6. Catharine E. Beecher and Harriet Beecher Stowe, *American Woman's Home* (New York: JB Ford and Co, 1869; reprint, New York: Library of Victorian Culture, American Life Foundation, 1979), 293

7. Melanie Dawson, "The Miniaturization of Girlhood: Nineteenth-Century Playtime and Gendered Theories of Development," in *The American Child: A Cultural Studies Reader*, ed. Caroline Levander and Carol Singley (New Brunswick: Rutgers University Press, 2003), 68.

8. "Nettie's Dollhouse," June 1, 2016, Small Talk Blog, the National Museum of Toys/Miniatures, https://toyandminiaturemuseum.org/toys/netties-dollhouse/.

9. "A Dollhouse Like No Other," November 22, 2016, Small Talk Blog, the National Museum of Toys/Miniatures, https://toyandminiaturemuseum.org/toys/inside-dollhouse-like/.

10. "Furnishing the Doll House," *American Motherhood,* quoted in Forbush, *Manual of Play.*

11. Cross, *Kids' Stuff,* 72.

12. Ibid., 403–12.

13. Ibid.

14. "11 Enchanting Dollhouse Sets to Encourage Imaginative Play," Fractus Learning, https://www.fractuslearning.com/dollhouse-sets-imaginative-play/.

15. Cooley, "Dollhouses Weren't Invented for Play."

CHAPTER 42

1. Gary Cross, *Kids' Stuff: Toys and the Changing World of American Childhood* (Cambridge: Harvard University Press, 1997), 68.

2. Nina Ranalli, "Tea Sets and Play," The Decorative Arts Trust Blog, no date, https://decorativeartstrust.org/tea-sets-and-play/.

3. "Tea-Table Manners," *Youth's Companion* 72 (1898): 607.

4. "Decorated Tea Set and Tray," *Ladies Home Journal,* December 1886.

CHAPTER 43

1. "Hair Grower?" *The Saint Maurice Valley Chronicle,* January 11, 1962, 5, https://news.google.com/newspapers?nid=728&dat=19620111&id=PMsvAAAAIBAJ&sjid=tkEDAAAAIBAJ&pg=1230,1090727.

2. Sally Kevill-Davies, *Yesterday's Children: The Antiques and History of Childcare* (Suffolk, England: Antique Collector's Club, 1991), 244.

3. William Clarke, *The Boy's Own Book: A Complete Encyclopedia of All the Diversions, Athletic, Scientific, and Recreative, of Boyhood and Youth* (Boston: Monroe and Francis, 1829; reprint, Bedford, MA: Applewood Books, n.d.), 179 and 181 (page citations are to the reprint edition).

4. Sarah Zielinski, "The Rise and Fall and Rise of the Chemistry Set," *Smithsonian Magazine*, October 10, 2012, https://www.smithsonianmag.com/science-nature/the-rise-and-fall-and-rise-of-the-chemistry-set-70359831/.

5. Gilbert Chemistry Outfit.

6. Rosie Clark quoted in Zielinski, "The Rise and Fall and Rise of the Chemistry Set."

7. Ruth Peck McLeod, "Hobbies as Vocational Tendencies," *Virgin Islands Daily News*, February 17, 1941, 3, https://news.google.com/newspapers?nid=757&dat=19410217&id=CDVOAAAAIBAJ&sjid=ki4DAAAAIBAJ&pg=6385,1477034.

8. Dave Lyons and Lucille Prince, "Gift Telescope Started FSC Prof on His Career," *Times Daily*, June 28, 1968, 11.

9. "Teen Girl Takes Top Prize in Science 'Talent Search,'" *Star News*, March 31, 1972, https://news.google.com/newspapers?nid=1454&dat=19720331&id=7MEsAAAAIBAJ&sjid=wAkEAAAAIBAJ&pg=796,6299854.

10. Jennifer A. Kingson, "Practical to Career-Oriented to Just Plain Fun," *New York Times*, December 24, 2012.

11. Rosie Cook, "Chemistry at Play," *Distillations* (Spring 2010), https://www.sciencehistory.org/distillations/magazine/chemistry-at-play.

12. Katherine Wollard, "Gifts to Look at the World: Science Toys as an Alternative," *Victoria Advocate*, December 17, 1986, 7D.

CHAPTER 44

1. Alton Brown, "Alton Brown's Mega Bake Video," *Popular Science*, accessed January 15, 2019, https://www.dailymotion.com/video/x40gg8l.

2. Ibid.

3. Ibid.

4. Scott Eberle, *Classic Toys of the National Toy Hall of Fame: Celebrating the Greatest Toys of All Time* (New York: Running Press, 2009), 217.

5. "Couldn't Cook on Toy Stove," *Herald-Journal*, January 10, 1956.

6. Eberle, *Classic Toys*, 213.

7. "The Evolution of the Easy Bake Oven Infographic," Partselect, accessed January 15, 2019, https://www.partselect.com/JustForFun/Easy-Bake-Oven-Infographic.aspx.

8. "Easy Bake Commercial—1972," Robert Zimmerman YouTube Channel, March 25, 2007, accessed January 15, 2019, https://www.youtube.com/watch?v=VpFjQoWMUoU.

9. Kenner Easy Bake Oven advertisement, *The Fredericksburg Free Lance-Star,* December 7, 1967, 18.

10. Diette Ward, author's Facebook Page, January 16, 2019.

CHAPTER 45

1. "Meet Alexis Puyleart '19," St. Norbert College website, https://giving.snc.edu/givingstories/alexis.puyleart.html.

2. "1940s Popular Vintage Children's Toys," The People History, http://www.thepeoplehistory.com/40stoys.html.

3. "Sears Roebuck advertisement," *The Tuscaloosa News,* November 2, 1952, 6.

4. William Grimes, "Lynn Pressman Raymond, Toy Executive, Dies at 97," *New York Times,* August 1, 2009, https://www.nytimes.com/2009/08/02/business/02pressman.html.

5. M. J. Field and R. E. Behrman, editors, "Patterns of Childhood Death in America," in *When Children Die: Improving Palliative and End-of-Life Care for Children and Their Families* (Washington, DC: National Academies Press, 2003), https://www.ncbi.nlm.nih.gov/books/NBK220806/.

6. Ricki Lewis, "Vaccine Memories: From Polio to Autism," DNA Science Blog, July 17, 2014, https://blogs.plos.org/dnascience/2014/07/17/vaccine-memories-polio-autism/.

7. Lewis, "Vaccine Memories."

8. Grimes, "Lynn Pressman Raymond."

9. Peter Stockley, *The Scallywags—Memories of a Rascal's 1950s Childhood* (London: John Blake Publishing, 2016).

10. Ibid.

11. Walt Disney's Mickey Mouse Medical Kit, The Strong National Museum of Play, object ID 112.6549.

12. "Women in Medicine: A Review of Changing Physician Demographics, Female Physicians by Specialty, State, and Related Data" (Irving, TX: Staff Care, 2015), https://www.amnhealthcare.com/uploadedFiles/MainSite/Content/Staffing_Recruitment/Staffcare-WP-Women%20in%20Med.pdf.

13. Rachel Giordano, quoted in Lori Day "The Little Girl from the 1981 LEGO Ad Is All Grown-Up and She's Got Something to Say," Women You Should Know website, February 11, 2014, https://womenyoushouldknow.net/little-girl-1981-lego-ad-grown-shes-got-something-say/.

PART X

1. Jane McGonigal, quoted in Kamaila Sanders, "Here's How You'll Get Smarter by Playing Video Games," *Business Insider,* January 17, 2012, https://www.businessinsider.com/heres-why-experts-think-playing-video-games-actually-make-you-smarter-2012-1.

2. "October 1958: Physicist Invents First Video Game," *APS News* 17, no. 9 (October 2008), https://www.aps.org/publications/apsnews/200810/physicshistory.cfm.

3. "History of Video Games," Video Game Sales Wiki, https://vgsales.fandom.com/wiki/History_of_video_games.

4. Eugene Provenzo, quoted in Howard Chudacoff, *Children at Play: An American History* (New York: New York University Press, 2007), 98.

5. Dr. Benjamin Spock, quoted in Chudacoff, *Children at Play*, 174.

CHAPTER 46

1. Jeremy Saucier, "Coin-Op Century: A Brief History of the American Arcade," Play Stuff Blog, May 9, 2013, accessed February 23, 2019, https://www.museumofplay.org/blog/chegheads/2013/05/coin-op-century-a-brief-history-of-the-american-arcade.

2. Ibid.

3. Jon-Paul Dyson and Jeremy Saucier, eds., *A History of Video Games in 64 Objects* (New York: Dey Street, 2018), 2.

4. Daniel Reynolds, "The Pinball Problem," *Refractory: A Journal of Entertainment Media,* no date, http://refractory.unimelb.edu.au/2010/07/18/the-pinball-problem-daniel-reynolds/.

5. Laura June, "For Amusement Only: The Life and Death of the American Arcade," *The Verge,* January 16, 2013, https://www.theverge.com/2013/1/16/3740422/the-life-and-death-of-the-american-arcade-for-amusement-only.

6. "Pinball Seizures Pushed by Police," *New York Times*, January 23, 1942, 40.

7. "Judges Denounce Pinball as Gambling, but Reserve Decision in Jersey Case," *New York Times,* October 9, 1941, 13.

8. Ibid.

9. "Pinball in Jersey Banned by Court," *New York Times*, February 25, 1942, 40.

10. Ibid.

11. "Pinball as 'Racket' Fought by Mayor," *New York Times,* January 29, 1942.

12. "Pinball Machines Ruled as Gambling Devices," *The Southeast Missourian*, March 7, 1949, https://news.google.com/newspapers?nid=1893&dat=19490307&id=OhEpAAAAIBAJ&sjid=8tYEAAAAIBAJ&pg=5175,7805.

13. "County Prosecutor Orders Ban on All Gambling as of Monday," *Mt. Adams Sun,* January 10, 1963.

14. "Outlaw of Pinball Machines Urged," *Ellensburg Daily Record,* February 20, 1969, 9.

15. Tom Buckley, "About New York," *New York Times,* April 4, 1975.

16. Roman Mars, "Why the City of Oakland *Finally* Legalized Pinball Machines," Gizmodo, October 9, 2014, https://gizmodo.com/why-the-city-of-oakland-finally-legalized-pinball-machi-1644249060.

CHAPTER 47

1. Don Rawistch, quoted in Kevin Wong, "The Forgotten History of 'The Oregon Trail,' As Told by Its Creators" *Motherboard*, February 15, 2017, accessed January 28, 2019, https://motherboard.vice.com/en_us/article/qkx8vw/the-forgotten-history-of-the-oregon-trail-as-told-by-its-creators.

2. Paul Dillenberger, quoted in Wong, "The Forgotten History of 'The Oregon Trail.'"

3. Wong, "The Forgotten History of 'The Oregon Trail.'"

4. "The Orgeon Trail," in Jon-Paul Dyson and Jeremy Saucier, eds., *A History of Video Games in 64 Objects* (New York: Dey Street, 2018).

5. Anna Garvey, "The Oregon Trail Generation: Life Before and After Mainstream Tech," Social Media Week, April 21, 2015, accessed January 28, 2019, https://socialmediaweek.org/blog/2015/04/oregon-trail-generation/.

6. "The Oregon Trail: IRL," https://do303.com/the-oregon-trail, accessed August 1, 2019.

CHAPTER 48

1. Joanne Friedman, "What was (sic) your memories of Pac-Man," answer on Quora.com, July 8, 2017.

2. Matt Peckham, "This Is What *Pac-Man's* Creator Thinks 35 Years Later," *Time Magazine,* May 22, 2015, http://time.com/3892662/pac-mans-35-years/.

3. "Pac-Man," in Jon-Paul Dyson and Jeremy Saucier, eds., *A History of Video Games in 64 Objects* (New York: Dey Street, 2018), 132.

4. Tegan Jones, "The History of Pac-Man," Todayifoundout.com, August 16, 2013.

5. Toru Iwatani, quoted in *A History of Video Games in 64 Objects*, 132.

6. Christine Champagne, "How 'Pac-Man' Changed Games and Culture," Fast Company Website, May 22, 2015, https://www.fastcompany.com/1683023/how-pac-man-changed-games-and-culture.

7. "Pac Man Maker Forced to Fight Imitators," *Reading Eagle,* March 13, 1982 https://news.google.com/newspapers?nid=1955&dat=19820313&id=49MxAAAAIBAJ&sjid=-uMFAAAAIBAJ&pg=3236,2075541.

8. "Pac-Man Fever (album)," Wikipedia, https://en.wikipedia.org/wiki/Pac-Man_Fever_(album).

9. "Letters to Santa," *The Malakoff News*, December 23, 1982, 10A, https://news.google. com/newspapers?nid=1032&dat=19821216&id=v8Y1AAAAIBAJ&sjid=vBEGAAAAIBA J&pg=1822,524303.

10. Jonathan Silverstein, "Pac-Man: Ten Things You Didn't Know," ABCNews.com, March 8, 2011, https://abcnews.go.com/Technology/GameOn/pac-man-10-secrets/ story?id=13084900.

CHAPTER 49

1. Paul Lilley, comment on the author's Facebook page, February 24, 2019.

2. Tom Cadwell, answer on Quora "Why Is Tetris So Popular?" October 29, 2012, https://www.quora.com/Why-is-Tetris-so-popular.

3. "Tetris," in Jon-Paul Dyson and Jeremy Saucier, eds., *A History of Video Games in 64 Objects* (New York: Dey Street, 2018), 178.

4. Ibid.

5. Ibid.

6. "New Software Game: It Comes from Soviet," *New York Times,* January 29, 1988, D1.

7. William R. Beardslee, "Children's and Adolescents' Perceptions of the Threat of Nuclear War: Implications and Recent Studies," in *The Medical Implications of Nuclear War,* ed. F. Solomon and R. Q. Marston (Washington, DC: National Academies Press, 1986).

8. Ibid.

9. George Gallup, "Teens Are Proud to Be American," *The Free Lance-Star*, July 2, 1981, 25.

10. Ibid.

11. Tetris advertisement, appearing in Drew Robarge, "Tetris: Fun in the Cold War?" O Say Can You See Blog, National Museum of American History, November 6, 2014, https://americanhistory.si.edu/blog/2014/09/tetris-fun-in-the-cold-war.html.

12. Tom Stafford, "The Psychology of Tetris," BBC Future, October 23, 2012, http://www. bbc.com/future/story/20121022-the-psychology-of-tetris.

13. Lilley.

14. *A History of Video Games in 64 Objects,* 179.

CHAPTER 50

1. Tom Huddleston Jr., "'Super Mario Bros.' Debuted 33 Years Ago," CNBC.com, September 13, 2018.

2. "Q&A: Shigeru Miyamoto on the Origins of Nintendo's Famous Characters," NPR All Tech Considered, June 19, 2015, https://www.npr.org/sections/alltechconside

red/2015/06/19/415568892/q-a-shigeru-miyamoto-on-the-origins-of-nintendos-famous-characters.

3. Howard Chudacoff, *Children at Play: An American History* (New York: New York University Press, 2007), 218.

4. "Nintendo May Pose Health Hazard," *Lodi News-Sentinel*, May 17, 1990, 4.

5. Ibid.

6. A. Craig Purcell, "Video-Game Mania: Passing Phase or Permanent Addiction?" *New York Times*, December 11, 1988, 38, https://timesmachine.nytimes.com/timesmachine/1988/12/11/issue.html.

7. Ibid.

8. Ibid.

9. "Super Mario Bros," in Jon-Paul Dyson and Jeremy Saucier, eds., *A History of Video Games in 64 Objects* (New York: Dey Street, 2018), 191.

AFTERWORD

1. Jessica Joelle Alexander quoted in "Families That Play More Are Happier, but Even Children Say They Are Too Busy for Fun and Games," Roar Rude Trangbaek, August 22, 2018, https://www.lego.com/en-us/aboutus/news-room/2018/august/play-well-report.

2. Howard Chudacoff, *Children at Play: An American History* (New York: New York University Press, 2007), 237.

3. Robert Preidt, "Play Is Key to Kids' Health, US Pediatricians Say," *WebMD*, August 21, 2018, https://www.webmd.com/children/news/20180821/play-is-key-to-kids-health-us-pediatricians-say#1.

4. Jessica Joelle Alexander quoted in *LEGO Play Well Report 2018*, 2018.

5. Chudacoff, *Children at Play*, 216.

6. Michael Yogman, Andrew Garner, Jeffrey Hutchinson, Kathy Hirsh-Pasek, Roberta Golinkoff, "The Power of Play: A Pediatric Role in Enhancing Development in Young Children," *Pediatrics* 142, no. 3 (September 2018), https://pediatrics.aappublications.org/content/142/3/e20182058.

7. Ibid.

8. Chudacoff, *Children at Play*, 218.

9. Claire McCarthy, "6 Reasons Children Need to Play Outside," May 22, 2018, Harvard School of Health Blog, https://www.health.harvard.edu/blog/6-reasons-children-need-to-play-outside-2018052213880.

Index

About the Author

Susan A. Fletcher is a Colorado Springs native. She grew up on a peaceful street surrounded by her best friends, and they had all sorts of marvelous adventures together. You can read more about her childhood exploits in this book. She currently serves as the Director of History and Archives for The Navigators. She is the co-editor of *Dawson Trotman in His Own Words* and has written numerous chapters on Colorado for the Pikes Peak Regional History Book Series. Her work also appears in *Springs Magazine* and *The Colorado Collective.*